The Changing Landscape of Plant Sciences: Taxonomy and Ecology

The Changing Landscape of Plant Sciences: Taxonomy and Ecology

Vaibhav Suri

CYBER TECH PUBLICATIONS
4264/3, Ansari Road, Daryaganj, New Delhi-110002 (India)
Ph.: 011-23244078, 011-43559448 Fax: 011-23280028
E-Mail: cyberpublicationsdelhi@yahoo.com
Website: www.cybertechpublications.com

THE CHANGING LANDSCAPE OF PLANT SCIENCES: TAXONOMY AND ECOLOGY

Vaibhav Suri

First Edition 2010

Published by :

G.S. Rawat for **Cyber Tech Publications**
4264/3, Ansari Road, Daryaganj, New Delhi-110002 (India)
Ph.: 011-23244078, 011-43559448 Fax: 011-23280028
E-Mail: cyberpublicationsdelhi@yahoo.com
Website: www.cybertechpublications.com

Printed at: Asian Offset Printers, Delhi-53

Preface

This book is written to provide a unique plant science text that emphasizes understanding the role of the environment in plant growth and development instead of the more traditional focus topics of analyzing the industries and surveying important crops. By emphasizing the scientific principles associated with the biological effects that the various environmental factors have on plant development, I hope that the reader will be better equipped to understand current and emerging technologies that modify the environment to improve plant production. The overriding philosophy of this text is that conceptualization and evaluation are more important than memorization, especially when trying to understand and direct biological responses and organisms.

To set the stage and provide some background information, *Principles of Plant Science: Environmental Factors and Technology in Growing Plants* begins with an overview of the plant sciences, including the role of plants in the development of societies, industries, and science. Its emphasis in plant science is on non-forest agricultural crops. A primer on plant growth and development follows that includes information on photosynthesis and respiration, plant hormones, and ecology. The influence of the environment on agricultural plant production constitutes the remainder of the presented material and is the primary emphasis of the text.

The environmental factors that affect plant growth and development are discussed in one of two broad categories: the aerial environment or the rhizosphere. The factors covered in the aerial environment section include irradiance (light), temperature, gases, air pollutants, and mechanical disturbances. The factors covered in the rhizosphere section include water, mineral nutrients, soil organisms, and allelochemicals. Although some of the environmental factors (e.g., temperature, water, atmospheric gases) may affect both the aerial environment and the rhizosphere, for discussion they were placed in the section that their effect was considered greater.

Material on each environmental factor covered is presented in three sections. This book is designed for use in plant science (or horticulture) courses that would be taken before a student enrolls in the various advanced plant production courses such as agronomy, crop science, vegetable crops, small fruits, pomology, and floriculture. The material may also be utilized for plant growth and development or applied introductory plant physiology courses taught at universities, junior colleges, or community colleges.

The primary emphasis of this book is on the environmental factors and their role in plant growth and production. Its intent is to provide sufficient introductory material on the various environmental factors and examples of effects of these environmental factors on plant growth and development to facilitate further discussions and study.

Complete and exhaustive discussions on the fields of plant science and the influence of the various environmental factors on plant growth are beyond the scope of any single textbook. Further information on the plant sciences can be gleaned from other introductory textbooks on plant science, crop science, and horticulture. Information from local extension services should serve as important sources of current location-specific marketing and crop production information. More in-depth information on the environment and plant growth can be obtained from plant physiology, plant ecology, and plant ecophysiology texts and/ or articles on specific topics in scientific journals.

—Author

CONTENTS

1

Introduction

Edaphic environmental stresses impose a constant constraint on stable plant production worldwide. Plant adaptability and productivity to a large extent are governed by response plasticity to short- and long-term multiple abiotic stresses. The plant response problem is complicated by the interaction of and simultaneous exposure to multiple stresses, such as acidity and drought, Al-Mn phytotoxicities, and Ca-Mg-P-K-Mo deficiencies, soil acidity and biotic agents (insects, diseases), soil acidity constraints, and plant genetic traits. Examples of the latter erratic constraints include compacted layers or high bulk density soils versus genetically controlled plant rooting volume and density; phytotoxic availability of specific ions in the soil versus plant nutrient uptake efficiencies for deficient elements, and tolerance to toxic levels of certain elements.

Plant response, or plasticity, to constantly changing environmental conditions (wet ”! dry, cold ”! hot) in stressful environments ultimately governs productivity and persistence over time. Most plant response plasticity mechanisms are genetically controlled and theoretically can be manipulated in breeding/genetic improvement programs. However, significant genetic improvements to complex abiotic stresses have been limited. DNA can be rearranged in response to environmental stress (Cullis, 1990). Systematic improvements in specific components of a stress complex (Al and Mn tolerance in certain crop species and on certain acid soils) have been successful; however, overall quantitative tolerance to the entire acid soil stress complex has been difficult to achieve. Many of the component genetic advances have been accomplished without a clear understanding of plant acid soil stress tolerance mechanisms and their interactions with specific acid soil complexes.

Field evaluation at multiple acid soil sites is the ultimate determinant for enhancing the long-term adaptation of a plant species and for improving plant productivity under fluctuating stresses. Selection environments affect patterns of genotypic response to varying environments. The ever-changing environment has posed significant problems for many abiotic stress tolerance field-based breeding programs, from basic genetic resource evaluations within species to development of effective breeding strategies. This review attempts to highlight success stories and offer suggestions for future research enhancement for acid soil stress improvements in breeding programs.

CROP STRESS RESPONSE PLASTICITY

Crop evolution and plant adaptation to stress environments are synonymous. Man and the environment have constantly applied direct or indirect selective pressure on plants, resulting in adaptive responses to the specific environments. The choice of selection environments affect both the response of genotypes to changing environments and the performance of genotypes in specific environments. In general, wild progenitors are much more plastic than their cultivated counterparts. Landraces exemplify an excellent example of repetitious, long-term selection for stable performance in stress environments. The landraces are also characterized by important stable agronomic traits that can be exploited in stress tolerance breeding programs. Stress arising from unpredictable environmental variation cause partitioning changes in the plant that are plastic, but the degree of response is under intra- and interspecies genetic control. When the environmental stress is relatively predictable over the life span of the plants, responses to the stresses become genetically fixed in the plant, leading to evolution of ecotypes or landraces.

Consequently, stress responses will govern the level of tolerance, ultimately affecting productivity and temporal stability to less than optimal habitats. Stress responses can be classified into morphological and physiological types. When the environment has a low frequency of disturbance and productivity is high, the plant response strategy may be toleration or avoidance (i.e., escape, or adjusting sensitive vegetative or reproductive growth stages to periods of reduced stress).

Plant Tolerance to Acid Soil Constraints

Morphological plasticity will be the dominant form of plant response in such cases. Morphological plasticity of the mitotic apparatus in cell and organismal development can produce new directions for growth. Mitotic plasticity governs the molecular basis of mitotic architecture and is a mechanism to compensate for mitotic apparatus asymmetry or deformation that developmentally impacts cell division. Mitotic apparatus morphology and alignment have a genetic basis. One aspect of a dynamic property of the mitotic apparatus in plants is the plant's ability to respond to its immediate erratic environment, especially any stresses imposed on the cell wall. The plant responsiveness and the epigenic machinery used in the response are products of evolution. Since several mechanisms governing Al-Mn toxicity, tolerance/susceptibility, and CaMg-P-K deficiencies are operating at the cell wall membrane interface, morphological plasticity becomes essential to survival.

Under stable conditions of extremely low productivity imposed by various stresses, biomass normally changes very little, and tissues are exposed to a regimented sequence of seasonal stress conditions. The dominant stress response is cellular acclimation. The functional characteristics and "hardiness" of plant tissues change rapidly through membrane and organelle biochemical adjustments. Phenotypic plasticity (phenotypic variation of an individual genotype under variable environmental conditions) is a mechanism whereby plants may adapt to a spatially or temporally heterogeneous environment. This plasticity is under genetic control and subject to selection and modification. The evolutionary and ecological significance of plasticity compared to genetic homeostasis (tendency of a physiological system to react to an external disturbance in such a way that the system is not displaced from its normal responses, or maintenance of genetic variability in a population when subjected to forces acting to reduce it) can be separated. Hypotheses that account for plasticity differences (pattern or direction of response and amount) within taxa and among individual genotypes include:

1. Heterozygosity: Inversely related phenotypic plasticity and genotypic variability are alternative response mechanisms that plants use to adapt to environmental heterogeneity.
2. Ecological factors: Plant groups with contrasting ecologies should differ in both pattern and amount of plasticity.
3. Relatedness: Plasticity profiles of more distantly related plant groups should be more variable. Different plasticity patterns are not ecologically or evolutionarily significant, but the patterns are by-products of genetic differentiation because either selection or random drift were operating on entirely different traits. The degree of genetic similarity and congruence of plasticity profiles are directly related, regardless of the ecological similarity for each plant group.
4. Specialization: Under some environmental conditions, specialist plant groups (landraces and ecotypes) may exhibit higher plasticity magnitudes than generalist plant groups (species, populations, and genotypes).

The ecological hypothesis is gaining support as the primary reason for evolution of stress-tolerant plants. Plasticity profiles manifest the historical integration of many evolutionary processes and are not the simple consequence of heterozygosity levels. Higher plasticity is expected in habitats dominated by short-term unpredictability, which prevents environmental tracking of specific environmental changes. Climate is a key factor in influencing differentiation patterns for morphological and phenological species traits. Populations adapted to more moderate climates have greater plastic phenological schedules (with specific associated morphological traits) that allow exploitation of temporarily favorable environmental conditions. The pattern of plant population differentiation for plasticity is congruous with the pattern of genetic differentiation, according to isozyme analysis.

Various aspects of a specific trait can be governed by different genetic systems, operating independently of one another during evolutionary divergence of populations and thereby reflecting the influence of a variety of selective forces including neutral processes. Climatic factors exert a strong selective influence on the evolution of phenological and morphometric traits and on intraspecific competition intensity and consistency, which may be critical ecological parameters accounting for stress tolerance plasticity differentiation. This type of evolutionary discussion provides a strong argument for conducting breeding programs involving multiple stresses and complex interactions of multiple tolerance traits, leading to subsequent repeated selection strategies in specifically targeted stress field environments.

GENETIC CONTROL OF ACID SOIL STRESS RESPONSE

Edaphic stress tolerance improvement requires some knowledge of biochemical and physiological aspects of gene action, i.e., epigenetics. Tolerance to the overall acid soil response complex is quantitative; but various components of genetic control vary from dominance to recessiveness to additivity, depending on species, level of soil acidity used in evaluation, and specific parental background of the cultivars that were evaluated. Generally, one to three genes (± modifiers) with either dominant, recessive, and/or additive gene action are controlling Al toxicity tolerance. For Mn toxicity tolerance, one to four genes with varying degrees of dominance or additivity are operating. Calcium efficiency involves two to three genes with additive effects. Magnesium efficiency usually involves one or more genes and additivity, and Mg substitution at critical sites in the cell is proposed as the principal mechanism through which Al expresses toxicity. Phosphorus efficiency is multigenic and additive, while potassium efficiency can vary from single recessive gene action to additivity.

The challenge for the breeder is to know the limitations of the specific soil constraints being targeted in the program and to combine appropriate breeding strategy with improvement of as many components of the acid soil tolerance complex as possible. Multitrait stress tolerance can be achieved either through pleiotrophy (single gene providing tolerance to one or more mineral stresses), or co-tolerance (selection for one mineral stress tolerance associated with simultaneous selection at another locus that provides tolerance to another stress). Co-tolerance to Al and Mn stresses has been demonstrated in wheat, carrots, and barley. The "opposite Al-Mn tolerance" phenomenon has also been documented for various crops. Nutrient deficiency effects on plant growth may be controlled by a centralized, hormonally induced stress response system.

BREEDING TECHNIQUES FOR ACID SOIL STRESS TOLERANCE

Advances in the overall acid soil tolerance complex using field-stressed sites have involved pedigree-backcross techniques (with individual adapted parental lines) or some form of recurrent selection involving populations. Variable soil pH blocks, generally e"5.0 and d"4.9, have been established in the field to enhance the breeding/developmental effectiveness.

Near-isogenic lines offer an alternative approach to enhancing the understanding of genetically controlled tolerance mechanisms. With toxicity and efficiency traits involved in the overall acid soil tolerance complex, multiple trait selection becomes very important in development of tolerant cultivars. Several schemes are available for multiple trait selection:

1. Modified convergent improvement: Different trait-specific populations are crossed using phenotypic recurrent selection during three cycles of selection, with interpopulation crosses after each selection cycle.

2. Tandem selection: Sequentially repeated cycles of selection can be used for selecting a series of individual traits.
3. Index selection: Simultaneous selection can be used on a series of traits.
4. Independent culling: Sequential selection of a series of independent traits in the same population can be used.
5. Strain crossing and multiple strain crossing: Two or more populations, each containing a unique and high frequency trait, are simultaneously crossed. Breeding gain per cycle was highest using modified convergent improvement and independent culling for traits controlled by recessive genes.

Selection of traits controlled by dominant genes or additivity was highest using independent culling. Modified convergent improvement was superior to independent culling when gene frequency was low ($q = 0.04$–0.12) in the selection of traits controlled by additive or recessive gene action. Modified convergent improvement was the superior selection method for multiple traits selected in dissimilar environments (which often happens in acid soil tolerance selection programs) and during initial cycles of germ plasm development.

For aluminum toxicity tolerance improvement, in vitro selection, various forms of solution culture or soil-pot bioassays, backcrossing involving specific parents, and population breeding, recurrent selection techniques have dominated developmental/improvement approaches. Manganese toxicity tolerance improvements have generally been handled through soil-pot bioassays, nutrient solutions, or artificial soil methods. Pedigree-backcross techniques are utilized in the improvement programs. Methods used to screen and select various forage legume species for acid soil tolerance are summarized in Devine et al. (1990).

Phosphorus efficiency enhancement has involved backcrossing, in vitro selection and somaclonal variation, pot culture, and various nutrient solution techniques. Backcrossing is commonly used to facilitate the genetic improvements. Calcium deficiency improvements have generally involved laboratory soil bioassays and backcrossing. Some breeding programs have utilized in vitro screening and somaclonal variation: Al toxicity tolerance; acid soil tolerance complex, P efficiency for stress tolerance improvements. A good review of the successes from this breeding methodology can be found in Duncan (1996).

GENETIC RESOURCES

Field stress evaluation and categorization of acid soil stress tolerance response among some crop species has been published for a few collections: sorghum, wheat, Old World bluestems, amaranthus, white clover, lotus, rice, alfalfa, soybean, and ryegrass. An additional 34 species and 87 cultivars have been assessed for Al-stress response. An alfalfa core collection has been screened specifically for acid soil tolerance. A summary of plant ecological distributions, as well as adaptation ranges for pH, moisture, and temperature can be found in Duke (1978).

SELECTION CRITERIA

The dilemma of what selection criteria to use in specific soil stress breeding programs has been a constant problem for breeders. Identifying and utilizing appropriate field stress evaluation sites has been a further challenge. However, technology is available for improving selection efficiency in stress environments through identification of optimal screening and evaluation nursery sites. Selection using alternative generations under differential stresses, selection for stability, or selection simultaneously for multiple types of environments (stressed, intermediate, and nonstressed) using rank summation, selection indices, and mean productivity are indirect selection techniques that can be used.

A breeding strategy combining direct selection in marginal environments (specific adaptation) and use of locally adapted germ plasm (landraces) is 28 times more efficient than a selection strategy encompassing high-yield environments and non-landrace material. The heterogeneous nature of stressed soils, coupled with other environmental interactions, intraspecies genetic variability, plant developmental stage of progression, evaluation criteria, and multiple abiotic interactions govern how successful the selection program will be. Ion and water balances, cell wall membrane integrity, hormonal balances, and inducement of stress response proteins all interact to influence growth and development of plants grown under abiotic stresses. Multiple selection criteria, as well as multiple-stage breeding strategies are necessary for trait improvement, with parallel selection of components that govern productivity. Erosion of this latter component does not have to be sacrificed during the stress tolerance improvement program.

For Al toxicity, selection for specific organic acids, stress-induced proteins, and specific Al-induced genes is possible. For Mn toxicity, evaluation of chlorophyll content and stress-induced proteins can be used in the selection program. Specific genes are selectable for Ca deficiency. Sugar content can be used to select for P uptake efficiency, while enzyme synthesis can be used in the selection program for P use efficiency. Screening for a stress-induced protein can be used to overcome K deficiency. A good review of stress-induced proteins can be found in Ho and Sachs (1989).

Highly correlated physiological and biochemical markers are critically needed for abiotic stress tolerance if improvements are to continue. Environmental interaction effects can be minimized and genotype–phenotype correspondence under abiotic stresses can be improved by use of appropriate standardized tolerant and sensitive indicator checks, progressive selection under discerning controlled laboratory conditions followed by selection under differentiating field conditions, delayed selection in early segregating generations and bulking within families under the F5 generation to maximize the number of segregants for field-stress screening, and using specific experimental designs. Genetic sterile-facilitated recurrent selection and shuttle (alternating selection cycles in stressed and nonstressed environments) breeding programs should include replicated evaluations at multiple locations (and acid soil stresses) to maximize breeding advancement. Reconstitution of the best stress-tolerant parents with advancing generations will eventually lead to quantitative stress tolerance trait improvement over time. Selection indices of 1–5% (percentage of total plants that were selected for tolerance response) in field-stress environments can be effective in developing productive, stress-tolerant genotypes.

RHIZOTOXICITY AND ROOT GROWTH UNDER STRESS

One of the most neglected aspects of breeding programs to improve plant tolerance to the acid soil complex is rhizosphere improvement. All nutritional imbalance components (rhizotoxicity, rhizodeficiency) occur in the root zone and ultimately affect overall growth and development. Stress response induction is functioning at the soil chemical, physical, environmental, and biological interfaces. Plant roots modify their development in response to environmental stimuli, changing direction of growth through signal transduction, alteration in gene regulation and protein/enzyme activity, and modification of cell division, expansion, and differentiation. The root apex is the primary site of Al-induced root growth inhibition. Genotypic variation in root systems has been documented. Different types of roots are functionally, developmentally, and genetically unique.

Genetic variability in various root types can be exploited in breeding programs. Root architecture (complex spatial configuration of the root system) encompasses geometric deployment of individual root axes, appearance of daughter (lateral) roots along root axes, direction of root axis elongation, senescence of root axes, and plasticity response of these processes to environmental stresses.

Morphological and physiological plasticities result from genotype × environment interaction-enhanced changes in plant root systems. Plants need these plasticity responses for survival in diverse and stressful soil environments. Significant genotype × environment interactions for field-grown root traits offer the potential for a broad genetic base that could be exploited in stress tolerance breeding programs. The interaction component creates problems in identifying genetically controlled spatial and temporal variability in rhizosphere factors, but AMMI (additive main effects and multiplicative interaction) statistics can be used to analyze root plasticity and characterize physiological, morphological, and genetic components. Soil chemical factors that limit root growth are well documented. Roots respond to nutrient excesses and deficiencies both physiologically and morphologically.

Aluminum rhizotoxicity has received extensive research coverage. In addition, water-deficient physiologically stressed effects on root extension, molecular and biochemical analyses of root-expressed genes involved in morphological characterization of root development, soil physical impedance, and P response plasticity (ability to sense and respond to localized changes in P availability, i.e., acquisition efficiency) have been investigated. Rhizosphere microsite monitoring using such techniques as the agar dye indicator method to determine genotypic capability for induction of root zone pH changes, microelectrode method to quantify the spatial variation of specific root developmental zones, maximum root growth monitoring in sequential experiments via direct measurements of individual root elongation, and root volume seasonal cycling are being used in stress response research programs. Seedling phenological root screening can be used to eliminate less vigorous plants in a population prior to field assessment.

Adventitious root growth can improve persistence of perennial legume species and divergent phenotypic selection can be used to improve crown growth and adventitious root volume. The mechanistic causes for Al rhizotoxicity and intraspecies tolerance differences have not been definitively determined. Even though tolerance may be governed by possible rhizo-exclusion mechanisms, whether apoplastic or symplastic compartmentation or actual cellular/ cytoplasmic exclusion is involved, has not been resolved. Dose-dependent root elongation response studies to characterize differential genotypic sensitivity have indicated the following temporal response to Al challenge: induction ’! 4-hour lag period post-exposure before elongation rates are depressed ’! 12-hour inhibition phase ’! acclimation or nonacclimation (sensitive types) period '! acclimation magnitude plateauing or attainment of a certain level of recovery. The magnitude of Al stress may be acute or chronic, while intraspecific differences to Al tolerance may be constitutive (shock–recovery) or inducible (expression of specific genes) responses.

TOLERANCE ENHANCEMENT AND GENE DEPLOYMENT

Quantative trait loci (QTLs) controlling Al tolerance in diploid alfalfa have been identified using restriction fragment length polymorphisms (RFLPs) (Sledge et al., 1996). Putative inward-rectifying K-channel protein genes KAT1 and AKT1 have been isolated, cloned from Arabadopsis, and homologous sequences determined. Specific environmentally stress-induced shock proteins that govern adaptation to different ecogeographic conditions have been isolated and cloned. A major QTL (RZ318) associated with root penetration ability into compacted soils has been located on chromosome 2 of rice, indicating marker-assisted selection for complex root traits is possible. A recombinational linkage map for Al toxicity tolerance has been developed in slash pine (Pinus elliotti var. ellioti). Five Al-inducible genes have been isolated and characterized in wheat: wali 1 '! 5.

Two additional genes (wali 6 and 7) have been characterized and complete nucleotide sequences determined. The nucleotide sequence of a protein associated with Al toxicity in wheat roots is also available.

The utility of mapping functionally related abiotic stress-responsive genes in a common linkage map for determination of relationships among clones of other genes has been proposed for wheat. Genetic analysis techniques will be essential for locating quantitatively controlled stress tolerance genes and for eventually enhancing the selection efficiency of desirable genotypes within segregating populations.

Hopefully, additional biotechnology-oriented research will help us to formulate a clearer picture for the genetic control of the overall acid soil stress tolerance complex. Ancestral evolution of stress-related genes from wild relatives and other sources can be tracked and cloned, and the genome co-regulation can be studied. Comparative mapping technology will help in elucidating stress tolerance genes and hopefully lead to their use in marker-assisted selection programs. Transformation of these stress tolerance genes and their functional implementation to the point of enhanced productivity of crop plants in stress environments is the ultimate goal.

CONCLUSIONS

Plant tolerance to acid soil stress involves multiple elemental toxicity and deficiency traits, multiple genes and stress responses, as well as root growth parameters. Breeding programs must encompass multiple breeding methodology and selection strategies on actual field-stressed sites to be effective. Escalation of breeding programs will come through effective biotechnology tools, such as gene isolation, comparative mapping, and transgenesis. However, traditional breeding methods will continue to drive the enhancement of abiotic stress tolerance in plants in the future.

2

Drought Resistance of Plants

INTRODUCTION

Water availability is limited in many parts of the world. Drought restricts plant growth and crop production more than any other single environmental factor. Drought stress affects nearly every aspect of plant growth and most physiological processes. The numerous functions of roots, including water and nutrient uptake, synthesis and translocation of hormones, and respiration processes are sensitive to drought stress. Roots are critical for plant survival in dry environments. Because of their direct contact with drying soil, roots may mediate drought resistance through various major physiological processes.

For example, water uptake is one of the primary functions of roots, which facilitates maintenance of the plant's internal water status; roots synthesize hormones such as abscisic acid (ABA), which may act as a chemical messenger relaying stress signals from roots to shoots. Reduction in water loss through the transpirational process can be accomplished by stomatal closure, which is at least partially controlled by chemical signaling sensed by roots in the drying soil. In spite of their importance in whole plant responses to environmental stresses, roots have received much less attention than aboveground parts because soil limits their accessibility. Root responses to drought have been reviewed by several authors during the past two decades. This chapter focuses on discussion of root traits that confer drought tolerance and the importance of root growth and functioning in whole-plant resistance to drought.

WATER UPTAKE IN RELATION TO DROUGHT RESISTANCE

Water uptake from the soil is a crucial function of a root system and largely determines the water status of the shoot. Therefore, effective water uptake is an important determinant of drought resistance. Water uptake capacity depends on root morphological characteristics (e.g., root length density and root distribution) and physiological properties (e.g., viability, osmotic adjustment, and hydraulic conductivity).

Root Morphological Characteristics

Root Length Density

Drought-resistant plants generally are characterized as having extensive, wellbranched, deep root systems. The extensiveness of a root system can be quantified by root length density (RLD), which is defined as root length per unit soil volume (cm root cm"3 soil). Monocotyledonous crop plants in general have greater RLDs than dicotyledonous crops. For example, Allamaras et al. compared RLDs of maize (Zea mays) and soybean (Glycine max) and found that RLDs in the upper 1.3 m of soil averaged 0.22 cm cm"3 for maize and only 0.08 cm cm"3 for soybean. Taylor and Klepper found that RLDs of maize ranged from 3.7 to 6.2 cm cm"3 in a 1.8-m profile, whereas RLDs of cotton (Gossypium hirsutum) ranged from 1.1 to 1.8 cm cm"3 . The RLD also varies with species within either the monocot or dicot group. Carrow found that zoysiagrass (Zoysia japonica Steud.) produced few roots and had lower root length density than tall fescue (Festuca arundinaceae Schreb.) at soil depths below 20 cm. Root length density is generally at a maximum in the surface soil layers. Gerwitz and Page found that root dry weight density decreased exponentially with depth in 71 of 101 case histories. Soil drying can affect this density–depth pattern. Smucker et al. reported that root density declined in the surface drying soil because many roots in the top 20 cm of the soil profile died, whereas many roots began to branch profusely at successively greater depths. Water uptake rate of root systems generally is considered to be proportional to RLD.

Using this assumption, Taylor and Klepper and Herkelrath et al. found that they could satisfactorily distribute water uptake of a root system among various soil layers. However, the relationship of total RLD to water uptake may not hold in some cases, depending largely on plant species, soil water availability, and soil depths. Mason et al. reported that sunflower (Helianthus annuus) extracted as much water from irrigated clay loam as maize and sorghum (Sorghum bicolor), despite having only half the total RLD of the cereals. Many studies have indicated that water uptake is positively correlated with RLD when soil is moist but not well correlated when soil is dry, especially when water is available only deeper in the soil profile. Under soil drying conditions, water uptake correlates better with rooting depth than with RLD.

Hamblin and Tennant suggested that a rapid rate of root elongation and maximum root depth would be better parameters for the selection of drought resistance than RLD when water is limited in the soil. Greater RLD at depth is highly correlated with water uptake and with drought resistance. Plants with greater RLD in deep soil layers are better able to maintain water status and stomatal conductance during soil drying than those with lower RLD. For example, tall fescue cultivars with a greater RLD at a depth of 60 cm are less prone to leaf wilting during drought periods than those with lower RLD. Greater RLD at a deeper soil profile facilitates the maintenance of higher leaf water potential for a longer period during drought for a drought-resistant hybrid of maize than for a drought-sensitive one.

Root Distribution

Deep rooting has been considered an important trait of drought resistance in various species and has been used in drought-resistance breeding programs. Lehman and Engleke reported the deep-rooting characteristic of creeping bentgrass (Agrostis palustris Huds.) to be heritable, suggesting that drought resistance could be improved through breeding programs based on rooting depth. Marcum et al. reported that drought resistance in zoysiagrass has been associated with rooting depth, weight, and branching deep in the soil profile. Differential ability to avoid drought stress among bermudagrass (Cynodon dactylon) genotypes is the result of different abilities to distribute roots downward in the soil profile. Buffalograss [Buchloe dactyloides (Nutt.) Engelm.] is more tolerant to surface soil drying than zoysiagrass, mainly because of its deep root system.

Qian et al. also reported that the deep-rooted buffalograss exhibited superior drought resistance compared to the shallow-rooted zoysiagrass, when the entire soil profile was subjected to drought stress. Development of a deep root system could be related to a faster elongation rate of roots under drying conditions. Selecting cultivars or species for faster extension rates might delay onset of moderate water stress, because this would allow more time for roots to increase at depths where water remains available. Deep rooting increases water uptake from deeper soil profiles. For example, water extraction rates in the deeper soil profile were greater for the deep-rooted buffalograss than the shallowed-rooted zoysiagrass when the soil was dried gradually from the surface.

Water uptake pattern was closely related to root distribution pattern. Gallardo et al. similarly reported that wild lettuce (Lactuca serriola), with a deep root system, extracted more soil water from deeper profiles than cultivated lettuce (L. sativa), with a shallow root system, when the upper soil was drying. However, when limited soil water is stored in deeper soil profiles, faster root extension into deeper soil profiles may be detrimental for plants because of rapid depletion of water. In contrast, water will be conserved if the plant has a sparse and poorly permeable root system with a slow rate of extension. Deep roots not only enhance water utilization in deeper soil profiles but also appear to act as a water transport system and can deliver water absorbed from deep in the soil profile to the surface dry soil at night (hydraulic lift). In an experiment involving two perennial grasses, the nighttime increases in water content in the surface dry soil were more pronounced for the deep-rooted buffalograss than for the shallow-rooted zoysiagrass.

Hydraulic lift in buffalograss improved surface soil water status and nitrogen uptake from the dry surface soil. The deep root system of drought-resistant plants commonly is formed by reallocation of root growth to the deeper soil during drought. The ability of plants to avoid water stress by rapid reallocation of root growth into deeper moist zones under heterogeneous soil moisture conditions is defined as root plasticity. Drought-resistant plant species are better able to reallocate root growth during soil drying. Root growth below 40 cm of wet soil is enhanced significantly with surface soil drying for two turfgrass species differing in drought resistance. However, greater root length in the deeper moist soil layers is observed for drought-resistant seashore paspalum (Paspalum vaginatum Swartz) than for the drought-sensitive zoysiagrass.

Root Hair Development

As soil dries, root hairs have been found to increase in length and number per unit root length in tall fescue and other species. The promotive effect of drying on root hair development is unclear. Homes reported that ABA, which accumulates in drying soil, applied at high concentration increased root hair growth in maize. Increases in root hairs in dry soil have a pronounced effect on total root surface area. This response may be an adaptative mechanism to maintain liquid continuity around the growing roots and to provide greater root surface for nutrient absorption, because the rate of nutrient diffusion to the root decreases in drier soil. Green and Beard found significant differences in root hair development among seven turfgrass species under nonlimiting soil moisture. However, cultivar difference in root hair development is not detected in tall fescue in drying soil. Root hairs can be sites for extensive mucilage production. Mucilage can enhance the ability of the hair to attach to soil particles and thereby prevent air gaps from developing between the soil and root surface when the soil dries, reduce water efflux from plants into drying soils, and ultimately delay root desiccation. Extensive development of root hairs could enhance water uptake and facilitate water retention under soil-drying conditions.

Root Physiological Adaptation

Root Osmotic Adjustment

Most plants adapt to water stress by either avoiding or tolerating cellular dehydration. One of the major ways of tolerating cellular dehydration is by accumulating organic and inorganic solutes, which lowers the osmotic potential of the cell to maintain cell turgor at low water potential (osmotic adjustment). Osmotic adjustment of leaves helps to maintain leaf turgor and thereby stomatal conductance and photosynthesis and is positively correlated with drought tolerance. Roots of many plant species have a substantial capacity for osmotic adjustment in drying soil. Osmotic adjustment helps roots to maintain turgor and longitudinal growth in drying soil. Turgor maintenance in roots by osmotic adjustment may be more effective in sustaining growth than is the comparable process in leaves.

Osmotic adjustment also facilitates water extraction from the drying soil. Osmotic adjustment capacity and turgor maintenance of roots vary with plant species differing in drought resistance. Roots of relatively drought-resistant cocksfoot (Dactylis glømerata) maintain higher turgor than those of susceptible perennial ryegrass (Lolium perenne) under drying conditions. Parker and Pallardy reported that black walnut (Juglans nigra) seedlings from Ontario, Canada, exhibited osmotic adjustment in roots, whereas some seedlings from New York showed no detectable osmotic adjustment.

Oosterhuis and Wullschleger found that cotton and sorghum exhibited the largest osmotic adjustment in roots; sunflower (Helianthus annuus) exhibited a moderate ability to adjust; wheat (Triticum aestivum) had very little adjustment; and soybean had none. Tschaplinski and Tuskan examined osmotic adjustment in several clones of eastern cottonwood (Populus fremontia) and found only one that displayed osmotic adjustment in roots.

Root Viability

Drought stress often is suggested as the primary cause of root death, especially in the surface soil. Death of roots in surface drying soils would prevent root penetration into a deep soil profile where water might be available and, thus, reduce water uptake capacity. The successful penetration of even a few main root axes through dry upper soil layers could be of considerable advantage for the establishment of an adequate root system. Sustained growth of roots in drying soil is of obvious importance for seedling establishment because of the vulnerability of surface soil to drying. In addition, surviving roots play an important role in rapid water uptake in the period immediately after dry soil is rewetted with water. Therefore, maintaining viable roots during drought would be beneficial for water uptake during and after drought periods, especially in habitats where drought stress is a temporary phenomenon and water often is supplied through irrigation. Root persistence of perennial grasses is a characteristic that greatly enhances their adaptation to semiarid and arid climates. However, many native species adapted to prolonged drought in desert climates shed fine lateral roots while maintaining main roots when the soil is dry and then produce fine roots rapidly following light rainfall.

In tall-grass prairie sites dominated by big bluestem (Andropogon gerardii), Hayes and Seastedt examined root production and death during a 58-day drought with only 28 mm of precipitation. They found extensive root mortality, especially in the top 10 cm, within the first 2 weeks of drought. Using a minirhizotron system, Smucker et al. found considerable death of maize roots in the top 20 cm of the soil profile after 21 days of drought. In a rhizotron study, Klepper et al. found that cotton root length declined by more than 50% in the 15-cm soil depth after exposure to dry soil for 21 days. Considerable death of fine roots under drought also occurs in many other species, including soybean, Agave deserti, and turfgrasses. Imposition of drought on the entire root system increased root cortical cell death and increased root shedding. Some species however, exhibit much more tolerance of dry soils. Some roots have been known to survive and even grow in soil at water potentials well below the conventional wilting point ("1.5 MPa). In citrus, few roots die even after more than 60 days of drought.

Root length densities of maize and wheat did not diminish after the plants had been growing in drying soil for weeks. The great variation in root viability among species reported in the literature suggests the possibility of widespread genetic variability in root mortality in response to drought stress. Variable patterns of root viability in response to dry surface soils have been observed in several turfgrass species differing in drought resistance. For example, when roots in the top 40 cm of soil were exposed to drought for 26 days while the lower 20 cm of soil was maintained at field capacity in a greenhouse, root death in the surface 20-cm layer was about 80% for relatively droughtsensitive "Emerald" zoysiagrass but only 30% for the relatively drought-tolerant PI509018 paspalum and "Tifblair" centipedegrass.

Root viability or persistence is an important trait in drought resistance under these experimental conditions. Apparently the presence of root mass or length does not necessarily correlate with physiological health or viability, although most studies attribute differences in water uptake to total root length as discussed above. Many factors can influence root survival in drying soil. Osmotic adjustment can sustain root growth in drying soil as discussed above. Root mortality could also be related to the fineness of roots or specific root length (SRL). Thinner roots tend to have shorter life spans than thicker roots. Limited comparisons of cold desert shrubs and tundra species indicated that small-diameter roots often die sooner than coarse roots.

Huang et al. reported that root fineness or SRL varied among turfgrass species; zoysiagrass with greater SRL had greater root mortality than the other grasses with smaller SRL. Drought induces production of finer roots, which may contribute to more root death, because finer roots could be more susceptible to desiccation in dry soil.

Zhang and Davies suggested that stress-induced fine root branches are less effective at maintaining turgor during soil drying. North and Nobel reported more extensive decomposition of cortical tissue in fine laterals than in the nodal roots in desert succulents. Because less carbohydrate is required to develop and maintain the finest roots and because smaller roots of annual plants or perennial grass species lack the secondary thickening essential for tolerating water stress, the finest roots probably are the most vulnerable to soil desiccation.

Root viability in drying soil may also be influenced by the succulence of the roots or tissue density. Note that variation in SRL may be caused by variation in root diameter, tissue density, or both. Ryser contrasted perennial grass species that were adapted to either infertile sites or fertile sites. Grasses adapted to infertile sites tended to be slower growing and have roots with higher tissue densities than those adapted to more fertile sites. In a common garden experiment, Ryser found that tissue density was correlated with root longevity after two growing seasons. Species that produced roots of lower tissue density tended to be faster growing than species that produced roots of high tissue density, but their roots had a shorter life span.

Thus, an important tradeoff may exist between having a highly plastic root system that grows rapidly in moist regions of the soil and one that can readily tolerate the low soil water potentials in dry regions of the soil. Suberization has been shown to enhance plant tolerance to drought by reducing water loss from plant roots. Suberization of the cortex occurs sooner in dry than in wet soils. An increase of suberization in dry soils may represent one mechanism for surviving drought.

Unsuberized roots disappear quickly under unfavorable soil conditions, whereas large, suberized roots are more resistant to decay. Ares found that 30 to 50% of young unsuberized roots of buffalograss died within a few weeks of elongation during initial spring growth. In many grasses that lack a suberized hypodermis, most of the cortex readily dies when exposed to a short period of drought. In species with a suberized hypodermis such as maize, the cells often die back radially beginning with the epidermis and continuing centripetally, with the outer cortical cells dying first.

Marshall found only low (and insignificant) root mortality in Douglas fir [(Pseudotsuga menziesii (Mirb.) Franco] caused by drought alone, but when drought was coupled with shading the shoot, 30 to 40% of the roots died. He suggested that starch and sugar depletions (carbohydrate imbalance) were the primary causes of root death in dry soil. A reduction of about 80% in carbon allocation to surface fine roots of citrus trees has been observed when roots are exposed to localized soil drying. However, Hallgren et al. found that drought had no effect on carbohydrate depletion related to root mortality in loblolly pine (Pinus taeda) seedlings. Root death can also increase following canopy loss in woody species.

However, rapid root shedding following defoliation is less evident in grasses. Root death during drought could be due to direct cellular desiccation, especially for grass species without a suberized hypodermis. Although dehydration tolerance involves many different aspects, cell membrane stability may be a basic requirement for the maintenance of physiological functions in plants and can be influenced by both cell water potential and carbohydrate status. Stress-induced loss of cell membrane integrity is associated with an efflux of solutes including electrolytes. Electrolyte leakage from cells or tissues during water stress can be used as a measure of dehydration tolerance. Huang et al. observed dramatic electrolyte leakage from grass roots grown in the surface 20 cm of drying soil, although the deeper soil layers were moist. Roots of drought-resistant centipedegrass and seashore paspalum had much less electrolyte leakage under water stress than did those of other relatively droughtsensitive grasses.

Root Hydraulic Conductivity

Hydraulic conductivity (Lp) is a coefficient relating the driving force, usually a drop in water potential or in hydrostatic pressure, to water flow, such as the volume of water crossing a root's surface area per unit time. Root Lp can represent two-thirds of the limitations on water movement within a plant. Thus, it can have a major influence on leaf water status and, in turn, on plant growth in both moist and dry soil. Root Lp varies with plant species, ranging from 0.1 to 70 × 10"8 m s"1 "1 when measured by applying a hydrostatic pressure gradient to the roots MPa and from 0.5 to 8 × 10"8 m s"1 MPa"1 when measured using osmotic pressure gradients. Hydraulic conductivity also varies with root age even within a species.

It decreases with root age in many species. It changes in different patterns with positions along the root axis and with root ages between monocot and dicot species. For example, for a monocot species, Agave deserti, Lp decreases with root age in both lateral roots and main roots. Along an individual lateral root, it decreases basipetally. The reduction in Lp with root age or distance from the root tip is due to the increase in the number of suberized hypodermal and endodermal cells, which have low permeability to water, especially under dry conditions. For two dicot species, Ferocactus acanthodes and Opuntia ficus-indica, Lp of main roots increased with root age, reaching maxima of 3.9 × 10"7 m s"1 MPa"1 for F. acanthodes and 5.2 × 10"7 m s"1 MPa"1 for O. ficus-indica, and then declined with increasing age for both species.

Along an individual lateral root for both F. acanthodes and O. ficus-indica, Lp increases with distance from the root tip. Differences in root Lp among species could result in differences in water transport to shoots that could influence plant growth and physiological responses during drought stress. Hydraulic conductivity of an entire root system correlated positively with the vegetative growth rate of citrus. Relatively vigorous rootstocks tend to have higher root Lp , stomatal conductance, and transpiration rate than the less vigorous rootstocks.

Root Lp generally decreases as soil moisture availability decreases and has been observed in many species, including A. deserti, F. acanthodes, O. ficusindica, rough lemon (Citrus aurantium), soybean, and cotton. The reduction of Lp is attributed to the suberization of endodermis, hypodermal, and peridermal cells, formation of air lacunae in the cortical tissue; and embolism of xylem vessels. Suberin deposition in the cell walls of the endodermis and hypodermis reduces water permeability, and formation of air lacunae interrupts radial water flow from the root surface to xylem vessels and, thus, limits radial hydraulic conductivity.

Xylem embolism or cavitation restricts water movement in the vessels, reducing axial hydraulic conductance. The decreases in Lp in desert succulents during prolonged periods of soil drying have been found to limit water flow from plants into the drying soil, because roots and shoots of these species can have a higher water potential than the soil for prolonged periods. For other species grown under temporary drought conditions, the decline in Lp may limit water acquisition. Variations in root Lp between species or cultivars that differ in drought resistance have rarely been examined. Syvertsen compared Lp of entire roots systems of four citrus rootstocks and concluded that variations in drought resistance between rootstocks could be explained at least partially by the differences in the Lp of the root system.

Rough lemon, a relatively drought-tolerant rootstock, had a root system with a higher hydraulic conductivity than that of sour orange (Citrus aurantium), a less-drought-tolerant rootstock. So and Jayasekara found that when the surface soil was drying while the lower soil profile was moist, Lp was higher in roots of a drought-tolerant sorghum hybrid than in those of a drought-sensitive one, which contributed to the greater ability of the tolerant hybrid to extract water from the deeper soil horizons. Saliendra and Meinzer also reported that the drought resistance of sugarcane (Saccharum officinarum) genotypes was related positively to root system hydraulic conductance. In contrast to the preceding reports, Rieger and Duemmel found no difference in root Lp of several Prunus species from divergent habitats and suggested a lack of importance of this trait for drought resistance.

The discrepancy in correlations of root Lp with drought resistance may be due to variations in drought severity, duration, and container size in different studies. In an environment where drought is temporary or soil water is often supplied by irrigation, high root Lp may be advantageous for rapid water uptake and plant growth in dry soils. Competition for water is most effective with an extensive, highly conductive root system. In a drought-prone environment where crops rely heavily on water stored deep in the soil profile, Passioura and Fischer have suggested, plants must use water sparingly during their vegetative growth, so that sufficient water is left in the soil at anthesis to enable them to fill grain. Richards and Passioura suggested that low Lp in wheat root systems could reduce early water use by plants growing on limited stored soil water and, thus, could sustain plant growth through prolonged periods of drought.

CHEMICAL SIGNALS FROM ROOTS IN RELATION TO DROUGHT RESISTANCE

As discussed earlier, root morphological and physiological characteristics play important roles in water uptake and supply to shoots. Limited water uptake capacity of roots can restrict stomatal conductance and shoot growth. However, roots affect shoot growth and plant responses to stressful environments in other ways. Gollan et al. reported that when roots of wheat and sunflower plants were placed inside a pressure chamber and pressurized to maintain leaf turgor as the soil dried, the stomatal conductance decreased whether or not leaf water content and leaf turgor were maintained. Similarly, in other studies, leaf elongation has been shown to decrease as the soil dries, even when leaves were maintained in a fully hydrated state by increasing the pressure applied on the roots. Many split-root studies indicate that stomatal conductance and leaf growth rates are reduced even though leaf water potential and turgor of the half-watered plants are no lower than those of well-watered plants. These studies suggest that roots influence shoot water relations and growth not only by supplying water, but also by providing a feed-forward signal to the shoots. Abscisic acid (ABA) in roots has been found to be the chemical messenger that mediates plant responses to drought. Stomatal closure can be induced by increases in leaf epidermal ABA content. There is evidence that this ABA originates in the roots in drying soil. Roots have the capacity to synthesize ABA.

Water-stressed roots accumulate ABA more quickly and with greater sensitivity than leaves. Various studies have showed that soil drying stimulates a substantial accumulation of ABA in roots, and that ABA synthesized in root tips in response to soil drying can move through the transpiration stream to the leaves, where it induces stomatal closure. Roots seem to be able to "measure" the degree of soil drying and send a chemical message to the leaves where stomatal conductance and transpiration are reduced. Not all the ABA in the xylem is necessarily produced in the root, because ABA is also produced in shoots.

However, production in shoots does not preclude the roots of plants in drying soil from acting as the primary sensors of soil water content and ABA acting as the primary root-to-shoot messenger. Also, ABA may not be the only hormone sending messages from roots to shoots, but it may be the major hormone detecting soil water deficit and providing the signal of drying soil conditions. The cytokinin supply from the roots is also reduced by soil drying, which may also act as a chemical signal. In spite of great interest in the role of ABA in whole-plant drought tolerance and its application to crop production, the direct involvement of ABA in plant responses to drought stress is still unclear. Because ABA induces stomatal closure, the natural assumption is that high ABA accumulation would save water and, therefore, improve drought resistance.

Work with maize and sorghum showed that drought-resistant genotypes tended to accumulate more ABA in wilted leaves than less-resistant genotypes; consequently, high ABA accumulation was a marker for drought resistance. However, the classification of the different genotypes for their relative drought resistance or the mechanisms involved are not well substantiated. Innes et al. invested much effort in isolating high and low ABA-accumulating lines of wheat. When lines are grown under mild drought stress, a yield advantage is claimed for the high ABA lines over the low ABA lines. However, this advantage is not significant statistically, nor does it occur in all experiments. Research with sorghum revealed that drought-resistant genotypes (in terms of the least reduction in grain yield under drought stress) tended to accumulate less ABA in wilting leaves than droughtsusceptible ones.

Lu et al. approached the issue of osmotic stress effects on the yield of wheat by screening for ABA-insensitive clones under osmotic stress. They found that the ABA-insensitive clones had better growth, less leaf senescence, and higher yields under drought stress than did more ABAsensitive clones.

This study demonstrated that variation for ABA insensitivity in wheat is genetic and that it is somehow associated with sustained productivity under drought stress. Genetic variation for ABA insensitivity has also been found in maize, Arabidopsis thaliana, and barley. Root ABA accumulation leads to stomatal closure and water conservation in drying soil and, thus, may enhance drought tolerance. Accumulation of ABA in roots of maize enhances their growth in drying soil, which may also contribute to drought tolerance by sustaining water uptake in drying soil.

ROOT RESPIRATION IN RELATION TO DROUGHT RESISTANCE

An extensive, well-branched root system is important for water acquisition during drought stress. However, the amount of carbon required in forming and maintaining such a root system can be substantial.

Major carbon costs of roots are associated with respiration, tissue construction, and carbon allocation. Carbon costs associated with different resource capture strategies are of fundamental importance for plant growth and survival. For plants adapted to limited water availability, survival during drought requires a considerable investment of carbon below ground. Nicholas et al. found that biomass allocation to roots was unchanged during drought stress in a drought-intolerant genotype of wheat and increased in a drought-tolerant genotype. Increasing carbon partitioned to roots in dry soils has also been observed in dryland wheat. Therefore, efficient carbon expenditure in roots may play an important role in coping with drought stress.

Respiration costs are substantial and can account for approximately 25% of the current photosynthates, 30 to 65% of the carbon partitioned to the root system, and up to 13.5% of the root weight of ryegrass (Lolium multiflorum). This percentage increases as the growth rate of plants decreases because either the species has an inherently low growth potential or it is growth restricted by stressful environmental conditions. Although the energy and catabolic intermediates produced by respiration are essential for the basic functions of the plant root system, minimizing respiration probably would increase and prolong root survival during extended drought.

Results of studies on the response of root respiration to water stress vary. Dhopte and Ramteke and Dhopte et al. reported increased root respiration under water stress, especially for drought-sensitive genotypes.

However, a rapid decrease in root respiration with soil drying has been observed by many researchers, but the extent of reduction varies with species and cultivars. Nicolas et al. reported that root respiration rates decreased in both drought-tolerant and drought-sensitive wheat genotypes during drought, but respiration became more energy efficient, particularly for the drought-tolerant genotype, because less root respiration took place via the alternative respiratory pathway.

Responses of root respiration to drought stress vary with species that differ in drought tolerance. Nicolas et al. found that a drought-tolerant wheat genotype exhibited lower root respiration than a sensitive one under drought stress, which contributed to more sugar accumulation in shoots and roots of the tolerant genotype.

Dhopte and Ramteke similarly reported lower root respiration rate in a drought-tolerant peanut (Arachis hypogaea) genotype than in a sensitive one during drought. However, Rice and Eastin found that a drought-tolerant sorghum hybrid had higher root respiration rates than a sensitive one under drought stress. Eissenstat and associates have examined the relationship of root survivorship in drying soil to root construction and maintenance respiration in citrus rootstocks and have suggested that a reduction in root respiration could be related to root survival and could contribute to drought tolerance.

In a study using rootstock seedlings selected for their wide range of specific root length (14–32 m g"1), seedlings exposed to dry surface soil for 84 days exhibited less than 3% root mortality. Using 14 C, they showed that carbon imported to the roots was reduced by approximately 80% during the drought period with little difference among rootstocks.

Further research comparing respiration and survivorship of the fine roots of mature trees with those of seedlings confirmed the large reduction in root respiration and low mortality of surface roots in dry soil. During exposure to dry soil, surface roots of citrus are essentially unable to provide appreciable benefit in terms of nutrient uptake but can greatly diminish carbon expenditures by reducing respiration and carbon allocation.

SUMMARY

Roots play important roles in plant adaptation to drought stress. Water uptake and movement to the shoots are primary functions of roots and are essential for the maintenance of shoot water status and plant survival during drought stress. Many root characteristics help to prolong water uptake. Root hair development and osmotic adjustment may help reduce root dessication and facilitate water uptake and survival of roots in drying soils.

Root length density and hydraulic conductivity are related closely to water uptake capacity when soil moisture is available. Under drought stress conditions, especially when soil moisture is distributed unevenly in the soil profile, root distribution and viability may be critical factors controlling water uptake. However, the relationship of root hydraulic conductivity and root viability to drought tolerance warrants further investigation. Roots also affect shoot growth and responses to stressful environments in other ways. Abscisic acid produced in roots serves as a chemical messenger that signals soil drying to shoots, promotes stomatal closure, and, thereby, enhances water conservation.

Although respiration is essential for producing energy and catabolic intermediate products, maintaining low respiratory costs may increase the possibility of plant survival during prolonged periods of drought. Further research is needed to examine interspecific and intraspecific variations in ABA synthesis and accumulation and respiration of roots with respect to drought tolerance. Such information is useful for improving drought resistance of plants using biotechnology or traditional breeding programs.

3

Mineral Nutrition

INTRODUCTION

Plant mineral nutrition is certainly one of the major environmental factors to which plants respond. The supply and absorption of mineral elements and their metabolism are affected by soil and climatic conditions that are specific to the locale of the plant and change dynamically during the growing period. This chapter discusses plant response to the supply of inorganic nutrients in all ranges from deficiency to toxicity. Those considered are nitrogen (N), phosphorus (P), potassium (K), calcium (Ca), magnesium (Mg), copper (Cu), iron (Fe), zinc (Zn), boron (B), and molybdenum (Mo), in that order. New to this second edition is nitrogen (N). The chapter reviews plant mineral responses to deficiencies and toxicities.

Each element is introduced giving general information from two reviews, followed by more recent literature. Subheadings under each element include uptake and translocation, physiology, and interactions. Emphasis is placed on the research topics of most interest during the past decade. These include vesicular-arbuscular mycorrhizae (VAM) research in relation to P nutrition, Ca amelioration of Al toxicity, effects of increases in the CO_2 pressure in the atmosphere, and physiderophore (SID) effects on Fe and other micronutrients. Because of the recent concern over environmental issues, more plant nutritionists are turning away from deficiency research to study effects of toxicity. Finally, a recent trend is to study varietal differences with respect to ion uptake and utilization mechanisms.

NITROGEN

Uptake and Translocation Plants show dramatic response to N amendments, since N is a major building block of amino acids and proteins. Plants are 2 to 5% N by dry weight. Nitrogen is taken up both as nitrate and ammonium, and both are metabolized, although more nitrate is taken up at a low soil pH and ammonium is taken up at neutral pH values. Nitrate uptake is active, but it is unknown whether ammonium is taken up actively or not.

The N deficiency threshold in cotton was found to vary according to plant age from a high of 5.2% N at the first pinhead square to 3.3% N at cutout. Some 80% of applied foliar urea was absorbed by cotton leaves on 20-day-old leaves, and this dropped to 38% for 60-day-old leaves, with more N being translocated to the boll at the later times. Nitrogen uptake is affected by many environmental stress factors including day/night cycle, drought, and waterlogging. Nitrogen uptake in soybeans decreased 30 to 50% 2 to 6 hr after the lights were turned off due to inhibition of NO_3 influx, which is under feedback control. In prairie grasses, N is translocated from the leaf to rhizomes and roots during drought, with %N in the leaves varying according to drought tolerance of the species.

Waterlogging also leads to N deficiency in corn due to denitrification and leaching of the fertilizer N and to decreased absorption and translocation of N and protein synthesis. Low availability of ammonium N to soybeans led to lower nodules per gram of root DW, but the plants were able to compensate and produce more total plant nodules, which increased plant growth. A new area of inquiry in N mineral plant nutrition has been the effect of atmospheric NO_2 on plant N.

The contribution of total N in barley from NO_2 polluted air was 5 to 6%, with an additional 3 to 5% coming from other gaseous sources. Free amino acids as mostly asparagine and glutamine increased in wheat exposed to NO_2.

The uptake of N from NO_2 was found to be higher in soybeans that were supplied with nitrate than those supplied with ammonium. The decrease in ammonium-N uptake was attributed to a decline in proton concentration resulting from the reduction of nitrate and nitrite from NO_2 absorption. In spring wheat, it was found that the energy required to metabolize the N from NO_2 to protein resulted in a lower proportion of carbohydrate and a higher amount of protein in the grain.

Physiology

Nitrogen supply to cereals affects not only N uptake but also nitrate and nitrite reduction production. Nitrogenase activity in soybeans was regulated by both C and N levels, which occurs through sensing changes in plant N by way of phloem translocatable compounds. Leaf N in soybeans, along with shading, was found to be strongly associated with starch content of the leaf. Starch and sucrose were higher in N-deficient leaves of spinach and soybean than N-sufficient controls. This increase in starch and sucrose was accompanied by a decrease in soluble protein, chlorophyll, and anaplerotic metabolites (malate and phosphoenolpyruvate) in the leaflets, suggesting that the enzymes of the anaplerotic carbon metabolite pathway were lower under N deficiency.

Nitrogen uptake is regulated by various mechanisms. Ammonium uptake in wheat is suppresses by the amino acids asparagine and glutamine, although it is not known whether they are acting outside the plant or through an endogenous pool. Nitrate exercises a feedback mechanism in barley roots to control its own influx. Nitrate induces polypeptides, which are linked to nitrate transport across the tonoplast and plasma membrane to reduce nitrate uptake in corn. In N-deficient wheat chloroplasts, the chlorophyll content reached a maximum on day 7 in the first leaf and declined more rapidly than for N-sufficient plants. In wheat and maize plants, the respiratory oxygen consumption by roots was 1.4–

and 1.6-fold larger for ammonia-fed than for nitrate-fed plants, respectively.

Interactions

Nitrogen nutrition is affected by the availability of other inorganic nutrients. Nitrate influx was decreased by transient P deficiency for squash and barley. The movement of ureide and other N constituents in soybeans was impaired by a decrease in energy status and carbohydrate utilization brought on by a deficiency of P. Decrease in N transport under N deficiency limited protein synthesis and elevated amino acid contents in tobacco. The amino acid in excess was asparagine, because of feedback control and limited ATP availability. The decreased transport is caused by changes in membrane properties, which cause concomitant effects on upward flow of water in the plant.

Barley N content increased with increased S rate on an alkaline soil. For wheat, the addition of N rates increased the S utilization percentage. In soybean leaves, the loss of S with age was inversely related to the level of N nutrition. There is likely a common mechanism for the export of S and N from mature leaves, which is inhibited at high levels of N, even under S deficiency. Copper uptake is increased at higher N levels in cereals by the release of amines into the root apoplast and rhizosphere. Under Cu-sufficient conditions, these may mobilize Cu by formation of soluble Cu-amine complexes. The activity of nitrate and nitrite reductases showed no correlation with Cu concentrations except at the highest Cu levels in rice. The leaf capacity to reduce nitrate to ammonia may be limited by the capability of the chloroplast photochemical reactions to generate reducing power. Boron at sufficient levels produced the highest N fixation for soybeans; however, nodules from the basal portions of the primary roots contained sufficient B for N fixation even under B-deficient conditions.

A new area of research in the past decade has been the effect of increased CO_2 on plant growth. The addition of CO_2 increased N uptake but actually lowered N concentration in the shoots of wheat. Lower-leaf N resulted in decreased N translocation to the grain, which lowered grain quality. Also, the proportion of the plant N allocated to the uppermost leaves was reduced under high-CO_2 atmospheres. The N allocated to ribulose-1,5-bisphosphate carboxylase/oxygenase (Rubisco) was also reduced and placed into other soluble proteins. The reason for the C:N imbalance is that under CO_2 enrichment, the C concentration in the plants increases while the N concentration decreases. Some results show that elevated CO_2 did not interact with N supply or that it increased total biomass and grain yield of wheat under optimum N supply.

PHOSPHORUS

Uptake and Translocation

The levels of P in plant tissue are generally between 0.3 and 0.5% of the dry weight to be considered in the sufficiency range. Unlike N and S, which are in the reduced form in plants, P is found in oxidized form as inorganic orthophosphate and pyrophosphate. Phosphorus uptake is active, the concentration in the xylem sap being 100 to 1000 times that in the soil solution, and P is involved in many metabolic processes, especially energy transfers linked to adenosine triphosphate (ATP). In the past decade, the influence of VAM on P uptake and availability has been of considerable research interest. Critical level research continues, especially for cereals. The critical deficiency values for wheat grain were between 0.19 and 0.23% P; for 90% maximum grain yield, they were between 0.21 and 0.24% P. However, the lower critical value for the last fully expanded leaf in wheat was 2.8 mM (0.043%), which was determined to be the best plant part to sample.

At higher P availabilities, the efflux neutralizes higher P influx such that the nonlimiting P concentration is mainly controlled by efflux. Plants have been shown to change the rhizosphere to obtain P as a function of plant species, soil type, and soil management history. Rape secretes acid phosphatase and wheat secretes dehydrogenase. Rice roots may secrete protons, which would solubilize acid-soluble soil P. Following the same line, Saleque and Kirk found that P depletion near the root coincided with acidification, presumably from oxidation of Fe^{2+} by oxygen and protons released from the roots. Much current P research centers on VAM. Pigeon pea and wheat benefited from VAM colonization, which increased P uptake and plant weights. Although VAM did not increase leaf P concentration in barley, it did result in higher rates of photosynthesis associated with higher stomatal conductance and increased P-use efficiency. However, VAM infection did increase P uptake in barley but not in wheat or rye; in another study, it affected P-use efficiency negatively. For safflower and wheat, VAM did not alter hydraulic properties of the plant/soil system, causing no differences in leaf turgor during drought.

Even though translocation of elements to grain is a usual mechanism of reallocation, it was found that for soybeans, seed development may occur independently of P remobilization from the leaves. Under P deficiency, wheat plants allocate resources toward maintaining root growth by limiting or delaying shoot proliferation. The efficiency of P use in wheat was directly proportional to water availability, with no evidence that selections could be made for efficiency of water use. In another study, it was found that water stress in wheat had no effect on plant development and changed P allocation very little.

Physiology

Phosphorus is stored in soybean seeds as phytic acid, which accounts for 70% of the seed P. Starch in soybean is affected by P stress to the degree that the starch-N relationship may be useful in identifying plant P deficiency. However, neither P deficiency or high P availability markedly affected starch or sucrose metabolism in soybeans. Phosphorus deficiency caused increased starch in soybean leaves due to an increase in free amino acid-N in arginine and asparagine. Transport processes in barley concentrate P absorbed by root cells, keeping the P concentration in the xylem exudate constant.

Phosphorus deficiency lowers leaf photosynthetic rates and stomatal conductance, leading to lower leaf total soluble protein. Photosynthesis and stomatal conductance are reduced by P deficiency and, conversely, increases P increased photosynthesis. Quantum yield of CO_2 uptake was decreased under P deficiency, but increasing the CO_2 concentration restored yield. Elevated CO_2 concentrations increased phosphatase activity, which is a factor in increasing P mineralization of soil P. Phosphorus deficiency decreased either the amount or activity of Rubisco in wheat, maize, soybeans, and potatoes. A reduction of photosynthetic rate in sugar beets with P deficiency was attributed to decreased Rubisco regeneration rate rather than Rubisco activity.

Low P affected leaf orientation in soybeans, due to lower Rubisco-specific activity and content. Phosphorus deficiency in tobacco led to low levels of hexose phosphates and 3-phosphoglyceric acid (3-PGA) in shoots and roots, while sucrose synthase and protein content increased in roots. Phosphorus concentrations in leaves and stems of wheat were decreased due to waterlogging, but it increased P in roots. In rice, hypoxia decreased root growth; this was attributed to the capacity for oxygen transport to roots. Under P deficiency, root porosity increased for rice. For soybeans, the rate of O_2 uptake was only 35% of control values when P was deficient, but nodule nitrogenase-linked O_2 uptake was 210% that of the control plants. Phosphorus deficiency leads to lower nodule growth for soybeans and alfalfa and reduced acetylene activity and nitrogenase. For P-deficient soybeans, the oxidative phosphorylation in the plant cell fraction of nodules was decreased to a much greater extent than it was in the bacteriods; it was concluded that P deficiency decreased specific nitrogenase activity.

Interactions

Interactions of other nutrients, VAM, and toxic elements like Al continue to be subjects of research. High P supply to wheat interfered with Mn uptake and/or translocation. Increasing external Cu concentration caused lower P in shoots and roots of wheat.

Where Cu was at a toxic range for rice, plants with Fe plaque on the roots had lower P in the leaves than plants without Fe plaque. The lower P should increase active Fe in the leaves and increase heavy metal tolerance.

An interesting interaction takes place in corn in that higher N increases plant Zn concentration and decreases plant P concentration, thus improving the P:Zn ratio to a more optimal range. In wheat, the increase in P concentration in Zn-deficient plants was mediated through a shoot effect of Zn rather than a root effect. This same effect of higher P concentration with Zn deficiency is found in corn shoots, but in roots only the inorganic forms of P were increased while organic P forms were decreased. When P is added at high rates, it causes decreased shoot Zn, Cu, and Fe concentrations. Adding VAM to maize supplied with low levels of P and Zn increased dry matter (DM) yield about fourfold, whereas at sufficient P and Zn, it increased yield only about 1.5 times.

However, for wheat, Zn concentration and uptake were decreased by both P and VAM amendments. It was shown that VAM enhances translocation of Zn and P to grain from roots. Additions of VAM to pigeon pea increased both P and Zn concentration and the P/Zn ratio, resulting in improved growth. As for other elements, there has been considerable effort to study the effects of atmospheric CO_2 levels on P nutrition of plants. For wheat and rice, the uptake of P has been increased by increased concentrations of CO_2. Increasing CO_2 pressures for maize, sorghum, cotton, and wheat does not enhance growth and photosynthetic rates under P deficiency, possibly due to effects on the leaf sugar partitioning and transport systems. Grain yield of rice was increased up to 58% by additional CO_2 even with P deficiency, but leaf P was unaffected by CO_2 concentration.

Aluminum toxicity has been a very active research topic during the last decade, even though such research has slacked off in recent years. Phosphate combines chemically with Al to produce unavailable solid forms and, in solution, to decrease the amount of free trivalent

Al, the form toxic to plants. For example, phosphate ions ameliorated Al toxicity in wheat and sorghum in nutrient solution studies. Phosphorus promotes the rate of root growth into acid subsoils; low P availability, even at levels that will not result in P deficiency, can greatly reduce a plant's tolerance to acidic subsoils. In solution, Al actually enhances P uptake by binding to plasma membrane phospholipids, forming a positively charged layer that enhances the movement of anions to binding sites of transport protein.

POTASSIUM

Uptake and Translocation

Potassium is the element with the highest concentration in plants, making up about 80% of the total cationic content of the phloem. The rate of K absorption by the root increases in proportion to the K concentration in the soil up to a point. This rate is linked to the ATP content of the root cells, which supplies energy for transport into the cells in the form of ATP. Plants get much of their K supply from exchangeable soil K, but it has been shown that plants can exploit the nonexchangeable K pool. The ability to utilize nonexchangeable soil K varies by plant species; for example, wheat is more efficient than sugar beets because of the relative differences in root density. The uptake by wheat from nonexchangeable and mineral sources increases with increasing temperature but is not influenced by water potential (94). A major function of K in plants is to regulate osmotic potential. In unstressed plants, the main effect of K application is to increase leaf water content and slightly decrease its osmotic potential.

For wheat under K deficient conditions, water-soluble carbohydrates, Ca, and Mg were higher in the press sap, indicating that they were substituted for K in its role of osmotic regulation. Potassium substitution in soybeans is accomplished by cations, anions, sugars, and amino acids. As K is supplied to barley, the shoot tissue moisture content increases along with specific leaf area as a result of increased moisture content and cell size as well as number of mesophyll cells. Under moisture stress, the K concentration in the leaves of soybeans increases, supplied by the roots and stems, which act as K reservoirs, especially in developing xylem vessels. High temperatures decrease K influx to sorghum and barley roots. Rice species which take up more K had higher oxygen exudation under K stress than those taking up less K. Species of soybeans differed in their ability to take up K during grain filling. Full-season hybrids continued to take up K during seed filling, while double-crop hybrids depended more on K translocated from other plant tissues. B. Physiology Potassium influx is regulated by root membranes through various mechanisms. A group of polypeptides associated with K influx was identified; these were unaffected by either N or P deprivation.

Following K deprivation, these polypeptides were synthesized in increasing amounts and are thought to form a part of the high-affinity K transport system in barley roots. In wheat, K influx was mediated by hyperpolarization-activated K-selective ion channels in root hairs that are important in the low-affinity K uptake mechanism and act as regulators of membrane potential. C. Interactions Research on interactions for K has continued to be active in recent years. Leaf K increased with increased N supply in wheat. Also, the net K translocation in wheat was increased by increasing nitrate availability. With increasing K supply, N uptake increased in soybean, but nitrogenase activity was not affected. In barley, K acts as a counter ion that has a role in partitioning nitrate reduction between shoot and root. Potassium affects Fe indirectly through effects on protons and phytosiderphores. For strategy I plants, high K levels increase proton flux due to accumulation of organic acids.

In strategy II plants, higher K influences transport of the Fe-phytosiderophore complex and plays a role in the mugineic acid biosynthetic pathway. Increased availability of K helps to ameliorate the toxic effects of Fe-toxic soil, and it decreases the bicarbonate content in soils, which, in turn, will lower the immobilization of Fe in soybeans by bicarbonate. Added K has been shown to ameliorate both Zn deficiency in rice and Mn deficiency in wheat. Aluminum inhibits K influx by forming a positively charged layer by binding to plasma membrane phospholipids. Wheat uptake of K decreased in the presence of NaCl, as it did for barley. Adding Ca to barley greatly decreased the effect of NaCl on K uptake and translocation. For rice, K also helped to alleviate salt stress by improving the ratios of K:Na, K:Mg, and K:Ca. As mentioned above, a new area of inquiry is the effect of increased CO_2 pressure on plants. Doubling CO_2 pressure increased biomass and grain yield for wheat, except that with K deficiency, this effect was cut in half. Elevated CO_2 decreased K uptake in wheat due to the smaller volume of water reaching the root surface. The effect may be offset by increased root density and by greater soil moisture, which would increase diffusion.

CALCIUM

Uptake and Translocation

Calcium uptake is passive; thus the high amounts in plants are due to high amounts in the soil solution. The Ca sufficiency range for plants is between 0.1 and 5.5% of the dry weight. Calcium functions outside the cytoplasm in the apoplast, where it stabilizes the cell wall. Calcium is used more efficiently by grasses (C_4 plants) than by legumes (C_3 plants); in fact, one of its functions in the more efficient cereals is to redirect foliar metabolites to grain filling. Since legumes are less efficient at Ca utilization, Ca deficiency has many physiological effects on legumes, as in peanuts, where it lowers the phospholipid content of the fat body, increases the simple lipid content, reduces the triglyceride content of the simple lipids, and increases the diglyceride content. Calcium deficiency in soybeans grown in nutrient solution led to optimal bacterial growth and attachment to the root hair surfaces. These effects were reversed with increasing Ca supply.

Physiology

Calcium supplied at high quantities to wheat can interfere with stomatal conductance, but it has been found that long-term high Ca supply does not affect the stomatal mechanism, and no explanation is available. Calcium has a role in soybean germination that has been linked to membrane stabilization. Adding Ca or Mg to the germination medium can improve germination of Ca-deficient seed. In rice, Ca enhances the activity of enzymes involved in sucrose-to-starch conversion, including sucrose synthase, invertase, pyrophosphate-phosphofructokinase, uridine diphosphate–glucose pyrophosphorylase, and adenosine pyrophosphorylase. Calcium has also been shown to be necessary to stabilize the structure of barley alpha-amylases in the endoplasmic reticulum. Calcium deficiency affects the secondary and tertiary structure, thus inactivating the enzymes.

Interactions

There are strong interactions between Ca and N, with Ca being important in N uptake and use. Supplemental Ca for wheat and barley and maize and rice increased NH4 -N plant use and efficiency by increasing absorption, tillering, metabolite deposition in the seed, and possibly photosynthesis. Higher Ca also results in higher NH4 in soil solution and increases in the diffusion coefficient for NH_4. Calcium deficiency reduced' nitrate influx in barley by 40% and in squash by 10% after 48 hours. High Mg availability reduced wheat yield by inducing Ca deficiency. The cause is apparently not impairment of membrane function by Mg but is more likely associated with a competitive ion effect, with high Mg levels competing with Ca in transport from the roots. The inhibition of K by high NaCl levels for barley were greatly alleviated by increasing the Ca supply. Likewise, Ca additions alleviated salt stress in barley, but more so for a cultivated variety than for wild species. Calcium deficiency in rice was remediated by B additions.

In rice, Si additions decreased Ca content and uptake, but the effect could be overcome by increasing the Ca supply. Increasing the CO_2 pressure for wheat decreased Ca content. One of the major areas if research on plant mineral nutrition in the past decade has been that of aluminum toxicity to plants and methods to ameliorate the effects of aluminum, which is prevalent in the soil solution of acid soils.

In general, Ca can be used to help overcome the effects of Al toxicity. The effect is not limited to Ca only but also includes Mg and other ions, such that the ratio of activities of cations in solution is a good measure of the variation in plant weight due to Al toxicity. In soybeans, Al inhibited the length of lateral roots more than that of tap roots, and adding Ca would achieve similar relative root length as for tap roots.

In Al-sensitive wheat cultivars, high Al levels inhibited Ca uptake, but they did not do so for Al-tolerant varieties. The mechanisms of the interaction of Ca and Al have presented an interesting line of research, with several mechanisms proposed and proponents and opponents of each. One mechanism is that Al acts to block Ca channels at the plasma membrane, as found for tobacco.

In a review, Rengel et al. suggest that differential blockage of Ca channels by Al may be the major factor in differential tolerance to Al. However, others have found that differential response to Al is not due to differences in Ca channels but to an ability to reduce Al activity in the rhizosphere. Another mechanism proposed is that the Al binds to plasma membrane phospholipids, forming a positively charged layer that decreases Ca influx. However, other groups feel that the theory fails and that amelioration of Al toxicity by cations occurs due to decreased membrane-surface activity of Al. For wheat, root growth could be greatly inhibited by Al concentrations that did not decrease Ca uptake, so Al does not inhibit root growth by decreasing Ca uptake. Again, the same group showed that displacement of Ca from the apoplasm by Al was not the explanation for reduced root growth but that tolerance in certain species was a caused by a reduction in Al accumulation.

MAGNESIUM

Uptake and Translocation

The content of Mg in plants is about 0.5%, being lower than that of either Ca or K. Cations that compete with Mg in uptake (K and NH_4) can lead to Mg deficiency. In nutrient solution studies, when Mg supply was stopped, Mg was translocated from old leaves to younger leaves. Under constant deficient Mg supply, deficiency symptoms appeared on young leaves and the concentration of Mg in the youngest emerged blade was closely related to Mg concentration in the nutrient solution. Waterlogging reduced the concentration of Mg in leaves and stems of wheat. Irrigation water that contained $Mg(CO_3)_2$ impaired the dry-matter yields of maize shoots and roots to a much greater extent that $MgSO_4$ or a mixed salt solution, presumably due to high pH (9.0) and nutrient imbalances.

Interactions

Wheat grain yields were reduced due to a Mg-induced Ca deficiency when highMg irrigation water was used. Calcium was also found to interfere with Mg transport from the roots in wheat, lowering the shoot and root Ca due to a competitive ion effect. However, in barley, Mg did not strongly interfere with Ca function in membrane integrity, but it did increase K leakage. Magnesium was found to enhance soybean seed germination when the seeds were Ca-deficient. Magnesium has an ameliorative effect on Mn toxicity where the ratio of Mg:Mn in the shoot tissue of tomato rises above 3.4 to 6.5:1 or, for wheat, above 20:1.

The Mg was found to increase tolerance of the plants to high Mn concentrations and to discriminate against Mn ions in translocation of nutrients from roots to shoots. Nitrate increased the uptake of Mg by wheat plants, whereas ammonium did not increase Mg uptake as much.

However, the increased nitrate lowered the translocation of Mg, such that shoot Mg concentrations were decreased. High P levels decreased the K:Mg+Ca ratios in wheat. This finding has implications for grass tetany for grazing ruminants. Uptake of Mg by wheat was increased by increasing the pressure of CO_2. Magnesium has an ameliorative effect on Al toxicity in wheat, as it adds to the cations that, when the activities are taken together, account for a high percentage of dry weight increases under Al toxicity.

SULFUR

Uptake and Translocation

The sufficiency range for S in plants is between 0.2 and 0.5% of the dry weight. Uptake of S is not related to pH, as is nitrate, the form taken up is the sulfate form. Other ions cause little interference in S uptake by plants. It has been determined that in order to avoid yield reductions in wheat due to S deficiency, it is necessary to apply S before symptoms become evident. Thus, critical tissue levels must be checked and the critical deficiency levels for different species must be known. For lupins, the critical S-deficiency concentration in young leaves is 0.28%; the N:S ratio must be 22. For wheat, the values are 0.14 to 0.31% S and an N:S ratio of 9 to 19 in the young leaves, but the values change with age. Total S concentrations in wheat grain ranged from 0.94 to 1.81 mg/g and in barley from 0.94 to 1.55 mg/g.

The grain from milling wheat contained more S than feed wheat, but feed and malting barley contained similar concentrations of S. The baking quality of wheat was increased by adding S to S-deficient wheat . The S uptake and translocation in tobacco was positively related to S supply, but xylem loading was inversely related to S supply. The S nutrition of tobacco, then, was considered to be controlled by xylem loading. Sulfur is transported or remobilized in various plants. Up to 75% of the S in barley was reexported and at least some of the S was exported from fully expanded leaves to developing leaves. It has been found that cytoplasmic S turns over rapidly in various species, but vacuolar turnover is too slow to support plant growth, which accounts for the apparent low mobility of S in mature leaves. Sulfur sinks were found to be the root and shoot for the short term in soybean seedlings, but as growth proceeded, the stem was the dominant sink for remobilized S.

Physiology

Photosynthetic assimilation decreased in S-deficient wheat plants, which was found to be an effect of S on the carboxylase efficiency rather than altered stomatal conductance or leaf internal CO_2 concentration. It was also found that S deficiency in soybeans led to a linear decline in the Rubisco fraction from nearly 50% to <10% of soluble protein as soluble protein in the leaf declined. This decline in the Rubisco fraction may be a function of the relative importance of certain enzymes as protein levels decline or a down-regulation of Rubisco synthesis as carbohydrates increase under S deficiency. At least two research groups have been studying glutathione in relation to S nutrition. Glutathione in tobacco is a signal agent that controls S nutrition. Reduced glutathione inhibits sulfate transport, but the process is reversible by adding protein-synthesis inhibitors, such as cycloheximide or puromycin. At low N levels S, glutathione in soybeans is metabolized to homoglutathione, which is important as a transport compound for exporting organic S.

Interactions

There are strong interactions between plant N and S. For barley, plant N content increased as S supply increased. The uptake of both S and N increased synergistically; as both were supplied to wheat and the fertilizer, the percentage of S use increased as N rates increased. With N deprivation in soybeans, there was a net loss of S, which was attributed to a proteolysis involved in the export of S and N from mature leaves. The decrease in N translocation from sulfate-deprived barley was associated with increases in both asparagine and glutamine in roots, but no such increases in the leaves were found. Sulfur has been found to help alleviate the symptoms of Zn toxicity in soybeans and to increase translocation of Zn from roots to the shoots. Increased CO_2 pressure had little effect on S uptake by wheat.

MANGANESE

Uptake and Translocation

Manganese uptake is active; therefore other ions of the alkali earth cations (Ca and Mg) and the transition metals (Zn and Fe) can interfere with uptake and translocation. Manganese can substitute for Mg in physiological reactions because of its lability with respect to binding. Although deficiency ranges for most plants are rather narrow, toxicity ranges are quite wide. Manganese research in recent years seems to center on Mn toxicity. Although Mn is taken up in greater quantities than Cu or Zn by wheat, the toxicity of Mn is lower than that of Zn, B, Fe, or Cu. The tolerance of soybeans to high Mn was increased at higher day/night temperatures, where the total leaf Mn was increased while stem concentration was reduced, indicating that the tolerance was not due to growth dilution in young tissues. Rice exposed to high Mn at various pH values in solution culture formed brown coatings (plaque) of oxidized Mn on the roots, which increased at higher pH and Mn concentrations.

This plaque, along with Fe and Al oxide plaque, reduces the rice tissue's ability to absorb nutrients from soils and causes deficiencies of P, K, Ca, and Mg. Increases in Mn supply to tobacco callus decreased callus formation and shoot regeneration. At high Mn concentrations, soybean callus was more sensitive to Mn toxicity than intact plants, giving a lower critical deficiency level but a higher critical toxicity level. The critical Mn toxicity levels have been determined for a number of species and given as milligrams of Mg per kilogram of dry weight in subterraneum clover, balansa clover, serradella, greater lotus, wheat, burr medic, murex medic, Persian clover, and lucerne. The critical deficiency level for barley was set at a log(Mn) of "9.8 for barley in a chelate-buffered nutrient solution. VAM has effects on Mn nutrition for several plant species. The Mn concentration in rice was higher with VAM than without VAM at all growth stages irrespective of soil fertility or water regimes.

For soybeans, it was found that VAM increased foliar uptake of Mn under deficient supply and decreased Mn uptak , under Mn toxic conditions. For barley, it was found that Mn was higher in concentration in the roots in inefficient plants due to immobilization, which may be an important mechanism for Mn efficiency. In wheat, Mn was remobilized from the roots and stems during grain filling, but not from the leaves.

Physiology

Physiological research on Mn nutrition concentrated on differences among varieties as to tolerance to toxicities. Various organic acids in wheat—including aconitic, malic, and citric acids—increased at high Mn levels in Mn-sensitive varieties but did not change in Mn-tolerant varieties. Increases in aconitate, alpha-ketoglutarate, and succinate in Mn-sensitive wheat varieties were found by another group, but this increase was a response to Mn toxicity and not a mechanism of Mn tolerance. In tobacco, the activity of peroxidase increased while that of catalase decreased under Mn toxicity. Also, it was found that toxic Mn did not affect the Rubisco concentrations in tobacco. Mn-tolerant soybean varieties had the highest peroxidase activity under Mn deficiency, but higher enzyme activity at high Mn concentration was found for Mn-sensitive varieties.

In peanuts, Mn deficiency led to decreased nitrate reductase activity, but ascorbic acid oxidase activity increased with increasing Mn up to toxic levels. Manganese toxicity decreased the rates of photosynthesis per unit chlorophyll for Mn-sensitive wheat cultivars but not for Mn-tolerant varieties. In rice, pigment concentrations decreased in plants with excess Cu due to the roles of Fe and Mn in chlorophyll and to carotenoid synthesis. It has been found that the Mn concentrations in wheat necessary for biosynthesis of phenolics and lignin are lower than those required for optimum growth. Wheat varieties that are tolerant of Mn deficiency are able to alter chemicals and biological properties of the rhizosphere to increase the availability of Mn. In rice, the formation of Fe plaque on roots was found to block micronutrient uptake. The uptake of Fe and Mn was positively correlated in eight plant species, leading to the conclusion that they were mobilized by similar root processes.

Interactions

The interactions of Mn with N, P, and K were discussed above under the respective elements. Magnesium interacts with Mn to increase the tolerance of plants to Mn toxicity. This subject is discussed under magnesium. Iron application interferes with Mn nutrition in soybeans, apparently by restriction of Mn translocation from the soil to the root or the root to plant shoots. In barley, this interaction was different in that Mn interferes with Fe nutrition by selectively replacing Fe^{2+} on endogenous chelators that transfer Fe to the sites of porphyrin metabolosm or by replacing Fe^{2+} in the active sites of enzymes involved in tetrapyrrole synthesis. This interaction can be helpful in that high Mn rates will alleviate Fe toxicity in rice. Increasing Cu can interfere with the Mn nutrition of plants. The highest yields of barley were found at Mn:Cu ratios of 8 to 13. Shoot Mn and Fe concentration in rice decreased at >0.05 mg Cu/L, but it was found that Cu affects Fe and Mn translocation by different mechanisms. Salinity causes a Mn deficiency in barley by reducing the photosynthetic rates and growth. This salt-induced Mn deficiency can be overcome by adding supplemental Mn. Shoot uptake of Mn was increased by increased CO_2 pressure in the atmosphere.

COPPER

Uptake and Translocation

The sufficiency range for Cu in plants is between 2 and 20 mg kg"1 of the dry weight. As for Mn, uptake is active and can be inhibited by other transition metals such as Zn. Copper binds with organic ligands both in soil solution and in the xylem sap of plants. Copper deficiency symptoms for wheat include rolling and wilting of young leaves and twisting and terminal dieback. Significant correlations were found between Cu concentrations in the leaves and grain yield and floret fertility, indicating the importance of Cu in wheat fertility. For rice and barley, the same response to Cu deficiency was found in that sterility occurred. In wheat and triticale calluses and tobacco leaf disc cultures, additional Cu stimulated shoot regeneration. Wheat grain and dry-matter yields were depressed by half at Cu content in the flag leaves of 25 μg/g of Cu due to toxicity. The critical toxicity level in the shoots of wheat were reported to be 0.075 mg Cu/kg dry matter. Compared with other micronutrients (B, Fe, Mn, and Zn), Cu was taken up at the highest rates and proved to be the most toxic. Copper concentrations were higher in rice with VAM than without VAM at all growth stages irrespective of soil fertility or water supply. The VAM organism was found to have a direct contribution to plant Cu nutrition in wheat.

Physiology

Copper has a role in many enzyme systems that are affected under both Cu deficiency and toxicity stress. Toxic amounts of Cu in soybeans induced an increase in superoxide dismutase (SOD) by affecting cystolic Cu,Zn-SOD synthesis. Since the mRNA of SOD did not increase with Cu treatment, the Cu-induced increase in SOD activity is likely caused at the level of translation. In rice, the activities of ascorbate oxidase, o-phenol oxidase, and diamine oxidase increased as Cu increased. The latter two enzymes play a role in the inhibition of growth induced by Cu toxicity. Nitrate reductase activity in groundnuts was decreased by both Cu deficiency and toxicity, whereas ascorbic acid oxidase activity was decreased at deficient Cu levels and increased with increasing Cu up to toxic levels. Additional Cu causes ethlyene biosynthesis in both tobacco and soybeans.

Besides ethylene, additional Cu induces proline production, which is believed to have a role in metal tolerance in wheat. Increasing Cu increased both the histidine and methionine content of protein fractions of rice. Toxic levels of Cu affect photosynthesis in wheat by slowing the electron transport as a result of a reduced requirement for photosynthesis products. The same explanation was given for the effects of Cu toxicity on rice, with electron transfer being inhibited mainly before the 1,5-diphenyl-carbohydrazide donation site in photosynthesis II. For both rice and oats, excess Cu affected chlorophyl and carotenoid biosynthesis.

In oats, Cu decreased the activities of catalase and ascorbate peroxidase. Thus, excess Cu causes rapid senescence in plant leaves through oxidative reactions with light. C. Interactions Copper interacts with other elements in its role in plant nutrition. Excess P application to corn resulted in decreased Cu content in the shoots, and additional

N for wheat also lowered Cu to the point of deficiency. On the other hand, as Cu concentration increased for wheat, the P concentration was depressed in shoots and roots. The critical Cu:N ratio for barley was independent of the N level, indicating that Cu remobilization in the older leaves does not occur even when N is deficient. Copper concentrations did not have any effect on nitrate or nitrite reductases in rice. Fe coatings on rice roots resulted in ameliorating Cu toxicity and affected the patterns of metal uptake and accumulation. The interactions of Mn and Cu are discussed above, under Mn. The Zn:Cu ratio was better related to the activities of enzymes in rice than their individual concentrations in rice. Zinc uptake by plants were enhanced by increasing Cu supply, which was a result of the Cu making the Zn more plant-available.

IRON

Uptake and Translocation

The past decade has seen many advances in research concerning phytosiderophores (SIDs), which are non-protein-forming amino acids produced by plant roots to mobilize soil Fe and other micronutrients. Microbial siderophores can act in a manner similar to plant phytosiderophores and are also considered in micronutrient nutrition. Plants take up Fe from the soil solution, in which it is often at very low concentrations. The release of root exudates is enhanced under nutrient-deficient conditions. Marschner et al. provide a brief review of research on root exudates, including amino acids, sugars, phenolics, and other phytosiderophores from various plant species to mobilize Fe and Zn. Plants have two mechanisms to mobilize Fe and other metals in soil. Grasses release SIDs and utilize Fe^{3+} (strategy II), whereas dicots release protons to lower the rhizosphere pH and utilize Fe^{2+} (strategy I).

Thus, the critical Fe^{3+} activities required by barley (strategy II) were found to be much higher than that of soyabean and tomato (strategy I). Barley releases SIDs that compete for Fe^{3+} in nutrient solution, while soybeans and tomatoes reduce Fe^{3+} to Fe^{2+} at the epidermal cell membranes. The efficiency of oat varieties to utilize

Fe was measured by quantifying the amounts of SIDs they produce. Plant uptake of Fe is complicated by microbes, which not only degrade the SIDs but also compete with higher plants for Fe. For barley and sorghum, it was found that the major effect of microbes in their interference in Fe availability is the degradation of SIDs rather than the immobilization or uptake of Fe. Phytosiderophores were compared in their chelating ability to the synthetic chelate DTPA, and it was found that Fe is mobilized to the same degree by both, whereas Mn was much lower for the SIDs.

A similar line of research revealed that mugineic acid (a common SID) from barley roots complexed Fe^{3+} to a much greater degree that for Cu or Zn. Mugineic acid of plant origin enhanced Fe uptake more than 100 times compared with the synthetic chelators EDTA and HEDTA due to the specific recognition mechanism by the transport system in barley roots.

It is interesting that under some circumstances SIDs from one plant will act as Fe carriers for another. The SID from oat solubilized Fe in nutrient solution making it available to corn, acting much like a chelating agent. Likewise, the Fe uptake by corn was higher from a barley SID that from ferroxamine B, a microbial SID. These authors make the distinction between plant "phytosiderophores" and microbial "siderophores" and indicate that nutrient solution studies carried out under nonsterile conditions can be greatly confounded by microbial SIDs.

Oat SID was also shown to be an effective Fe carrier to melons and tomatoes but not to soybeans. In most cases the SIDs' main components are mugineic acids, which have a high affinity for Fe but not for other polyvalent ions such as Ca, Mg, and Al. The transport system is very specific, recognizing only the mugineic acidFe(III) complex and not other mugineic acid–metal or synthetic chelator–Fe(III) complexes, which indicates that the binding sites have a strict stereo structure recognition system located on the plasma membrane. It has been shown that in some cases the release of SIDs is in response specifically to Fe deficiency and is not induced by other deficiencies. For corn, the Fe uptake mechanism involves a specific chiral receptor in conjunction with reductive processes.

However, in other cases, the same SID (2 -deoxymugineic acid) was released in response to both Fe and Zn deficiency. The critical toxicity level of Fe in rice was determined to be 300 mg/kg, but the toxic effects were due to the formation of Fe oxide plaque on roots that inhibited the uptake of P, K, Ca, and Mg. The concentration of Fe was higher in rice cultured with VAM than without VAM at all growth stages and did not depend on soil fertility or water supply. For soybean roots, it was determined that plant roots had to be in direct contact with the Fe substrate in order for it to be mobilized by the roots. Bicarbonate in carbonaceous soils is known to exacerbate Fe deficiency in plants.

Adding bicarbonate to peanuts in nutrient solutions depressed Fe nodule formation much more than Fe deficiency alone. In studies with corn, barley, and sorghum, adding bicarbonate increased the accumulation of organic acid around roots and produced a decline in uptake and translocation of Fe, thus decreasing root growth. Much research has been carried out concerning the synthesis of SIDs. It was determined that, for barley roots, deoxymugineic acid is most likely the first SID to be synthesized in the biosynthetic pathway of mugineic acids.

However, other research indicated that the first step for barley is not Sadenosyl-L-methionine synthetase but nicotinamine synthase and that the second is nicotinamine aminotransferase. Nicotinamine synthase was induced by Fe deficiency in barley, sorghum, and corn and the level of the enzyme was associated with the amounts of SIDs secreted. The mugineic acid Fe transporter was induced by Fe deficiency in barley in its amount or activity and it was determined that it needed ATPase for movement. Iron transport from leaf veins to mesophyll cells carried by SIDs is light-regulated and Fe influx into chloroplasts is light-dependent, while Fe efflux occurs in the dark. B. Physiology Iron has a key role in plant enzyme systems, thus Fe stress can disrupt vital processes.

The bronzing of rice from toxic Fe concentrations was believed to be associated with peroxidase activity. Also, at deficient Fe levels in peanuts, the peroxidase and nitrate reductase activities were both low. Since bicarbonate additions lower Fe concentrations in plants, they were also found to decrease nitrogenase activity. Iron reductase isoenzymes did not serve as a good criterion for genetic selection in soybeans for resistance to iron-deficiency chlorosis. Plants respond to Fe toxicity and deficiency in various ways morphologically and physiologically. In tobacco, cellular damage from Fe toxicity is associated with oxidative stress. Peroxidase activity has been linked to the bronzing that is the Fe toxicity symptom in rice. In soybeans, Fe concentration had no effect on peroxidase activity even though high Mn concentrations gave high enzyme activity. Ferredoxin-like compounds in the roots of Fe-deficient tobacco have been associated with increased amounts of free riboflavin and flavin mononucleotide. Tolerance to Fe deficiency in soybeans is enhanced by the accumulation of Fe reserves in the root apoplast and by large amounts of translocation to the shoot under Fe deficiency stress.

Interactions

Interactions of Fe supply with other ions are a significant area of current research. High K supply to strategy I plants increase proton flux and Fe reduction, whereas high K in strategy II plants assist in producing high amounts of mugineic acid and in the transport of the Fe^{3+} -SID complex. Application of high K to soybeans depresses bicarbonate content in the soil, which, in turn, lowers the immobilization of Fe in the plant.

This effect was supported by results showing that adding either P or K to Fe-toxic soils will increase rice and yield and that adding P lowers Fe in the shoot of corn. In rice, toxic amounts of Cu decreased shoot Fe concentrations. Manganese additions have been found to interact with Fe activity in various crops, in some cases because both are mobilized by similar root processes. Supplementing Mn to rice corrected Fe toxicity. The reverse effect was found for soybeans, where additional Fe interfered with Mn nutrition by restricting Mn translocation from soil to root or from root to shoot. Manganese additions caused Fe deficiency in barley by binding to endogenous chelators, which transfer Fe to sites of porphyrin metabolism, or selectively replacing Fe in the active centers of enzymes involved in tetrapole synthesis. Iron often accumulates on plant roots, which may cause the inhibition of uptake of other nutrients. This effect can increase the tolerance of plants to high levels of available heavy metals.

ZINC

Uptake and Translocation

The sufficiency range for Zn in plants is between 15 and 20 mg kg”1 dry weight, while the critical toxicity range is 400 to 500 mg kg”1 dry weight. Unlike Mn and Fe, which are in various oxidation states in soils, Zn is taken up only as a divalent ion. Most evidence points to Zn uptake as being active, although there is literature to the contrary. Plant species show different susceptibility to Zn deficiency, as found for cereals, which decline in the order durum wheat > oats > bread wheat > barley > triticale > rye. Oats and barley were found to be tolerant of high Zn and were considered to have high potential for use in phytoremediation of Zn-contaminated soils. The ctitical Zn toxicity level in peanuts was found to be 240 mg kg”1 and the critical Zn deficiency level in peanut was set at 8 to 10 mg kg”1. In determining critical deficiency levels in chelate-buffered nutrient solutions, it was discovered that the free activity and the total amount of Zn must be considered and not just the free activity alone. Zinc nutrition has been implicated in the severity of wheat take-all disease.

However, in one report, Zn additions to Zn-deficient soil had no effect on the take-all fungus. Another group found that there was an inverse relationship between Zn efficiency of wheat genotypes and the length of take-all lesions on plant roots. Another disease, root rot, has been shown to be more severe under Zn deficiency conditions. Under toxic Zn conditions, Zn taken up by barley is adsorbed in to the extracellular matrix but taken into cells slowly.

The Zn taken into the mesophyll protoplasts appears in the vacuolar compartment. Toxicity damage was inversely related to apoplasmic compartmentation, so that it was concluded that compartmentation and transport are important mechanisms in Zn tolerance in barley. Likewise, Zn is taken into the vacuolar volume fraction in rye to a greater extent than in rice and wheat, such that the toxic effects are minimized.

Large amounts of Zn were remobilized in wheat from roots and stems, but not leaves, at grain filling. Zinc-deficient plants produce phytosiderophores (SIDs) to help mobilize rhizosphere Zn. Cereals (wheat and barley) produce SIDs in higher amounts; these are also more effective than dicotyledonous species. However, corn does not produce SIDs, as sorghum and wheat do, so that corn is more susceptible to Zn deficiencies under field conditions. Wheat species that are more efficient in utilizing low soil Zn are more able to produce effective SIDs than inefficient species. However, in bread wheat cultivars, root uptake and root-to-shoot transfer may be more important to Zn uptake efficiency than release of SIDs.

Physiology

Zinc has a role in various plant enzyme systems. Toxic levels of Zn decreased carbonic anhydrase activity more in peas than in oats. However, higher levels of carbonic anhydrase were found in wheat genotypes that were efficient in utilizing Zn under deficient conditions. At lower pH (5.5 vs. 6.5), Zn stimulated the activity of H^+ -ATPase more that Mn or Mg, leading to the conclusion that Zn, in combination with pH of the cytoplasm, has an important influence in regulating plasma membrane H^+ -ATPase and, therefore, the nutrient uptake of plants.

The activity of nitrate reductase was decreased under both Zn deficiency and toxicity in peanut. At high Zn supply, wheat retained Zn mainly in the stem, indicating that Zn was removed from the xylem sap but not loaded into the phloem in large quantities. At the high critical Zn level, phloem transport was strongly inhibited due to decreased phloem loading or to decreased mass flow in the sieve tubes and not by affecting phloem unloading or metabolism in sinks. Rye and wheat genotypes that are efficient in utilizing Zn under deficient conditions have higher amounts of physiologically active Zn in the leaves, and it was found that measuring Cu/Zn-SOD is a better way to determine Zn nutritional status than by just determining Zn concentrations alone. Another indicator of efficiency in Zn uptake and utilization is the amount of sulfhydryl groups in the roots.

Interactions

Zinc interacts with other nutrients, especially P. The P/Zn interaction has been investigated for the last three decades, and this activity continues unabated with the exception that more recently the effects of VAM are being considered. In corn, it was found that inorganic P was increased in Zn-deficient roots, but organic P forms were decreased.

However, increased P in Zn-deficient wheat plants was mediated through an effect of Zn in the shoots and not in the roots. At high rates of P to corn, the shoot Zn decreased. VAM infection and P additions both worked to decrease Zn concentration and uptake in wheat. The concentration of P in pigeon peas was increased linearly by VAM colonization, which, in turn, increased Zn concentration in the shoots. Phosphorus uptake rates by barley were decreased by increasing Zn concentrations in nutrient solutions.

The Zn concentrations in rice were increased by inoculation with VAM. Nitrogen applications increased the Zn concentrations in corn and decreased P concentration, thus improving the P:Zn ratio to a more optimum range. On the other hand, Zn deficiency in squash and barley decreased NO_3 uptake.

Potassium application was found to ameliorate Zn deficiency in rice. Likewise, increased S supply to soybean increased Zn translocation from roots to shoots, improving the effects of Zn toxicity. It was found that additional Cu increased Zn uptake in the shoot of plants under Zn-contaminated conditions.

BORON

Uptake and Translocation

Boron uptake is in the form of the undissociated boric acid and is present in the plant in the same form at the physiological pH. Although B is not an enzyme component, it is an important plant micronutrient that controls at least 15 plant functions, including phenols and lignin, which protects the forage quality of grasses. Boron uptake by sunflowers, squash, and tobacco has been determined to be a passive, nonmetabolic process mediated by nonexchangeable B complexes within the cytoplasm and cell wall. The critical B deficiency level for soybeans for normal seedling development in low-B soils was determined to be 14 to 20 mg/kg. The shoot critical toxicity level of B for wheat was found to be 0.4 mg/g dry matter.

The critical toxicity level of B in barley plants is 50 to 420 µg/g. Barley can accumulate relatively high concentrations of B and show leaf injury and other toxicity symptoms without significantly affecting the grain yield; thus shoots are not suitable tissue to diagnose B toxicity in barley. In barley, soil temperature had no effect on B content or concentration, and it was concluded that tolerance to high B levels came either through maintaining low tissue B concentrations or tolerance of high tissue B concentrations. Boron deficiency has an effect on fertility in grains. Although B deficiency did not lead to sterility in rice, it did in barley and wheat. Differences in the response of wheat genotypes to B deficiency are caused by differences in the effect of B supply on the germination of pollen in the stigma and style in wheat. This infertility can be overcome by B application directly on the ear on sterile male plants—a finding that could have utility in breeding programs using wheat with differing sensitivity to B deficiency. Plant species differ in their uptake mechanisms, which affect sensitivity to B deficiency.

Differences are due to reduced uptake in wheat, decreased B translocation in celery, or a combination of both in tomatoes. Among six plant species, the highest concentration of B was in the leaves and the lower third of the plant, suggesting that the best tissues to sample to determine B status are the most recently matured leaves in Brassica spp. and the young leaves in forage legumes. Boron content of branch leaves and seeds in soybeans led to the conclusion that B is more mobile than was expected; thus the main stem leaves are good for diagnostic testing for B in soybeans. Foliar diagnosis of B deficiency and toxicity is problematic because of the influence of water supply and transpiration on B concentrations in the leaves; which can vary 100-fold in the same leaf and can reach toxic values in older leaves while younger leaves are deficient. Increases in water supply and use caused B accumulation in leaf tips in barley; thus sampling for B status should not include leaf tips. The sensitivity of B concentration in leaves to water supply in wheat was not found for other elements (Ca, Cu, Mg, Mn, P, S, Zn).

Physiology

An increase in B uptake by soybeans resulted in a decrease in phenolic content of the leaves, thus indicating that B has a role in membrane maintenance. In squash and tobacco, B increased in the cell wall at the expense of the cytoplasm as the cells became B-deficient. The greater portion of the cell B was associated pectins in the cell wall. In a similar study, 90% of the cellular B was found in the cell wall, while very low amounts were in the membrane fraction. The cell wall B was bound to rhammogalacturonan II to form a dimeric complex. In soybeans, toxic levels of B decreased protein synthesis.

Interactions

Boron at sufficient levels enhanced N fixation in soybeans and in the nodules. Under B deficiency, large nodules from the primary roots contained sufficient B for N fixation, such that N fixation was not affected by B deficiency. Calcium chloride added to rice caused salinity problems that were overcome by B additions. In salt-affected corn, B application was found to exacerbate the toxicity. Even though B has been reported to help ameliorate Al toxicity in wheat, no improvement in Al toxicity was noted in nutrient solution even when the B content of the leaves was increased by increased B supply.

MOLYBDENUM

Uptake and Transport

The critical deficiency range for Mo is the lowest of any of the mineral elements at between 0.1 and 1.0 mg kg"1 of the dry weight. The variation between deficiency and toxicity is even higher than that for Mn at around 104 . Molybdenum is absorbed by plants as the molybdate ion. Molybdenum is important to legumes because it is a part of two enzyme systems—nitrogenase, which fixes atmospheric N, and nitrate reductase, which allows all plants to utilize the nitrate form of N. Molybdenum is also necessary to other organic constituents and enzyme activities in plants. Deficiency symptoms for Mo include a general yellowing of the leaves and rolling, curling, and scorching of the leaves. Molybdenum toxicity is a rare occurrence in the field due to the very low soil levels usually found. Diagnostic plant tissue for Mo status is the recently matured leaves in Brassica spp. and young leaves in legumes. Sterility was higher in both rice and barley at deficient levels of Mo, which was related to the acceleration of tiller development during later growth stages. It was found that wheat displayed more dormancy under Mo sufficiency than deficiency, which could be used as a way to decrease preharvest sprouting losses by adding Mo to Mo-deficient soils. Under Mo deficiency in wheat, the seed dormancy increase with Mo addition is associated with a concurrent increase in abscisic acid content in the seed. Molybdenum deficiency in wheat, then, leads to a lack of dormancy because of decreased synthesis of abscisic acid.

Physiology

When tobacco plants were grown hydroponically with sufficient Mo, the activity of nitrate reductase was increased, and was the total protein content over control. Where higher Mo than sufficient was added to the tobacco, the ammonium and nitrite content of the leaves and the protein content in the root increased, but the activities of nitrate reductase and nitrite reductase were not changed. The nitrate reductase activity was decreased in peanuts at deficient levels of Mo, while toxic levels led to a decreased peroxidase activity. In field-grown peanuts where Mo availability was low, N deficiency was found because the Mo did not meet the needs for N fixation. A frost-induced decline in NADH:HR activity in winter wheat was prevented by Mo application.

Interactions

In soybeans, the addition of Mo increased leaf N and the dry weights of shoots, roots, and nodules even though the mean photosynthesis, specific root nodule nitrogenase activity, and chlorophyll content did not change. The addition of P alone to tobacco did not increase Mo concentration, but when Mo was applied with P, the Mo concentration increased. The form of P fertilizer applied to peanuts has an effect on the Mo uptake and N nutrition of the plants. When single superphosphate is applied to peanuts, the Mo levels in the nodules decreases, as does the N concentrations in the shoots. However, when triple superphosphate is soil-applied or P is applied by foliar means, the N and Mo uptake increase. The addition of Mo to soybeans decreased nitrogenase activity when the CO_2 pressure was elevated, but there was no change in photosynthetic rate.

4

Root Plasticity in Exploiting Water and Nutrient Heterogeneity

INTRODUCTION

Soil resources are often unevenly distributed in space and time under field conditions. Many plant species respond to this heterogeneity with morphological and physiological plasticity. Root plasticity is the ability to exploit available resources by increasing root growth and/or physiological activity in enriched microsites or horizons of the soil profile. Specific plastic responses of roots include changes in root growth rates, architecture, and demography, water uptake capacity, nutrient uptake kinetics, mycorrhizal infection, exudation, and the form and density of root hairs.

Plastic responses of roots to a heterogeneous environment were first noticed in roots passing through different layers of soil in the field. These results were later supported by laboratory experiments in which roots and shoots of plants were subjected to controlled patchiness in supply of such resources as water and nutrients.

It is now widely accepted that plants can alter root distribution patterns and rates of nutrient uptake when a localized supply of nutrients is elevated. Root plasticity plays an important role in plant adaptation to heterogeneous environments. Plants exhibiting rapid and highly plastic responses in root growth and development may under certain circumstances be at a selective advantage, because they can rapidly utilize the available resources. Jackson and Caldwell have linked the rapid proliferation of new roots in nutrient-rich soil patches to the greater competitive ability of Agropyron desertorum (Fisch. ex Link) Schult. relative to its unresponsive neighbor, Pseudoroegneria spicata (Pursh) A. Löve (formerly Agropyron spicatum (Pursh) Scribn.). Although the relative importance of altered root morphology (root density, length, root hairs, etc) versus uptake kinetics is still debatable, it seems clear that many plant species are capable of rapidly adjusting both their morphology and physiology in the acquisition of limiting essential resources that become available in a localized patch of soil. In this chapter we will focus our discussion on how roots respond to spatial and temporal heterogeneity in water and nutrient availability, mechanisms controlling root plasticity, and costs and benefits associated with root plasticity in exploitation of heterogeneous environments.

ROOT RESPONSES TO SPATIAL VARIATIONS IN WATER AVAILABILITY

Soil water status varies vertically and horizontally. It is very common in the field that surface soil is dry while water is still available deeper in the soil profile. Horizontal heterogeneity of soil moisture also often occurs in patches in soil surface. In an attempt to simulate the heterogeneous water distribution in the field, researchers have often utilized split-root techniques, in which only part of the soil is dry while other parts are wet. In some studies the roots have been vertically separated, with half the roots kept adequately watered and half exposed to drying soil. An alternative system of large, horizontally segmented soil columns in which the soil is hydraulically separated into distinct layers better simulates varying water availability at different soil depths.

Morphological Responses

There are both genotypic and phenotypic components to root architecture. Root distribution, which is influenced by root birth, growth, and death, strongly responds to spatial variations in water availability. Phenotypically, roots tend to proliferate or extend in localized wet zones in a soil profile.

Species also exhibit distinct rooting patterns, which can have evolved in response to a particular climatic region. In hot deserts and other arid regions where the soil surface is wet periodically because of sporadic, light rainfall during the growing season, it is common to find that many plants have extensive, shallow root systems that appear to be appropriate for the adsorption of water following light rain. Prairie plants and cold desert plants growing in environments where there is often relatively abundant water at depth may have very deep root systems. When soil is dry at the surface, production of roots increases considerably in the lower layer where water is available in many species, including cotton (Gossypium hirsutum), lupin (Lupinus albus), soybean (Glycine max), lettuce (Lactuca sativa), maize (Zea mays), sorghum (Sorghum bicolor), and turfgrasses. However, the extent of morphological plastic responses may depend on growth stage.

Taylor and Klepper reported that young cotton plants developed much deeper root systems under conditions of gradual drying of a deep, moist soil profile compared with conditions of frequent superficial application of water to the surface soil. Carmi, Plaut, and Sinai reported that roots of mature cotton plants in the flowering stage failed to respond to wet soils deeper in the soil profile. The ability of roots to follow moisture into deeper layers of the soil profile conditions the ability of a plant to tolerate or avoid short and long periods of drought. Horizontal variation in soil moisture availability is also very common, largely due to nonuniform irrigation. For example, drippers or minisprinklers often wet only part of the root zone.

Pregitzer, Hendrick, and Fogel reported that the addition of water or water plus nitrogen to small areas in the root zone resulted in a significant overall increase in the production of new fine roots in the enriched areas. New root production was much greater in response to water plus nitrogen when compared with water alone, and the duration of new root production was related to the length of resource addition in the water plus nitrogen treatments. Roots produced in response to the additions of water or water plus nitrogen influenced both the proliferation of new roots and their longevity, with both proliferation and longevity related to the type and duration of resource supply. Morphological plasticity may have several components. Fine lateral proliferation in small zones of enriched resources may be accomplished by a plant producing many fine root branches quickly off a main nodal or parent root. Studies by Caldwell and Eissenstat indicated that the tussock grass species of greater specific root length (SRL) or finer roots tended to have more rapid root proliferation than the ones with high SRL or thicker roots in response to enriched nutrients. The positive correlation of SRL with root growth in moist soil patches has also been indicated in a comparison of six different citrus rootstocks.

Fitter also found that SRL (as indicated by mean root diameter) was positively correlated to root proliferation in four closely related species in the Caryophyllaceae family. The ability to proliferate in deep soil layers, however, may require production of large-diameter nodal or framework roots that can readily grow through dry soil layers of high soil impedance and serve as a reservoir of meristems for further fine lateral production. However, larger roots require greater quantities of carbohydrates to produce and maintain more root tissue. Many studies of drought tolerance have indicated that of large-diameter roots the ability to penetrate the dry surface soil layers is the principal characteristic associated with development of a deep root system and drought tolerance.

Sharp and Davies suggested that turgor maintenance accounted for continued root extension in drying soil, which may be responsible for sustained root growth in the drying soils and thus would account for growth in the deeper wet soil. In some species, there is a trade-off between production of numerous large-diameter framework roots capable of deep soil penetration and production of many fine laterals of high SRL.

Water Uptake

Many species have the ability to utilize localized supplies of soil water to maintain gas exchange, water status, and growth despite appreciable portions of the root system being in dry soil, but the extent of water extraction varies with species and cultivars. Root penetration into deeper soil profiles where water is available enhances water uptake from deep in the soil profile. Drought tolerant species or cultivars tend to have a greater ability to extract soil water from lower wet soil layers because of their more prolific root system at depth. Gallardo et al. reported that wild lettuce (Lactuca serriola) with a deep root system extracts more soil water from deeper profiles than cultivated lettuce (Lactuca sativa) with a shallow root system, when the upper soil is drying. In some species water absorbed by deep roots in moist soil can move through the roots and leak into the dry surface soil at night by hydraulic lift or by root pressure. Roots that proliferate rapidly into the deeper wet zones act as a water transport system that retrieves water deep in the profile and delivers it to the surface soil when the surface soil is dry.

Hydraulic lift can improve plant transpiration and alleviate water deficit. It also prolongs the activities of roots and root life span in surface drying soil by providing water to surface roots from deep roots when soil moisture is available only in deeper soil layers. In two C4 perennial grass species, prairie buffalograss and Meyer zoysigrass, 15 N uptake by roots in the surface drying soil layer is enhanced when the lower soil layer is watered compared to full-dried conditions, especially for prairie buffalograss. Water efflux from roots to the dry soil has also been reported in bermudagrass (Cynodon dactylon × C. transvaalensis L. Pers.) and Opuntia ficus-indica. Theoretical models of water movement also support the possibility of water movement from the plant into the soil if the gradient of water potential is in that direction.

Plants are also able to modify their spatial patterns of water uptake in response to variations in soil moisture availability in the root zone. Water uptake from wet zones can compensate for lack of uptake from dry zones. When one part of a root system is subjected to decreasing water availability while the other part is well supplied with water, absorption capacity by the well-supplied roots increases. Moreshet et al. found that roots in the wet soil of partially irrigated trees contributed almost 90% to the total seasonal transpiration, whereas just 10% came from roots residing in the drier soil. Tan and Buttery found the complete water requirements of peach (Prunus persica) seedlings could be met by supplying only half of the root zone with water. The increased water absorption capacity is commonly attributed to a reduction in root hydraulic resistance. A decrease in root water potential is another possible mechanism that may be used to explain the observed increase in water uptake by roots well supplied with water.

ROOT RESPONSES TO TEMPORAL VARIATIONS IN WATER AVAILABILITY

Sporadic light rainfall often occurs in many semiarid and arid regions following a prolonged period of drought, which can lead to brief periods of high soil water availability resulting in increased plant physiological capacity. Improved shoot growth after soil rewetting may be largely determined by the ability of the root to resume water and nutrient uptake. Therefore, how quickly root growth and water uptake respond to resupply of water following a period of drought stress is also an important aspect of growth plasticity of roots. Rapid regrowth of existing roots and production of new roots is important for rapid exploitation of water and nutrients following rainfall or irrigation events.

This ability may be expected to confer superior productivity under transient drought conditions typical in semiarid regions. Rapid water uptake resumption has been observed in desert succulents. Nobel and coworkers have characterized changes in root hydraulic conductance for several crassulacean acid metabolism (CAM) species during and following imposition of water stress. Hydraulic conductivity of existing young main and lateral roots of Agave deserti returns to the prestress level about 7 days after rewetting.

The increased radial hydraulic conductivity of main or lateral roots with new branches formed during rewetting is at least partially explained by the interruption of the suberized endodermis and adjacent cortical cell layers when branches have emerged. Resumption of axial hydraulic conductance is mainly attributed to decreases in xylem cavitation. Variations in water uptake resumption following soil drought have been reported for different barley (Hordeum vulgare) genotypes, indicating a potential for varietal selection or genetic modification to enhance efficiency of water usage in regions characterized by relatively light and/or infrequent growing season rainfall.

Resumption of water uptake capacity following soil drought may be a result of renewed permeability or functioning of existing roots as well as new root growth. The initial rapid response to addition of water following a drought is entirely due to uptake by existing roots. The rate of water uptake by existing roots of Bouteloua gracilis is sufficient to increase leaf water potential within 24 hours after rewetting. The continued response to increased water availability is made possible by the appearance of new roots. In some species new roots are produced within hours after rewetting. The new root growth increases the absorption rate and expands the root system, which increases contact with wet soil. New roots have a hydraulic conductance that is an order of magnitude higher than that in older roots. Limited information is available on root plastic responses to heterogeneous soil moisture conditions relating to drought resistance.

Plants in regions where rainfall events are short and sporadic may favor roots that can readily proliferate near the soil surface so that water can be captured before it is evaporated (e.g., hot deserts). Species adapted to relatively wet sites where mineral nutrients are strongly limiting and patchily distributed may also tend to build fine root systems of high SRL. On the other hand, areas where there are more distinct wet and dry seasons may favor root systems that promote development of a deep root architecture, which should favor substantial investment in large-diameter framework roots that can sustain growth through dry surface layers.

ROOT RESPONSES TO NUTRIENT HETEROGENEITY

Root responses to nutrient heterogeneity have received wide attention and have been reviewed by several authors. Nutrient concentrations vary widely in space and time. At an intensively sampled field site in sagebrush steppe, for example, soil phosphate varied threefold and soil nitrate varied twelvefold around individual plants. Nitrate patches in particular can be very ephemeral. At the same site, wetting dry soil doubled nitrate concentration in the surface soil layer (0–5 cm) in one day, but after seven days nitrate concentration was the same as that in control soil. Other studies have also documented short pulses of nitrogen following rewetting. The evolution of plants to nutrient heterogeneity can be considered in terms of evolution to predictable and unpredictable patches.

Highly predictable spatial and temporal patterns of nutrient heterogeneity include the typically higher nutrients at the soil surface or temporal flushes of nutrients in the springtime in temperate, boreal, and arctic climates. When nutrient-enriched patches are predictable, plants may have evolved specific physiological and morphological root characteristics to capitalize on the nutrient heterogeneity. For example, tundra graminoids have a strong photoperiod response to root elongation, presumably to establish sufficient root length to capitalize on nutrients released when the soil temperature increases in the spring.

The evolution of root architecture can also be strongly influenced by predictable and stable nutrient spatial patterns in the soil. Nutrient distribution and root distribution in the soil are often highly correlated, with both root length density and nutrient concentrations declining exponentially with soil depth. Evidence that predictable patterns in the vertical distribution of nutrients (and nonlimiting water conditions) can influence the evolution of root architecture is illustrated by genotypic variation among crop root systems. Crops such as common bean and lettuce, which have been selected for high yields under minimal drought stress, tend to grow a higher proportion of their total root system near the soil surface than less nutrient-efficient cultivars or wild species, even under uniform nutrient distribution. The more shallow growth can be caused by many factors, including more lateral root initiation near the soil surface and a shallower angle of lateral root emergence. Although roots clearly have evolved to predictable patterns of nutrient availability, most research has concentrated on the highly plastic responses of roots to unpredictable spatial and temporal patterns of nutrient availability. Under nutrient-limiting conditions, roots commonly proliferate in zones of ammonium, nitrate, phosphate, and magnesium enrichment but not potassium.

In maize and subterranean clover (Trifolium subterraneum), roots may proliferate to localized K enrichment, but only when the other half of the root system is growing in solution completely devoid of K. When even a minimal concentration of K is provided in the unenriched solution, little root proliferation occurs in the enriched solution. Because soil is never completely devoid of K, it is unlikely that root proliferation will occur in response to heterogeneity in K under field conditions. Many studies have shown that uptake rate per unit root mass or length is often higher for roots in nutrient-rich patches than those in uniformly rich or uniformly poor soil or solution (75% of the cases reviewed by Robinson.

Higher specific rates of uptake may be a function of both higher nutrient concentrations in the patch and higher uptake capacity (i.e., Vmax) of the roots in the patch. Only a few studies have specifically examined the nutrient uptake kinetics of roots in patches. Compared to roots in unenriched soil, roots growing in nutrient-enriched patches may exhibit elevated nutrient uptake capacity, as shown in some cold desert species. Roots in enriched patches have been shown to increase nutrient uptake capacity for phosphate and ammonium. Enhanced uptake kinetics for potassium resulted only from the addition of NO_4 NO_3 , not from the addition of KOH. These studies were conducted in soils high in K, but typically deficient in N and P. To our knowledge, the effects of nutrient heterogeneity on nitrate uptake kinetics have not been examined, although there is indirect evidence of enhanced uptake capacity.

Plasticity in uptake kinetics may contribute substantially to nutrient acquisition. The easiest way to examine the potential advantages afforded by enhanced uptake kinetics for nutrient acquisition from patches is by mechanistic modeling with soil solute transport models. Using the Barber–Cushman model for example, Jackson and Caldwell evaluated the importance of soil heterogeneity and root plasticity for nitrate and phosphate uptake of a cold desert tussock grass, based on previously measured plant and soil parameters. Plasticity in root proliferation and uptake kinetics accounted for up to 75% of nitrate and over 50% of phosphate acquired from enriched patches. Using an actual area of soil in the field to parameterize soil nutrient heterogeneity, they showed that plant acquisition of P was 28% higher with plasticity than without, while nitrate acquisition was 61% higher with plasticity.

Enhanced uptake kinetics and root proliferation contributed equally to phosphate acquisition from enriched patches, whereas increased uptake capacity accounted for nearly all the nitrate acquisition because it has greater mobility than phosphate. Nutrient acquisition from enriched patches was often greater than the magnitude of the difference in the nutrient concentrations of the patch and background soil. In threefold P-enriched patches, simulated P acquisition was three to four times higher in the patch than in the bulk soil; for the twelvefold N-enriched patches, N acquisition was 7–20 times greater in the patch than in the bulk soil. Plant variation in plastic responses to nutrient heterogeneity has been examined in both an ecological and agronomic context.

One prevailing hypothesis associated with plant species variation is that species that have evolved in more stressful environments are less plastic in relation to the growth of their tissue and exhibit a more conservative strategy in response to nutrient heterogeneity than those plants originating from fertile environments.

Original comparisons dealt with the stability of the root/shoot ratio but then were extended to nutrient foraging of patches. Grime and colleagues have argued that rapid-growing plants tend to exhibit high morphological plasticity with low foraging precision of nutrient heterogeneity, whereas slow-growing species exhibit higher precision (root proliferation only in the patch and not elsewhere) and the tendency for physiological (i.e., increased uptake capacity) rather than morphological shifts in response to nutrient heterogeneity. More recent experiments with grasses have tended not to support these theories. Fransen et al. compared five grass species of different potential growth rate that occur in habitats widely divergent in nutrient availability. Although faster-growing species produced significantly more root length density in patches than slow-growing species in this study, the proportion of total root length in patches was not clearly related to potential growth rate of the species.

Moreover, a species of intermediate growth rate (Anthoxanthum odoratum) exhibited the greatest benefit to nutrient heterogeneity in terms of whole-plant biomass, N content, and P content, apparently because of the physiological plasticity of its roots in the nutrient-rich patches. Hodge et al. also did not find species differences in the fraction of total roots in the enriched patch compared to control patches among five co-occurring grasses that differ in potential growth rate.

The fastgrowing species also exhibited precision of root growth in the enriched-patches similar to that of slow-growing species. There were also no species differences in N extraction among the patches or enhancement of plant growth due to nutrient heterogeneity (species × patch interaction). Lastly, Larigauderie and Richards found seven cool-desert grasses that differ in productivity and competitive ability to exhibit very similar responses to nutrient heterogeneity. Thus, at least among grasses, there has been a general lack of a relationship between potential growth rate and root responses to nutrient heterogeneity.

Indeed, Grime provides evidence that the inverse relationship of dominance to the precision of root proliferation is much higher in dicots than grasses. Broader species comparisons are needed to fully evaluate the linkage of potential growth rate of a species with root responses to nutrient heterogeneity. Other factors, such as plant phenology and specific root length, may be equally important in describing variation in species responses to spatial and temporal nutrient heterogeneity.

MECHANISMS CONTROLLING ROOT PROLIFERATION INTO ENRICHED SOILS

It is still not clear what mechanisms could be responsible for the localized proliferation of roots in soils with high water and nutrient availability. This plasticity may be related to changes in carbohydrate allocation between root and shoot or between different sectors of the root system or may take the form of changes in the architecture of fine roots. Root plastic responses may divert more carbon from shoots to roots for new root production within the rich patches. There may be a diversion of resources from roots in poor to those in rich patches, leading to a reduction in growth in the former. Split-root experiments suggest that the latter typically occurs, and a detailed series of experiments on pea (Pisum sativum) specifically to test this proposition has recently confirmed that.

However, tracing the movement of 14 C-labeled assimilates to the half-root system in drying soil in Picea has proved that more assimilates in fact have moved into the roots in dry soil than in wet soils. The rapid proliferation of roots in resource enrichment zones and the superior competitive ability for mineral nutrients exhibited by fast-growing species on fertile soils depends critically upon high rates of root dry matter production and high specific absorption rates and is not the result of greater flexibility in dry matter allocation between parts of the root system located in rich and poor sectors.

Increased production of roots in nutrient-enriched zones may also be related to substrate availability. Compared to slower-growing roots, rapidly growing roots would use substrates at a higher rate and their concentrations within these roots would be relatively low. As a result, these roots grown in nutrientenriched zones could be expected to be better sinks for substrates, thus growing faster than roots in poor soil. Granato and Raper demonstrated that localized uptake and reduction of nitrate by root apices contribute to proliferation of roots within zones of nitrate enrichment. The capacity for in situ nitrate reduction in the basal tissues of the roots with addition of nitrate enhanced the reduced nitrogen supplied for elongation of lateral root branches.

The alternative to carbohydrate or substrate diversion is a role for specific signals such as hormones that control root growth. For example, blocking the growth of taproots of Quercus robur seedlings, thus inducing a change in their hormone balance, caused thickening of the apices of the lateral primordia. Gersani and Sachs reported that enhancement of lateral development at one part of the root system was accompanied by a reduction in the other parts. They assumed that root proliferation is mediated by the hormonal balance of the various regions of the root. However, Sattelmacher and Thoms, and Bingham, Blackwood, and Stevenson dispute the auxin theory. They suggested that proliferation of lateral roots in response to localized soil conditions, such as nutrient patches, may be regulated by sugar, either directly through some form of signal transudation mechanisms or indirectly through an effect on metabolism.

Auxins are known to induce the initiation of new roots and to reach the roots primarily from the shoots. Where environmental conditions, such as the availability of water and nutrients, allow for rapid root initiation, the root may become the preferred sink for these auxins. The response to auxin distribution could be rapid, preceding rather than following overt development, and it could be relatively specific to the development of new root apices. In the case of cytokinins, they are known to be formed in developing root apices and to inhibit the formation of additional apices on the same plant. The sensitivity to cytokinins could be modified by local environmental conditions. Thus, it appears that known hormones are likely candidates for the role of integrating the local effects of the environment.

COSTS ASSOCIATED WITH ROOT PLASTIC RESPONSES

Studies concerning plant exploitation of soil heterogeneity have primarily focused on the morphological and physiological plasticity associated with rapid resource acquisition. However, as in most plant responses, there are trade-offs associated with rapid resource acquisition that should be considered. There is increasing evidence that there can be a considerable energy investment in patch exploitation. Root foraging can be accommodated by enhanced root growth, uptake kinetics, and mycorrhizal activity. All of these processes may require substantial inputs of current photosynthate. Indirect evidence that root foraging in patches is energetically taxing on the plant comes from shading experiments in the cold desert. For example, Cui and Caldwell examined the effects of partial shading on nitrate and phosphate (P) acquisition from soil patches in Artemisia tridentata and Agropyron desertorum seedlings growing in 60-L pots in the field.

The shading was designed to simulate the kind of light competition that can occur in shrub-steppe vegetation in the early springtime when nutrient acquisition is very important and when the sun is at a low solar angle. Patches were created using polyethylene wicks such that the enriched soil represented a soil column only about 2 cm in diameter. Shading reduced acquisition of nitrate and P for both species in both nutrient distribution treatments. Presumably because of its mobility, shading reduced nitrate uptake similarly in the patchy and uniform nutrient treatments.

For acquisition of immobile P, however, the effects of shading were much more pronounced in the patchy than the uniform treatment for either plant species. For example, unshaded Artemisia seedlings acquired 54% more P than shaded plants in the uniform nutrient treatment and 185% more in the patchy nutrient treatment. If shading only affected plant nutrient demand, then one would expect that shading would diminish P uptake similarly in the uniform and patchy nutrient distributions. Consequently, the data suggest that plants require substantial amounts of energy for root foraging for spatially heterogeneous immobile nutrients such as P.

Root proliferation in nutrient-rich patches is typically accomplished by increasing lateral branching, not increasing root elongation. Root lateral initiation is fundamentally linked to plant energy status. Bingham et al. found that whenever an increase in lateral root primordia was observed, it was associated with increased soluble sugars (glucose, sucrose, and low molecular mass fructans). Separate experiments associated with partial nitrate supply, root pruning, or exogenously applied glucose all yielded similar results. For example, seminal roots fed glucose (50 mM) exhibited an increase in primordia within 15 hours. The investigators concluded that lateral root proliferation in response to soil heterogeneity was signaled by an increase in sugar content in the parent root, rather the material cotransported with sucrose in the phloem, because glucose-fed roots had reduced 14 C-photosynthate compared to roots not fed glucose. Thus, physiological studies suggest that conditions that reduce plant energy status can directly affect the potential to initiate new lateral roots.

Field investigations support this view. Bilbrough and Caldwell found that in mature Agropyron desertorum plants, root relative growth rates (RGR) in N-enriched patches were reduced by more than 50% by short-term shading treatments, while root RGR in unenriched soil was unaffected by shading. The investigators found that roots had higher SRL in the enriched than unenriched patches, primarily because of increased production and length of higher-order laterals as a result of greater lateral initiation. Shading reduced initiation of lateral roots. Other investigators have also found that roots in patches have higher SRL than those in unenriched soil. When dry weight is used as an estimator of cost, this would suggest that construction of root length is cheaper for growth in patches than for growth in unfertile soil.

Moreover, species that tend to produce fine roots of high SRL may have greater capacity for root proliferation in resource-rich patches than those that tend to produce fine roots of lower SRL. Enhanced nutrient uptake kinetics associated with root foraging in fertile patches also can require substantial inputs of energy. Normally, plants with roots deficient in a particular nutrient have higher uptake capacity of that nutrient (e.g., Vmax) than roots of nutrient-sufficient plants. This pattern is consistent with the energetics associated with moving nutrients along an electrochemical gradient and the energy required to maintain an adequate proton-motive force through the action of the plasma membrane H+ -ATPase. However, root P concentrations and nutrient uptake kinetics were higher for roots in the high-P patches than those in relatively low-P soil.

Roots in ammonium-rich patches also can exhibit enhanced ammonium uptake capacity as compared with roots in unenriched patches, although in this study root N concentrations were not reported. The apparent pattern of roots in nutrient-rich patches having enhanced nutrient uptake capacity despite having higher nutrient concentrations suggests that roots in the rich patches require more energy for active uptake of a nutrient at a given nutrient concentration in the soil solution. This additional energy required for enhanced phosphate uptake capacity is not likely to be too large, considering the small amounts of respiration associated with P uptake; however, if the same pattern is true for ammonium and nitrate, then the energy requirements for enhanced uptake capacity may be appreciable. Field studies provide additional evidence that plants with reduced energy reserves have less potential to enhance nutrient uptake in fertile patches.

Unshaded Agropyron desertorum plants selectively increased P uptake capacity of roots in enriched patches by 73%, while shading eliminated any enhancement of uptake kinetics. Shade-induced reductions in P uptake capacity were linked to root total nonstructural carbohydrates (TNC) in only the first year of the two-year study, although shading substantially reduced shoot TNC in both years.

The efficiency of root proliferation and enhanced uptake kinetics into patches can be examined from an economic perspective. Although the benefits may be high in terms of enhanced nutrient inflows, the previous discussion clearly indicates that the energetic costs of root proliferation may also be high. Similar calculations can be made using P as the sole currency for cost and benefit. We can illustrate the costs of root proliferation by calculating the payback time for new root growth in a nutrient-rich patch using a solute transport model previously described. For example, assuming a root P concentration of 0.1% and a moderately rich patch (0.5 mM P in soil solution), simulation modeling of Volkamer lemon seedlings (parameter values and model described in 125) indicates that it would take about three days for the root to pay back the P investment of just that individual root. However, this calculation does not include the other plant parts (leaves, stem, and taproot) that must support the function of the fine roots but also depend on the fine roots for P acquisition.

If we use the fine root/whole plant P content ratio of these seedlings, which is about 7:1, to estimate plant support of the fine root system, then it would take approximately 21 days to pay back the whole-plant P investment in fine-root production in that patch. If P concentrations in the patch diminish, then the payback time would be even longer. Thus, it may take several weeks or more for new roots in P-rich patches to pay back the plant P investment. As illustrated in the preceding example, several factors may influence the advantages of patch exploitation. In terms of the patches, potential nutrient gain will be based on patch duration, patch contrast with the bulk soil, and patch size. Plant factors influencing benefit include changes of root physiology with root age and the longevity of the roots in the patch. Data on fine-root persistence in patches is sparse and inconsistent. From a root efficiency perspective, plants should retain roots in patches longer than those in the less-fertile bulk soil as long as root efficiency (the ratio of nutrient uptake to the costs of root maintenance and root construction) is higher for roots in the fertile patches. In mixed hardwoods, roots that proliferated in response to additions of water or water and nutrients lived longer than roots in unamended patches of soil.

On the other hand, localized water and nutrient addition diminished root life span in a pot study using four old-field herbaceous species. One factor that may potentially explain the mixed results associated with root survivorship in patches is root herbivory and root parasitism. When roots proliferate, there may be a dense population of young fine roots very close together. Young roots are often very vulnerable to attack by soil organisms. For example, the root-rot fungus, Phytophthora nicotianae, more readily infects young citrus roots. Root-knot nematodes (Meloidogyne spp.) normally infect rapidly growing roots by entering behind the root cap and Belonolamus and Longidorid nematodes feed on root tips (L. W. Duncan, personal communication).

Older roots and roots in a "resting" state are typically much more resistant to infection. Moreover, because organisms often have restricted mobility in soil, close proximity of young roots should greatly facilitate foraging of root-feeding organisms. To our knowledge, however, no one has directly examined the potential interactions of root proliferation with root herbivory parasitism. Up to now, we have only focused on the efficiency of patch exploitation. We argued that a plant might not directly benefit by patch exploitation if the photosynthate and mineral nutrient capital expended on roots proliferating in patches is not satisfied by a corresponding increase in mineral nutrient acquisition. But plants that are most fit are not necessarily those that acquire resources efficiently. When a plant has competing neighbors, it may be a more advantageous strategy to acquire resources rapidly, albeit inefficiently, so as to deprive neighbors of these resources. The benefits of rapid resource exploitation in a competitive context may better explain the apparent large-energy expenditures on root foraging of nutrient patches than resource acquisition efficiency.

SUMMARY

In natural conditions, water and nutrient availability in the soil is often heterogeneous. Plants can exploit available resources by increasing root growth and/or physiological activity in enriched microsites or horizons of the soil profile. Root plastic responses enable plants growing in heterogeneous environments to use limiting resources in ways that maximize the efficiency of water and nutrient acquisition. Root responses to soil heterogeneity can be separated into phenotypic/ morphological and physiological responses.

Morphological responses include shifts in lateral root initiation, elongation, and angle of growth, as well as changes in root diameter, root hairs, and mycorrhizal colonization.

Physiological responses include shifts in water and nutrient uptake kinetics and root exudation. The type and magnitude of plant responses to nutrient heterogeneity depend on plant species, characteristics of the patches, such as contrast, duration, size, and predictability. Although many studies of root responses to soil heterogeneity have been conducted, most have been done with isolated plants in pots under quite controlled conditions. Some of the root responses to water and nutrient heterogeneity observed under controlled conditions may be considerably dampened when considered in the context of other environmental stresses acting on an individual in the community. Thus, most generalizations concern potential plant responses. We still have relatively little understanding of the magnitude of plant responses to water and nutrient heterogeneity in a field context and their importance to plant growth, yield, or fitness.

5

Soil Constraints on Plant Mineral Nutrition

INTRODUCTION

Soils throughout the world are diverse, and plants grown on them invariably encounter many mineral stress problems. The nature of mineral stress problems that plants encounter may depend on the many soil chemical [e.g., acidity and alkalinity (pH), sodicity and salinity, elemental deficiencies and toxicities, organic matter] and physical (e.g., moisture, temperature, bulk density, texture) properties. Each of these factors has specific influences on the type and severity of mineral stresses that plants encounter. Discussing the importance that each of these factors has for plant mineral nutrition in various types of soil and ecosystems is beyond the scope of this article. Fortunately, some of these soil factors and their influence on mineral nutrition have been discussed in other articles in this book and in other articles of the earlier book in this series. This review discusses acidic and alkaline soil constraints affecting plant mineral nutrition of plants.

ACIDIC SOIL CONSTRAINTS

Factors that contribute to soil acidity are parent materials low in weatherable minerals, excess precipitation over evaporation, leaching and runoff water losses, leaf fall before winter under forest cover, accumulation of organic matter, atmospheric deposition of nitrogen

(N) and sulfur (S), intensive crop production removing large amounts of cations, addition of acid-forming N fertilizers, N_2 fixation by legumes, and time involved with each of these factors. Since acidic soils are prevalent throughout the world, many inherent mineral nutritional problems appear with plants grown in these soils. However, some regions of the world have more serious problems than others because of certain soil properties and amount and severity of acidity in soils of different regions. Acidic soils make up 26%, or 37.8 million square kilometers, of the global ice-free surface land area. Acidic subsurface soils make up slightly less area than surface soils but consist of 20%, or 29.2 million square kilometers, of the global ice-free land.

The region with highest amounts of moderately to high surface soil acidity (pH <5.5) is South America, with over half of the soils being classified in these categories. About 31% of North American and about 43% of European surface soils are moderately to highly acidic. Some soil orders are commonly associated with acidity [e.g., Oxisols, Ultisols, Alfisols, Andepts (Inceptisols)], and these soils have the potential to impose fairly severe mineral deficiencies/ toxicities on plants. The main chemical constraints limiting plant growth in acidic mineral soils are high available hydrogen (H), aluminum (Al), and manganese (Mn) concentrations (H, Al, and Mn toxicities), decreased basic cation concentrations, and reduced plant acquisition/availability of these cationic nutrients [magnesium (Mg), calcium (Ca), and potassium (K) deficiencies], decreased phosphorus (P) and molybdenum (Mo) solubilities (P and Mo deficiencies), inhibited root growth (mineral nutrient and water deficiencies and elemental toxicities), and increased leaching (mineral nutrient deficiencies).

Some soils may impose not just one but several of these constraints on plants at the same time, and interactions among one or more of these factors may occur simultaneously. The importance of each chemical constraint and/or interaction depends on such factors as soil pH and organic matter, soil type and horizon, concentration and species of nutrient/element, parent material, soil physical properties, plant species/genotype, and climatic conditions. Mineral deficiency and toxicity constraints related to soil pH commonly follow these general patterns:

(a) soils with slight acidity (pH 5.5 to 6.5) do not normally impose many problems to plant growth when adequate quantities of essential mineral nutrients are available, but these soils are relatively prone to acidification from improper management and/or environmental pollution [e.g., from application of high ammonium (NH+ -N) fertilizer and deposition of atmos4 pheric sulfur dioxide (SO_2) and nitrogen oxides (NOx)];

(b) soils with moderate acidity (pH 4.5 to 5.5) commonly impose basic cation (Mg, Ca, and K) and P deficiencies and Al toxicity on plants;

(c) soils with high acidity (pH 3.5 to 4.5) usually impose extensive and often severe Mg, Ca, K, and/or P deficiencies with dominant Al and sometimes Mn toxicities on plants; and

(d) soils with extreme acidity (pH <3.5) are usually acid sulfate soils containing pyrite that is oxidized to sulfuric acid from high H [iron (Fe) toxicity], contain few available essential mineral nutrients, and are usually highly toxic to plants.

The general method to alleviate mineral stress constraints for plants grown in acidic soils has been addition of limestone to raise soil pH and ameliorate H, Al, and Mn toxicities and addition of fertilizers to provide adequate nutrients to sustain/maintain optimal plant growth. Besides N, which is the most limiting mineral nutrient to many plants grown in any soil, the primary mineral nutrients limiting plant growth in acidic soils are P, Mg, Ca, and Mo.

Hydrogen

Acidic means relatively high H^+ concentrations, and most detrimental effects at low pH (<5.0 to 5.5) or high H^+ concentration are indirect because high H^+ increases solubility of toxic elements like Al, Mn, and Fe, decreases solubility of P and Mo, and decreases availability of Ca, Mg, and K. However, some direct effects of H^+ toxicity may occur. High H^+ concentrations reduce nodulation of leguminous plant roots and survival, activity, and multiplication of rhizobia and other beneficial microorganisms in acidic soil. Root infection with nodulating bacterial species appears to require higher pH (lower H^+ concentration) than survival of the bacteria involved.

In addition, high H^+ concentrations may inhibit root growth, increase plant requirement for higher Ca, and decrease the capacity of roots to retain cationic nutrients like Ca, Mg, Mn for average mineral concentrations in dry matter are for field crops providing optimal growth. These values would likely be different for many plants, and interested readers are referred to books/articles with reported mineral nutrient values in various plant tissues. Additional information and descriptions of deficiency symptoms on shoots and roots are provided by Clark, Fageria et al., and Baligar et al. zinc (Zn), and copper (Cu). Detrimental effects of high H+ concentrations have also been associated with impaired net extrusion of H^+ by plasma membrane–bound ATPase activity and decreased loading of polyvalent cations (e.g., Ca^{2+} , Mg^{2+} , Mn^{2+} , and Zn^{2+}) into the apoplasm of root cortical cells. Apoplastic loading of these nutrients enhances uptake of cations into the symplasm.

Aluminum

Aluminum toxicity is considered to be the foremost yield limiting factor for plants grown in acidic soil. This malady is normally alleviated once soil pH increases above 5.2 to 5.5. As soil pH decreases below 5.0 to 5.5, increasing proportions of cationic exchange sites on clay minerals become occupied with Aln^+ by replacing other cationic elements such as Mg^{2+} , Ca^{2+} , and K^+. As such, increased percentage Al saturation of soil cation exchange sites has been closely associated with decreased soil pH. Once cationic nutrients have been replaced from exchange sites, they are vulnerable to leaching, so that plant roots are often unable to obtain sufficient nutrients for optimal growth. In addition, Aln^+ becomes the primary exchangeable ion and roots are deprived of essential mineral nutrients because Al competes against these nutrients; furthermore, Al imposes direct detrimental effects on roots (e.g., inhibits cell extension to reduce root length, and roots can no longer explore large soil volumes to obtain needed nutrients and water to support plant growth). Aluminum, one of the most plentiful elements in the earth's crust and a major constituent of clay mineral lattices, is not required for plant growth but restricts root elongation and cell division and inhibits many plant metabolic functions.

Phytotoxic effects of Al on plants depend not only on restricted essential nutrient acquisition but also on other factors such as nature of Al species (Aln^{+}), quantity and ratio of Aln^{+} and complexed Al, and ionic strength of soil solutions to determine degree of phytotoxic effect of AL. That is, certain Aln^{+} are highly toxic [e.g., Al^{3+} , $AlOH^{2+}$, 'Al13 '], some are less toxic [e.g., $Al(OH)^{+}$, $Al(OH)^{0}$], and some are nontoxic [e.g., Al(OH)" , $AlF2^{+}$, AlF+ , 3 2 4 2 $AlSO^{+}$] to plants. Organic matter may also decrease Al toxicity in 4 acidic soil, and organic compounds common to organic matter (e.g., fulvic and humic acids) may ameliorate Al toxicity. In addition, organic acids often found in organic materials or exuded by roots may ameliorate Al toxicity, and the effectiveness of low-molecular-weight organic acids followed a sequence of citric = oxalic > malic > succinic. Plants grown with high and/or enhanced levels of other nutrients over Al are not as detrimentally affected by Al as plants grown with low levels of nutrients. This may be due in part to interactive effects some nutrients (e.g., P, Ca, and S) have for inactivating Al. Roots are detrimentally affected more by Al toxicity than are shoots, and Al-affected plants usually have stubby to coralloid roots with enlarged diameters because of reduced root elongation/growth. Because of shorter root systems, Al-affected plants commonly undergo not only nutrient deficiencies, especially P, but also water stress.

Manganese

Manganese, like Al, also becomes more soluble as soil pH decreases below <"5.0 to 5.5 (8–10), but Mn toxicity on plants is not usually as prevalent as that of Al toxicity. This is likely because Mn in many soils, especially when cultivated, is not at sufficient concentrations to induce plant toxicity compared to Al. Nevertheless, Mn toxicity has been considered to be the second most important growth-limiting factor after Al toxicity for plants grown in acidic soil. Of the many soil properties that influence Mn solubility and activity (e.g., high H^+ concentration, organic matter, microbial activity, anaerobiosis), redox potential is an important factor influencing detrimental Mn effects to plant growth.

Conditions common for Mn toxicity induction on plants are wetland and/or anaerobic conditions where microbial activity for Mn reduction prevail. Shoots are generally more susceptible to changes in growth compared to roots when Mn toxicity occurs. However, sorghum [Sorghum bicolor (L.) Moench] roots had greater changes and decreases at lower levels of Mn than did shoots when plants were grown with different levels of Mn in nutrient solution. In addition, sorghum tolerated relatively high Mn concentrations (<"6 mM in solution) before detrimental effects appeared. An example indicating that Mn toxicity is not as prevalent as Al toxicity in many acidic soils was noted in studies where bean (Phaseolus vulgaris L.), subterraneum clover (Trifolium subterraneum L.), and switchgrass (Panicum virgatum L.) were grown in many Appalachian soils. In each case, Al toxicity or some other factor was more important than Mn toxicity for limiting plant growth, even though many of the soils contained relatively high Mn. Extensive coverage of Mn chemistry in soils and Mn effects on plants is provided by Graham et al.

Iron

Iron toxicity ("bronzing") is not commonly reported for most plants grown in acidic soil but is common for rice (Oryza sativa L.) grown under wetland or poorly drained conditions. This disorder is considered to be the second most severe yield-limiting factor for plants grown under wet conditions. Even though genotypes and/or plant species vary in Fe concentrations when grown under wet/anaerobic conditions, plants normally accumulate relatively high Fe before the disorder appears [<“300 to 700 mg kg”1 for rice and <“1100 to 1600 mg kg”1 for dock/sorrel (Rumex)]. Activity of polyphenol oxidases is commonly enhanced to form oxidized polyphenols, which appears to cause the “bronzing”/“brown speckling” associated with Fe toxicity (and sometimes with Mn toxicity). In addition, Fe toxicity may be more severe when other nutrients like P, K, and Zn are low.

Trace Elements

The trace elements cadmium (Cd), cobalt (Co), chromium (Cr), lead (Pb), and nickel (Ni) are generally more mobile under acidic conditions, and increasing soil pH decreases bioavailability of these cationic elements. If parent materials of soils contain high concentrations of these elements or if soils are contaminated with these elements [e.g., high levels of sewage sludge (biosolid)/ amendment applications and soils near or at smelter, mining, manufacturing, or disposal sites], it should be recognized that plants could potentially accumulate sufficient quantities of these elements to be of concern to animal/human consumption of products from plants grown in these soils. The chemistry/interactions/properties of arsenic (As) and selenium (Se) (anionic trace elements) are similar to those of P and P and S, respectively, so plant accumulation of these elements and toxicity to plants might be of concern for plants grown under some conditions.

Deficiencies

Mineral nutrient deficiencies are also prominent for plants grown in many acidic soils of the world. This is usually because acidic soils lack sufficient quantities of essential mineral nutrients, and these nutrients are commonly unavailable for plant use.

1. Phosphorus

Phosphorus deficiency is common in nearly all acidic tropical soils. Fixation or inactivation of P is common in acidic soils because of strong P binding with relatively high Al and Fe oxides (sesquioxides) that often exist at surfaces of layer-silicate clay particles in low pH soils. Factors such as quantity and quality of clay minerals (exchange sites), colloid and Fe and Al oxide contents, exchangeable Al, and organic matter influence P fixation. In the decomposition of organic matter, organic acids (e.g., citric and oxalic) are released, which partially dissolve Fe and Al oxides and release bound P into soil solution. Organic acids can form stable metal ligand complexes in soil solution to increase P availability. In addition, Ca added to soil as lime can bind P, but not as strongly as Fe and Al oxides.

As lime is dissolved by soil acidity, Ca-P becomes readily available to plants. Added lime also increases soil pH and inactivates free Fe and Al oxides to prevent P binding. Since P remains relatively stationary in soil and does not readily move, roots must grow to sites where P is located or other factor(s) must be present to make P available and/or to supply P to roots. A major detrimental effect of Al is to reduce root cell elongation, so Al-affected roots may not grow to sites where P (and other essential mineral nutrients) may be plentiful and the immediate root rhizosphere becomes depleted of these nutrients. Aluminum also interacts strongly with P to reduce P availability. Even with poor mobilization of P in soil and inability of roots to grow to new sources of P, other processes associated with roots may be important to make otherwise unavailable P available to roots.

For example, P availability near root surfaces may be influenced by root exudation of H^+ /hydroxyl ions (OH^-) and organic acids (e.g., citric and oxalic) and enhanced root phosphatase activity. Other factors that may be just as or more important than root excretions and enzyme activities are mycorrhizae (beneficial soil fungi) and/ or other microorganisms associated with roots. For instance, mycorrhizae colonize/infect roots and enhance plant ability to acquire mineral nutrients, especially P. Enhanced mineral nutrient acquisition has been attributed primarily to ability of mycorrhizal hyphae to grow away from roots to extend effective surface areas that roots have for obtaining nutrients. Mycorrhizal hyphae also have the ability to transport nutrients fairly long distances and are smaller in diameter than most roots, so they can make contact with soil particles that roots per se would not otherwise contact. Some mycorrhiza are highly effective in low-pH soils to enhance ability of plants to grow and survive, and some species/isolates of mycorrhizae are more effective than others. For example, certain mycorrhizal isolates enhanced plant acquisition of essential mineral nutrients, restricted plant acquisition of toxic elements (e.g., Al, Mn, and Fe), and enhanced growth of switchgrass considerably more than other isolates when grown in pH 4 soil.

2. Calcium

Calcium deficiency per se is often difficult to identify in plants grown in acidic soil, and factors other than low Ca may be involved, especially Ca-Al interactions. Many studies have been conducted to provide evidence for absolute Ca requirements of plants grown in acidic soils and to better understand factors inducing Ca deficiency or elemental induced Ca deficiencies. In such studies, evidence for Ca requirement in plants or induction of Ca deficiency was provided by enhanced root growth of many crop plants when acidic soil had been treated with Ca sulfate ($CaSO_4$) at pH values known to induce Al toxicity (i.e., pH 4.3 and 4.7). Leucaena leucocephala growth was enhanced when Ca carbonate ($CaCO_3$) compared to strontium carbonate ($SrCO_3$) was applied to soil.

The increase in growth occurred primarily because of increased soil pH. Calcium deficiency was induced in barley (Hordeum vulgare L.) by raising soil pH with Mg carbonate ($MgCO_3$), and Ca deficiency appeared in bean when soil pH was 3.3. In addition, $CaSO_4$ decreased soil pH and enhanced growth, $MgCO_3$ eliminated exchangeable Al and induced Ca deficiency, and Ca hydroxide [$Ca(OH)_2$] raised soil pH, eliminated exchangeable Al, provided Ca, and increased plant growth. Calcium deficiencies were also induced on plants grown in subsoils to provide additional evidence for a Ca requirement by plants grown in acidic soils. In many cases, Ca-Al interactions were also apparent for plants grown in these various experiments. Apical meristem Ca deficiencies have also been documented for soybeans [Glycine max (L.) Merr.] and beans grown in acidic soil known to induce Al toxicity, and added Ca reduced Al induced root growth inhibition in maize (Zea mays L.).

Even though considerable evidence is available that plants require Ca when grown in acidic soil, results have been inconsistent for an Al-induced Ca deficiency in wheat (Triticum aestivum L.), and Ca deficiency was not a factor for cowpeas [Vigna unguiculata (L.) Walp.] grown with toxic levels of Al. Other evidence indicating Ca requirements for plants grown in acidic soil were obtained when soybeans and beans had reduced or delayed root nodulation with low Ca, and Ca was required for nodulation of cowpeas grown in solution culture with varied concentrations of Ca. Calcium requirements in most plants are low, and Ca at relatively high concentrations commonly found in plants may detoxify or exclude entry of other toxic elements to provide protection against some stress factors like drought and mechanical stress. Plants like peanuts (Arachis hypogaea L.), tomatoes [Lycopersicon lycopersicon (L.) Karsten], and apple (Malus spp.) require relatively high concentrations of Ca for development of pegs and fruits. Aluminum has strong competing effects against Ca uptake into root cells and Al may block Ca^{2+} channels in root plasma membranes. Because of the effective inhibitory effects that Al has on Ca uptake, Ca/Al ratios appear to be more important than Ca concentrations per se for predicting Al induced Ca deficiency.

3. *Magnesium*

Magnesium deficiency is also common for many plants grown in acidic soil and is accentuated even more when acidic soil is amended with high levels of Ca products such as gypsum ($CaSO_4 \cdot 2H_2O$) and calcitic limestone ($CaCO_3$). Enhanced Mg deficiency in plants from added soil Ca usually occurs because of Ca/Mg imbalances. Detrimental effects of excess Ca on acidic soils have been referred to as "overliming stress" effects. These effects relate not only to Mg deficiency and reduced Mg availability or fixation but also to other nutrient deficiencies and imbalances (e.g., reduced K absorption).

Ratios of Ca/Mg in soil greater than <"30/1 imposed Mg deficiency on maize grown in acidic soil amended with $CaCO_3$, $CaSO_4$, and gypsum-quality coal combustion products. Another problem that might arise with the addition of Ca to acidic soil may be displacement of exchangeable Al into soil solution to enhance Al toxicity effects. Acidic soils may reduce Mg absorption by roots and induce Mg deficiency in plants because of strong Al interactions with Mg. Magnesium concentrations were reduced more than those of any other mineral nutrient when maize was grown in nutrient solution with different levels of Al. Aluminum may also inhibit root Mg absorption by blocking plasma membrane cation binding sites. Added Mg to acidic soil may also alleviate Al toxicity problems on plants, as was noted for forest plants and for sorghum and soybean plants grown in acidic soil and nutrient solutions. Like Ca, Mg/Al ratios in plant matter appears to be a better parameter to predict Al toxicity than Mg concentration itself.

4. *Molybdenum*

Available Mo in acidic soil is often at levels that are too low to support plant growth. In acidic soils, Mo may be bound by Fe, Mn, and Al. Molybdenum deficiency is often alleviated by increasing acidic soil pH through liming. In addition, plants grown in acidic soil with either added Mo or lime could produce similar plant yields. Molybdenum deficiency has been reported for many crop plants, especially soybeans and alfalfa (Medicago sativa L.), which are grown in eastern and southeastern acidic soils of the United States. Seed contents of Mo have sometimes been sufficient to keep plants from undergoing Mo deficiency.

5. *Other Mineral Elements*

Even though P, Ca, Mg, and Mo deficiencies have most commonly been reported for plants grown in acidic soil, plants may suffer other nutrient deficiencies such as N, K, S, Zn, silicon (Si), and boron (B) in acidic soil when these nutrients are at sufficiently low levels. Although K uptake—in contrast to that of Ca and Mg—

is not affected extensively in acidic soil by the presence of Al, Al can restrict Ca and Mg uptake to increase K/Ca^{+} Mg ratios and aid in induction of Ca and/or Mg deficiency. Nitrogen deficiencies may occur in any soil and are not particularly related to low soil pH, but microbial activity (e.g., ammonification, nitrification, denitrification, and N2 fixation) is normally lower in soils at pH below 5 compared to those at higher pH. Adams and Martin summarized N availability relative to acidic soil conditions as follows:

(a) rate of organic N mineralization occurs over wide pH ranges but decreases progressively below pH 6.0 to 6.5;

(b) rate of nitrification is optimal at pH 6.6 to 8.0, and decreases progressively with decreasing soil pH and is negligible below 4.5;

(c) denitrification by microbes is optimal at pH 7.0 to 7.5, but much lower below pH 5;

(d) N_2 fixation associated with root infection by Rhizobium may occur over wide soil pH ranges, but some bacteria are more effective at high compared to low pH and vice versa;

(e) ammonia (NH_3) volatilization is accentuated above pH 7; and

(f) plants preferably absorb NH^{+} -N at high 4 pH and nitrate (NO" -N) at low pH.

Sulfur is normally less available at lower 3 than at higher soil pH values and has been related to high levels of soluble Al and Fe oxides in low-pH soils. Increasing soil pH with lime also enhances decomposition of organic matter to release organically bound S, which is a dominant fraction of S in soils. In addition, progressively more S became available with lime increment increases in an acidic subsoil horizon than without added lime. Another element that may be limiting to some plants grown in acidic soils is Si. Although Si has not been proven to be essential to plant growth according to the classic definition of essentiality established by Arnon and Stout, Si accumulates in some plants at concentrations equivalent of those of N and K and provides plants with many beneficial effects. Plants have generally been classified into three categories relative to Si accumulation:

(a) "wetland" grasses and ferns/allies [e.g., paddy-grown rice, sugarcane (Saccharum officinarum L.), and horsetail (Equisetum arvense) with 100 to 150 g Si kg"1];

(b) "dryland" grasses, gymnosperms, and some specific plants with 10 to 30 g Si kg"1 ; and

(c) dicotyledonous plants with <10 g Si kg"1. Rice and sugar cane particularly have been studied relative to needs for Si application to optimize production and quality of final product.

Silicon can interact with many essential mineral nutrients to enhance and/or inhibit them under specific conditions. Some major and important benefits of Si are its ability to ameliorate plant abiotic stresses (e.g., keep stalks erect to hold heavy weights and improve photosynthesis, delay leaf senescence, withstand water and salt stresses), ameliorate and/or provide ability of plants to withstand attacks by insects and/or disease organisms, and overcome Al, Mn, and Fe toxicities. Even though most benefits from Si are considered to be indirect effects, Si alleviation of mineral toxicities is of particular importance to plants grown in acidic soils. Zinc, B, Mo, and Fe deficiencies have been reported in highly weathered Oxisols and Ultisols. Histosols consistently induce Cu deficiency on crop plants that have high demand for Cu. Crop plants grown in Entisols often exhibit Zn, Mn, Cu, and Fe deficiency, primarily because these elements are strongly bound-onto clay or organic matter in these soils. Andisols commonly have low levels of Mo and B as these soils have high anion-fixation capacity, and plants grown in Oxisols often develop Mo and P deficiency.

ALKALINE SOIL CONSTRAINTS

Distinctions between acidic and alkaline soils are usually associated with differences in amount of precipitation compared to evapotranspiration. If precipitation exceeds evapotranspiration in most years, soils usually are leached, which leads to formation of acidic soils. If evapotranspiration exceeds precipitation, soils are usually neutral to alkaline. General differences between acidic and alkaline soils are boundaries between forests and prairies; in the United States, these boundaries generally follow where maize and small grains are grown as predominant crops. Neutral to alkaline soils prevail in subhumid, semiarid, and arid climates. These soils frequently contain fairly high soluble salts like K and Na and may often contain sufficient amounts of Ca as $CaCO_3$ to be termed calcareous. Strongly alkaline soils may have high sodicity and be termed saline or saline-sodic soils. For discussion here, soils with alkaline pH (>7.0) have been referred to as alkaline, calcareous, saline, and/or saline-sodic.

Calcareous soils make up <"30% of the earth's surface, and $CaCO_3$ levels in these soils vary extensively (e.g., 5 to 95%). Magnesium is often abundant in calcareous soils and may even be high enough such as in serpentine soils to interact with other elements and cause deficiencies. Alkaline soils commonly have abundant 2:1 layer clay minerals (montmorillonitic) compared to the 1:1 clay minerals (kaolinitic) so frequent in acidic soils, and 2:1 clay minerals usually provide fairly high ion-exchange-capacity properties to soil. Alkaline soils are also well distributed throughout the world, and various mineral deficiency and toxicity problems are commonly associated with alkaline soils (Mollisols, Vertisols, Aridisols). Regions with the most land area with moderately high to high alkaline/saline risk are west-central and mideastern Asia, northern Africa, and Australia. Major mineral nutritional problems associated with these soils are P, Fe, and Zn deficiencies, although Mn, Cu, and B deficiencies and B and salt toxicities may occur in some.

Deficiencies

1. Phosphorus

Solubility of P decreases as soil pH increases above <"6.5, especially as amount of soil Ca increases. Phosphorus is made unavailable to plants because of adsorption and precipitation reactions. Adsorption reactions of P generally dominate when soil solutions contain low P and precipitation reactions dominate when soil solutions contain high P. The usual adsorption reaction at low solution P concentrations is onto $CaCO_3$ particle surfaces, and various kinds of Ca-P compounds are formed depending on fertilizer formulation when P is added to soil at relatively high levels. The many compounds formed when added P reacts with soil constituents have been summarized by Sample et al.

2. *Iron*

The foremost mineral stress problem for plants grown in calcareous soil is Fe deficiency. It is not that Fe is limiting in these soils, since mineral soils on average contain <“2% Fe (40,000 kg ha$^{"1}$), but that Fe is essentially unavailable to plants. Plants remove minute quantities of Fe from soil annually for growth (<“1 to 2 kg ha$^{"1}$). Concentrations of Fe^{2+} and/or Fe^{3+} in soil solution for well aerated high pH soils is <“10”10 M, whereas concentrations of available Fe near root surfaces needed for optimal plant growth is <“10”6 to 10"5 M. Iron availability to plants is highly dependent on soil pH and redox potential. For example, Fe^{3+} concentration in solution decreases from 10"8 to 10"20 M as pH increases from 4 to 8 (1000-fold change per unit pH change).

Excess moisture in soil may reduce redox potentials and enhance Fe solubility. High bicarbonate (HCO”) concentrations may 3 also decrease Fe availability in calcareous soils. In addition, enhanced Fe deficiency often appears when soil aeration is poor from soil compaction, high water content, and low soil temperatures. Iron deficiency occurs frequently on plants grown in sandy, fine-textured mucks and peat soils, where pH is higher than 6.

Dissolution and precipitation of ferric oxide is the major factor controlling solubility of Fe in well-aerated soils. Many soil microorganisms affect availability of Fe by (a) releasing inorganic Fe ions during decomposition of organic matter, (b) immobilizing Fe by incorporating it into microbial biomass, (c) oxidizing Fe to less available forms, (d) reducing oxidized forms of Fe under conditions of limited oxygen, and (e) changing environmental conditions such as soil pH and oxidation potentials.

Susceptibility of plant species and/or cultivars within species to Fe deficiency often depends on plant root responses to Fe deficiency and/or HCO" as well as substances added to soil that may change pH near roots (rhizosphere) to complex/chelate Fe. For example, the severity of Fe deficiency in nongraminaceous species like soybeans, grapes (Vitis spp.), and apples correlates well with HCO" concentrations in soil, while gramina ceous species like sorghum, maize, and wheat do not. These plant species also have different strategies with which to cope with Fe deficiency (e.g., root ability to make Fe more available). Graminaceous species normally have Strategy II (enhanced root release of nonproteinogenic amino acids called phytosiderophores) while nongraminaceous species have Strategy I (increased reducing capacity of roots and enhanced root release of protons) mechanisms for acquisition of Fe.

Additional definitions and the importance of various Fe acquisition mechanisms by different plant species are summarized in Marschner. Rhizosphere soil pH can also influence availability of Fe to plants. Application of NH^+ -N versus NO" -N and K chloride (KCl)/K_2 SO_4 versus KNO_3/K phosphate (Kn Hn PO_4) to soil tends to decrease root rhizosphere soil pH and enhance Fe solubility. This occurs because roots excrete H^+ when NH^+ -N is absorbed to reduce rhizosphere soil pH. On the other hand, roots excrete OH" when NO" -N is absorbed to raise rhizosphere soil pH and decrease Fe_3 availability. Roots of some plant species also have greater ability to decrease or enhance rhizosphere pH than others.

Organic compound excretion by roots (e.g., malic, citric, and phenolic acids and phytosiderophores) can also complex or chelate Fe and enhance its availability to plants. These strategies for Fe acquisition provide many plants with a greater ability to resist Fe deficiency and otherwise tolerate Fe-deficiency conditions. Organic substances released into soil from decomposing organic matter (e.g., fulvic and humic acidic) may also be effective complexing agents of Fe and subsequently enhance its solubility. Iron interacts with several elements to enhance Fe deficiency. For example, high soil P may decrease Fe availability. Enhanced organic acids and excreted compounds by roots not only enhance Fe but also P availability, and enhanced P availability from organic compounds may interact with Fe to restrict Fe availability. Some plant species like cotton (Gossypium hirsutum L.) and sugar beet (Beta vulgaris L. subsp. vulgaris) with Zn deficiency also have enhanced Fe uptake, and Mn in the growth medium can interact with Fe to decrease its availability. Other studies have reported that K and Mo in the growth medium may interact with Fe to reduce its availability.

3. Zinc and Manganese

The availability of Zn and Mn, like that of Fe, decreases with increasing soil pH in neutral and alkaline ranges. Decreases in Zn and Mn concentrations in plant tissue with increasing soil pH may be more extensive than those of other nutrients that might be limiting (e.g., P and Fe) for plants grown in the same soil. Zinc deficiency in cereals has been considered to be one of the foremost mineral stress disorders these plants will encounter when grown in calcareous soil. Decreased availability of Zn to plants grown in calcareous soil has been attributed largely to Zn adsorption by soil constituents and to precipitation of Zn compounds. Zinc can be adsorbed by Al, Fe, and Mn hydrous oxides, but the nature of Zn precipitates is not well known. Zinc adsorption onto soil components increased <“10-fold when soil pH was increased from 5.5 to 6.5 and solution-Zn concentration was 0.1 M, but it increased <“45-fold when solution-Zn concentration was <10”7 M. Even though the amount of Zn needed by plants is relatively low, roots need to grow to or toward sources of Zn in soil, Zn must diffuse to roots, and/or root-microorganism associations must supply adequate Zn to plants. Relative to the latter, mycorrhizae were important in providing Zn to plants.

For example, 50 and 25% of total Zn was provided to white clover (Trifolium repens L.) and maize, respectively, by mycorrhizal hyphae. Root excretion of H^+ or other means for reducing rhizosphere pH (e.g., NH^+ -N fertilizer) were more effective in enhancing 4 Zn acquisition than root excretion of Zn chelating compounds. Zinc mobility in soil with high pH was reduced compared to that in low-pH soil, and Zn deficiency was more prevalent in higher- than in lower-pH soil. Although Zn interacts extensively with elements like Cu, Fe, Mn, K, and N in both soils or within plant tissue, the element that interacts most strongly with Zn is P, and many examples of P-Zn interactions have been reported. High-pH soil favored formation of insoluble oxide forms of Mn compared to low pH soils, which favored formation of divalent water-soluble Mn. Liming acidic soil also decreased Mn availability in soils.

Applications of acid-forming fertilizers often decrease soil pH and increase Mn availability. Band applications of ammonium sulfate $[(NH4)_2 SO_4]$ enhanced and urea decreased Mn acquisition by plants. Soil solution pH decreased from 8.1 to 7.3 with addition of $(NH_4)_2$ SO_4 and increased from 7.7 to 8.0 with addition of urea; additions of different sources of N changed the quantity of available Mn in soil. Addition of KCl also enhanced availability of soil Mn. Roots may excrete organic substances and organic matter decomposition may provide such substances, which can complex Mn and make it more available to plants. Mycorrhizal infected roots normally decrease acquisition of Mn by plants. However, availability of Mn may be enhanced in soils with reducing conditions that exist during submergence. Iron and Mo interact extensively with Mn to reduce Mn availability/acquisition, and both negative and positive P-Mn and Zn-Mn interactions have been reported.

4. Copper

Copper may be the most immobile of all the micronutrients in soil. Adsorption of Cu with soil constituents normally increases as soil pH increases, but Cu acquisition by plants has not related well with soil pH. Although reduced availability of Cu has been associated with high organic matter in soil, complexed Cu from organic compounds in organic matter (or microbial breakdown of organic matter) and root excretions normally enhanced Cu availability.

Copper acquisition by wheat grown in a large number of soils was not affected when organic C was <12 g kg"1 soil, but it increased when organic C was 12 to 64 g kg"1. Mycorrhizal colonization with roots and mycorrhizal hyphae associated with roots greatly enhanced Cu acquisition (60% of total) for white clover (178) and provided <"25% of the total for maize. Inappropriate growth media levels (usually high) of Zn, P, and N may decrease Cu availability to plants and induce Cu deficiency.

5. Boron and Molybdenum

Boron deficiency may occur on plants grown at high pH, since B availability decreases at high (pH e"7.5) compared to low pH. Liming and/or raising soil pH often decreases B acquisition by plants, which has been attributed primarily to presence of Ca but also to presence of Mg, K, Na, and N. In addition, B deficiency appears to be dependent on plant species as well as on many soil factors. Plants relatively sensitive to B deficiency are alfalfa, apples, beets (Beta vulgaris L.), celery (Apium graveolens L.), clover (Trifolium spp.), peanuts, cotton, and Cruciferae spp. Even though high soil pH enhances Mo availability and liming of soils often alleviates Mo deficiency, Mo deficiency may be enhanced by reducing soil pH with applications of acidifying fertilizers (NH^+ -N materials) and S.

Toxicities and Excess Salts

Plant toxicities from mineral nutrients essential to growth are relatively rare for plants grown in alkaline and calcareous soils, but some may occur under some conditions. Most of the conditions associated with elemental toxicities concern the amount of water in or added to soil. When water is limiting or evaporation exceeds water input, elements may accumulate at high levels in soil and plant toxicities may be induced. High salts added with irrigation water may accumulate in soil and be detrimental to growth. Salts in deeper soil profiles that are commonly immobilized may rise to the surface via capillary action when water is percolated and/or poor water management practices are used. As such, salts may accumulate in surface soil to reduce growth. The most common problems in alkaline or salt-affected soils are B, Na, and Cl toxicities.

1. Boron

Boron is essential to plant growth and has a narrow range between sufficiency and toxicity compared to other essential mineral nutrients. Boron toxicity may appear on some plants grown in particular soils or under certain conditions. For example, B toxicity normally appears on plants grown in arid and semiarid soils but may occur in plants grown in acidic to neutral soils if sufficient B is present. Boron readily leaches from soil if sufficient water is available for percolation and will accumulate similar to other soluble salts when water is insufficient to induce potential toxicity. Certain regions of the world such as the western U.S. states, especially California, and many soils in southern and western Australia and Israel have been recognized for B-toxicity problems. Conditions conducive for B toxicity in plants are for those grown in soils that contain naturally high B, use of irrigation water with high B, and overfertilization/application with minerals/substances high in B. Although plant species/cultivars differ in concentrations of B in tissue for induction of toxicity, B toxicity generally occurs when B concentrations in tissue exceed <“150 to 200 mg kg”^{1}.

2. Sodium and Chlorine

Many soils commonly accumulate high concentrations of soluble salts (saline, sodic, saline-sodic), which usually induce “salt toxicity” in plants. Soils are normally considered to be saline when electrical conductivity of saturated soil pastes exceed <“4 dS m”1 at 25æ% C (equivalent to <“40 mM NaCl L”1) and the sodium adsorption ratio (SAR) is <“13 to 15 [SAR = Na ÷ (Ca + Mg)/21/2]. When soils have SAR ratios >13 to 15, they are usually considered to be either sodic or saline-sodic, depending on salt accumulation. The pH of saline and saline-sodic soils may not be high (usually <8.5), while the pH of sodic soils may become quite high (usually >8.5). Saline soils may be nonsodic (nonalkaline) and may contain sufficient soluble salts to impair the productivity of many plants. It has been estimated that <“33% of irrigated land world-wide has been affected by salinity. Problems of salt-affected soil have arisen with many turfgrass (golf courses, sports fields, and lawns) sites because the sites are located near seacoasts, because of increasing use of effluent water for irrigation, and because of water intrusion and storm surge events.

Chlorine is an essential nutrient for most plants, and Na is essential to some plants. Deficiencies of these elements are hard to induce in plants because of their ubiquitous nature in the environment. These elements are normally associated with toxicities, especially in salt-affected soils. Major problems for plants grown in salt-affected soils are ion toxicity associated with excess accumulation of Na and/or Cl (and sometimes SO_4) and imbalanced nutrition from reduced uptake and/or translocation of essential nutrients, especially Ca. Water deficit (drought stress) can also be a common problem for plants grown in salt-affected soils. Except among some graminaceous plant species, Cl toxicity appears to be more widespread than Na toxicity unless Ca is low and soil aeration is poor. Many plants have the capability to exclude entry of Na into tissues or restrict its internal transport to sensitive tissues. Thus, Na toxicity may not appear even though plants may have been grown in relatively high salt conditions. However, plants grown in poorly aerated soils (e.g., waterlogged) do not appear to have the ability to restrict Na and Cl acquisition, so that toxicity symptoms will commonly appear. An important mechanism for salt toxicity has been associated with accumulation of salts in the apoplasm of leaves to enhance leaf dehydration and turgor loss leading to death. For example, rice grown in 50 mM NaCl solutions had 10-fold increases in Na^+ in leaf apoplasm to cause dehydration of cells, and differences in sensitivity of peas (Pisum sativum L.) and spinach (Spinacia oleracea L.) to salt toxicity were assessed as differences in regulation of leaf apoplastic Na^+ and Cl". In addition, toxicity of peas to NaCl was associated with higher generation of highly detrimental superoxide (O") radicals.

Chlorine instead of Na toxicity was associated with some plants, like grape and citris (Citrus spp.), grown in relatively low NaCl solutions and in deciduous and coniferous trees grown in or exposed to relatively high NaCl.

Many leguminous plant species such as peanuts, beans, and soybeans have also been reported to be sensitive to Cl. Some plants have also been observed to be sensitive to SO_4 compared to Cl, and reduced growth of sorghum was noted to be from reduced uptake of K and Mg when this plant was grown with high SO_4. Chloride may reduce NO" 3 N uptake to some extent, and reduced uptake of Mn and induced Mn deficiency were associated with high salinity in barley. Plants grown with high salt contents have also had reduced P uptake and induced P deficiency, enhanced P uptake (P toxicity), and high demand for K.

Improved plant tolerance to high salt and/or amelioration of high salt effects has been well documented when Ca has been added to salt-affected soils or high-salt growth conditions.

Examples of this have been found when increased Ca added to high NaCl solutions for growth of bean and citrus species decreased Na in leaves. In addition, soil amelioration of coastal salinesodic soils with gypsum ($CaSO_4$) decreased leaf rolling and bleaching of rice leaves, Ca amendments overcame Ca deficiency of wheat and barley grown in saline soil, added Ca decreased lettuce (Lactuca sativa L.) tipburn and tomato blossom-end rot in plants grown in saline soil, and an eightfold increase in salinity to Brassica plants did not affect fresh weight but enhanced tipburn from 0 to 80%.

In the latter case, the disorder was overcome by increasing overnight humidity, which was associated with enhanced Ca transport in plants. By adding Na to solutions containing low Ca, uptake of Ca was also decreased and Ca deficiency induced. These disorders may be associated with Na^+ displacement of Ca^{2+} on binding sites of plasm and intracellular membranes and transmission of salinity signals from roots to shoots (Ca^{2+} homeostasis).

CONCLUSION

Both acidic and alkaline soils can impose relatively severe mineral nutritional problems on plants. Overcoming these constraints may be expensive. The normal method has been by fertilizing soils to replenish availability of nutrients to overcome deficiencies and by amending soils to alleviate toxicity factors. These practices are good in many cases, especially when relatively inexpensive resources are available. Alternatives to expensive resources may be to use germplasm with high adaptability to mineral nutritional deficiency/toxicity constraints. Considerable germplasm with improved ability to grow and produce under many of these mineral constraints has been identified and developed. By growing adaptable germplasm in soils with chemical constraints, agriculturists could be helped to meet many desired plant productivity goals with limited fertilizer/ amendment inputs.

Other approaches for overcoming mineral nutrient deficiency/ toxicity constraints might be to take advantage of soil microorganisms such as mycorrhiza and beneficial bacteria/fungi and amendments of organic matter and organic-inorganic mixtures containing valuable nutrients and materials that will alleviate mineral nutritional problems. It is important to understand and recognize that many kinds of mineral stress problems can occur on plants in acidic and alkaline soils. Once these problems have been identified, means for alleviating such mineral stress constraints can be incorporated and more effective management strategies can be used to improve plant yield potentials.

6

Plant Stress Symptomatology

Biological research is a practice of conducting experiments wherein a single component is altered. Any changes in growth, for example, are, ipso facto, due to the one factor that was altered. Unfortunately, sometimes multiple uncontrolled factors are changed without recognition by the researcher. This can lead to confusion, which leads to much research, discussion, and dissension. The attached reports are an attempt to explain a presumed pesticide problem. Without access to the plant species originally exposed to deleterious conditions, we chose a sorghum cultivar [Sorghum bicolor (L.) Moench. cv GP-10] that experience has shown to be responsive to every stress we have utilized previously. By varying the culture medium (± organic matter), temperature, and fertilizer, it has been shown that the fungicide is relatively nontoxic even when applied at 5× registered application rates.

But the type of mineral nutrient fertilizer was determinative. The plant responses were identical to the symptomatology of plant growth in acid soils. These symptoms were totally reversed by the addition of magnesium (Mg^{2+}) to the culture medium. This reversal is a major diagnostic symptom for acid soils. Which factor was determinative? H^+ or pesticide? Excess H^+ in the rooting media (pH d"4.3) induces an acid-soil stress, with decreased magnesium and increased manganese and aluminum availability. The aluminum is toxic at virtually any soil pH. But, the quantity of aluminum ($Al3^+$) in the soil is extremely low at pH e"5.0.

Additionally, when fertilizers containing ammonium (NH^+) are utilized, the NH^+ is exchanged through the root plasma membrane for H^+. This exchange results in an acid soil. Thus, the cataloging of plant symptoms to a supposed pesticide influence [stubby (3-in.) black roots, chlorotic leaves with necrotic spots] must include the responses to changed cultural conditions. Response to other stress-produced symptoms are often indistinguishable. And in this case, acid soil–induced symptomatology was determinative.

TEMPERATURE AND FERTILIZATION INFLUENCE ON SORGHUM BICOLOR RESPONSE TO BENLATE DF AND WP

Benomyl[(methyl-1-butylcarbamoyl)-2-benzimidazolecarbamate]—or Benlate— is a systemic, soil-applied fungicide that has been used extensively in the greenhouse, container-grown, ornamental horticulture industry. Recently, extensive losses to that greenhouse, container-grown, ornamental horticulture industry have occurred, which have been putatively explained as being due to contamination of Benlate DF (dry flowable) with a herbicide, plant-growth regulator, or other foreign substance(s), or the Benlate DF itself. After extensive experimentation, the producers of Benlate DF stipulated that (a) they did not know what had caused the problem and (b) the problem was not due to contaminants in Benlate DF. Additionally, the symptoms of the damaged plants (i.e., chlorotic to necrotic foliage and shortened, black roots) could not be reproduced by Benlate applications in the same cultivars and in greenhouses in which the original problem developed.

These symptoms were present in isolated greenhouses and were not generally prevalent throughout the industry. Two methods of benomyl application were registered. One was a foliage spray of approximately 1 to 1 2 lb Benlate DF, which is a 50% benomyl a.i. material, in 200 to 500 gal water per acre. The second technique for use in ornamental container-grown crops in greenhouses was a soil drench at 1 lb Benlate DF per 100 gal water applied as 1 to 2 pints/ft^2. The latter application technique utilizes a 600-mg L"1 benomyl a.i. solution at <"2 pt/ft2 which approximates 54.5 lb of benomyl a.i. per acre (A). Since the water solubility of benomyl is 3.8 mg/L and 1 mg/L applied to the soil at 40 gal/A is approximately equivalent to 1 lb/A in the top 3 in. of soil, a considerable surplus of benomyl would be applied in the 60 mg/L.

The benomyl T1/2 in water approximates 7 hr, so that a single drench application would result in undissolved benomyl in the container for over 56 hr. The undissolved benomyl would be absorbed to the potting mix or any other adsorbent material in the rooting container. The major benomyl degradation products are methyl-1H-benzimidazolecarbamate (MBC) + n-butyl isocyanate (BIC). The latter degrades to n-butylamine + CO_2 with a T1/2 of 7 min. Presumably, the growers would use a commercially available fertilizer (CF). Two major fertilizers were extant and labeled analyses indicated that they were virtually identical in chemical composition. Benlate DF is not registered for use on sorghum [Sorghum bicolor (L.) Moench.]. Sorghum [Sorghum bicolor (L.) Moench. cv GP-10] was chosen as an assay plant because it has been shown to respond readily to chemical or environmental stress. Additionally, sand culture was chosen to permit the deletion of any confounding factors due to benomyl adsorption to soil and/or other potting medium characteristics. Therefore, we evaluated a CF and Hoagland-and-Arnon complete mineral nutrient solution on GP-10 sorghum grown at 38 and 32æ% C as well as ± Benlate DF and Benlate WP (wettable powder).

Methods and Materials

1. Experiment 1

At 38æ% C, ten GP-10 sorghum seeds were planted 1 cm deep in "white quartz flintshot" sand contained in 10-oz plastic cups (nestable, 9 cm diam; top, 13 cm deep). Fertilization was 100 mL/pot/week of Hoagland-and-Arnon complete mineral nutrient solution (H&A) or 500 mg/L (approximately 2 heaping tablespoons/gal deionized water). Pots were harvested at 1, 2, 3, and 4 weeks after planting (WAP) for shoot length (cm) above the sand and shoot and root fresh weight (FW) (g/plant). Five replications were used for each sampling date. Plants were watered daily with 100 mL deionized water.

2. *Experiment 2*

Grown in white quartz flintshot sand at 38æ% C using CF (100 mL/week of 50 mg/L) fertilizer. Benlate DF and WP (100 mL of 1200 mg/L) were applied at week 1, week 1 and 2, or week 1, 2, and 3. Plants were harvested at 4 WAP for shoot length (cm), and root and shoot FW (g/plant).

3. *Experiment 3*

Identical to Experiment 2 except that the plants were grown at 32æ% C.

4. *Experiment 4*

Identical to Experiment 2 except that the plants were grown at 32æ% C and fertilized with H&A weekly.

5. *Experiment 5*

At 32æ% C, plants were grown in sand culture (as above) and fertilized weekly with 100 ml/pot/week with (a) CF (500 mg/L), (b) CF (1000 mg/L), (c) H&A (pH 5.3), or (d) H&A (pH 3.5). After 4 weeks, plants were harvested for (a) number of plants/pot, (b) shoot length (cm), (c) shoot fresh weight (g/pot), (d) root fresh weight (g/pot), (e) shoot dry weight (mg/pot), and (f) root dry weight (mg/pot). All data were subjected to analysis of variance on a randomized complete block design. Standard errors per treatment are presented.

Results

1. *Experiment 1*

H&A induced greater shoot (cm) growth than CF for shoot FW (g/plant) and root FW (g/plant) (Table 1) at all levels of weeks of exposure except for root FW (g/plant) and root FW (g/plant)

(Table 1) at all levels of weeks of exposure except for root FW (g/plant) after 1 week's growth.

The commercial fertilizer (500 mg/L) pH was 4.0, while that of H&A was about 5.3. The CF was low in Mg, and deficient in Ca; the other ions were less concentrated than in H&A (Table 2). In H&A, the nitrogen was nitrate (NO"). In the CF, the nitrogen 3 (20% of total weight) was supplied as ammonia (3.96%), NO" (5.61%), and 3 urea (10.43%).

Growth Parameters of Sorghuma Shoot Nutrients H&A Week 1 2 3 4 1 2 3 4 cm 35.0eb 50.8c 57.8b 62.6a 26.6g 35.6de 38.0d 31.4f g FW/plant 321.6d 948.3b 1222.9b 1565.0a 202.0e 453.2c 541.8c 452.2e Root g FW/plant 593.0f 1030.3cd 1227.3b 1557.1a 610.1f 870.8e 1024.9de 890.2e

2. Experiment 2

When the plants were grown at 38æ% C and fertilized with 100 mL of 500 mg/L CF weekly, shoot length (cm) was slightly but significantly decreased by weekly massively excess applications of Benlate DF and WP (5.3 and 25.1%, respectively). Shoot FW (g/plant) was not significantly decreased by Benlate DF but root FW (g/plant) was decreased by a single massively excess application of Benlate DF (27%); multiple applications were more deleterious than a single application.

3. Experiment 3

Excessive application rates of Benlate DF did not induce a significant decrease in any growth parameter when the plants were grown at 32æ% C and fertilized with CF (Table 4). Multiple applications of Benlate WP did induce decreased growth in all three parameters.

4. Experiment 4

When plants were grown at 32æ% C and fertilized with H&A, massively excess application rates of Benlate DF induced significantly decreased shoot length

5. *Experiment 5*

Number of plants/pot was decreased by 1000 mg/pot CF. Shoot length (cm) was significantly greater in H&A than in CF. Shoot FW (mg/plant) was greatest in H&A (pH 5.3), decreased at H&A (pH 3.5), significantly decreased at CF 1000 mg/L, and least in CF 500 mg/L. Root FW (mg/plant) was equivalent in plants grown in CF (1000 mg/L) and H&A (pH 5.3), decreased in H&A (pH 3.5), and least in CF (500 mg/L). Shoot DW (mg/plant) and root DW (mg/plant) were greatest in H&A without any pH influence, decreased at CF (1000 mg/L), and least at CF (500 mg/L). Total plant FW (g/plant) was greatest in H&A (pH 5.3), significantly decreased in H&A (pH 3.5), which was equivalent to CF (1000 mg/L), and least in CF (500 mg/L). Total DW (mg/plant) was greatest in H&A (pH 5.3) significantly decreased in H&A (pH 3.5), which was equivalent to CF (1000 mg/L), and least in CF (500 mg/L).

Discussion

Sorghum responds readily to nutrient deficiencies. Plant growth under acid soil stress (pH d"4.5) has been studied extensively with sorghum.

Because CF (500 mg/L) supplies approximately one-half as much total N to the plants as is present in the H&A, a direct comparison of H&A (pH 5.3) and CF (1000 mg/L) (pH 3.5) shows that the CF is incomplete and does not permit plant growth at the same rate as does the H&A (pH 5.3). The differences due to pH in the CF (500 or 1000 mg/L) (pH 4.0 and 3.5, respectively) and H&A (pH 3.5) show that even under acid-soil–stress conditions the mineral ion incomplete CF does not permit optimum growth. The influence of acid soil stress is shown by the decreased shoot FW (mg/plant), root FW (mg/plant), and total plant FW (g/plant) in plants grown in H&A (pH 3.5) compared to plants grown in H&A (pH 5.3). The differences between plants grown with CF 500 and 1000 mg/L are, primarily, a total N supply response. Inadequate supply of Ca^{2+} and Mg^{2+} exacerbates the problem. CF (1000 mg/L) and H&A (pH 3.5) had equivalent N fertilization, yet growth in the H&A (pH 3.5) was significantly greater than with CF (1000 mg/L) in all growth parameters except root FW (mg/plant) and total plant FW (g/plant). Thus, two basic interacting parameters are demonstrated. These are (a) the supply of a complete mineral nutrient fertilization regime to the plants and (b) the pH of the solution applied. Both of these parameters have a long history of deleterious influences on plant growth. And these parameters are inextricably interactive. The differences in growth of sorghum exposed to H&A or CF is totally explicable on the basis of a combination of several factors: (a) low pH in CF, (b) low concentration of required mineral nutrients in the CF in comparison to H&A, (c) low Mg in the CF, (d) absence of Ca in the CF, and (e) the form of nitrogen applied in the CF.

In sorghum as in other plants, given equal water status, low mineral nutrition equals low growth. Calcium is not supplied by the CF and calcium has been shown to be requisite and to act as a cytosolic second messenger, so that deficiency or excess of Ca in the cytosol results in leaky plasma membranes that are visualized by black roots caused by the induction of polyphenol oxidase activity. Additionally, NH^{+} and 4 Mg^{2+} concentrations are highly correlated in sorghum grown under acid soil stress. Low Mg^{2+} fertility results in severe stress. Thus, these data demonstrate the influence of a multiple stress syndrome. If sufficient water is available, high temperature induces a high evapotranspiration. When the stoma were induced to open by one herbicide, increased water utilization resulted.

This increased water uptake resulted in the absorption of residues of a second herbicide to the extent that the residues of the second herbicide became deleterious or lethal in the presence of the first herbicide, but those residues of the second herbicide were not deleterious when the plants were not exposed to the first herbicide. Or, under high waterutilization conditions (i.e., high temperature) more of whatever was present in the rooting medium was absorbed by roots and translocated to the shoots in the evapotranspiration stream. Thus, at 38æ% C, Benlate DF influenced shoot length (cm), shoot FW (g/plant), and root FW (g/plant). But at 32æ% C, Benlate DF did not influence plant growth in any of the three plant growth measurements. Growth at 32æ% C was less than at 38æ% C. This is explicable as a response to total mineral nutrient supply differences at 38æ% and 32æ% C as influenced by total water evapotranspiration. This concept is corroborated by the greater growth of the untreated plants fertilized by H&A in comparison to those growth with CF.

Additionally, greater growth with H&A resulted in more root uptake of materials in the rooting medium and massively excess application rates of Benlate DF and WP induced decreased growth in all three growth parameters. Benomyl water solubility (3.8 mg/L) is low. The individual Benlate DF and WP applications utilized herein equaled 60 mg/pot. Benomyl degradation T1/2 is reported to be about 7 hr. Or, undegraded benomyl was present for at least 7 T1/2 , and those plants with a high evapotranspiration were constantly exposed to benomyl concentrations greater than the benomyl water solubility for >49 hr. Plants absorb benomyl. And those plants were subjected to nutrient imbalance when exposed to the CF. Therefore, root plasma membranes (PM) were exposed to conditions that resulted in leaky PM, which resulted in black roots that do not function selectively. Therefore, high temperature and fertility imbalances have been demonstrated to be a multistress syndrome where massively excessive applications of Benlate DF and WP can marginally influence plant growth.

INFLUENCE OF ADSORPTIVE SURFACE ON THE RESPONSE OF SORGHUM TO BENLATE DF AND BENLATE WP

The systemic, soil-applied fungicide benomy: (methyl-1-butylcarbamol)-2-benzimidazolecarbamate) has been utilized extensively in the greenhouse-lathhouse, container-grown, ornamental horticulture industry where losses have occurred which were postulated by the growers as being due to contamination in Benlate DF (dry flowable). The producer of Benlate DF has been unable to document contamination of the Benlate DF by any herbicide, plant-growth regulator, or other substance. The response of plants to massively excessive rates of Benlate DF has been shown, in sand culture, to be influenced by the temperature at which the plants were grown and the fertilizer utilized. A Benlate DF drench application presents benomyl at concentrations which would require >56 hr to degrade. The previously presented data were from plants grown in sand culture without any source of adsorptive surface other than the plant roots. Therefore, the question of presence or absence of an adsorptive surface in the treated pots arose. Could an adsorptive surface prevent the development of deleterious conditions in the root zone? And how would changes in ambient temperature or fertilization influence the response of plants to excessive Benlate DF or WP?

Methods and Materials

Ten sorghum [Sorghum bicolor (L.) Moench. cv GP-10] seeds were planted 1 cm deep in "white quartz flintshot" sand. Plants were grown at 32æ% C. Five replications were utilized. Fertilization was by 100 mL per pot per week of Hoagland-and-Arnon (H&A) complete mineral nutrient solution or 100 mL per pot per week of 500 mg/L commercial fertilizer (CF). Daily water applications utilized deionized water. Benlate DF or WP was applied at 100 mL per pot per week of 600 mg benomyl a.i. (0, 1, 2, and 3 applications). In addition, a duplicate set of pots were utilized in which 3 cm of granular charcoal was added to the top of the plant containers. Plants were grown for 4 weeks and harvested for number of plants per pot, shoot length (cm), shoot fresh weight (FW) (g/plant), and root FW (g/plant).

Eleméntal contents were analyzed by is explicable on the basis of a removal by the charcoal (or other adsorptive surface) of immediate root exposure to some substance and the maintenance of conditions without acid soil stress in the root zone (pH e" 5.0). The influences of soil type on benomyl uptake have been known for at least two decades. Presence of MBC (the major benomyl degradation product) in leaves of elm seedlings, as amended by planting substrates, was sand > silt loam soil > silt loam + perlite, and peat. Peat moss added to sand reduced benomyl uptake and benomyl was adsorbed to soil but not sand. In soils fertilized with ammonium-nitrogen (NH+ "N), roots induce an 4 increased hydrogen (H^+) ion efflux with a resultant decrease in soil pH.

The interaction of Mg deficiency in the presence of low soil pH induced Al stress has been shown to be highly cultivar-dependent. At soil pH 4.8, Al decreased Mg absorption without major root damage, but the Al induced highly toxic to the roots and shoots. A second problem associated with acid soil stress is the excess Mn^{2+} availability. Manganese is a requisite ion used as a cofactor in gibberellic acid (GA) biosynthesis. Yet different sorghum cultivars respond totally differently to Mn^{2+} concentrations, and while one cultivar is highly susceptible at low Mn^{2+} concentration and does not grow or dies, another cultivar is almost totally resistant to a high Mn^{2+} concentration. Additionally, high Mn^{2+} concentrations at the root surface have been shown to induce high indoleacetic acid (IAA) oxidase activity, which induces massively decreased root growth and is reversed by the addition of exogenous IAA supply. Therefore, the induction of an acid soil stress by repeated applications of fertilizer (pH 4.0) must be considered as a seriously detrimental influence on plant growth.

The overall damage to container-grown plants in the presence of massively excessive rates of Benlate DF has been shown to be a multistress syndrome in which synergistic responses to high temperature, fertilizer imbalance, low pH, and composition of the potting root medium are present. Reduction of any stress: growth of plants at decreased temperatures (40æ% C), balanced fertilizer at neutral pH, type of fertilizers, or presence of a highly adsorptive potting medium results in a greatly diminished plant response to this multistress syndrome. Comparison of Benlate-untreated plants ± charcoal indicates the degree of response of plants to this highly deleterious multistress syndrome.

REVERSAL BY MAGNESIUM OF SUPPOSED BENLATE DF–INDUCED GROWTH RESPONSES

Introduction

Benlate DF [dry flowable formulation of (methyl-1-butylcarbamoyl)-2-benzimidazole carbamate] has been putatively implicated in growth inhibitions in the container-grown, ornamental horticultural industry. Researchers have been unable to document this to be a response to any contaminant in the Benlate DF. Using a sorghum cultivar [Sorghum bicolor (L) Moench. cv GP-10] that is highly responsive to stress, plant growth was responsive to the type of fertilizer applied in sand culture, temperature, and presence of an adsorptive surface in the rooting medium (see Secs. I and II of this chapter). A commercial fertilizer (CF) commonly utilized in this industry has a pH 4.0 at 500 mg/L and pH 3.5 at 1000 mg/L; applications of fertilizer solution at this pH induces acid soil stress (3–15). Additionally, application of ammonium-nitrogen (NH^+ "N) fertilizers 4 induced an excess hydrogen (H^+) ion efflux by the roots, resulting in a low soil pH.

Growth parameters and mineral element analyses showed inhibitions of shoot length (cm), root fresh weight (FW) (g/plant), and shoot FW (g/plant) when plants were fertilized with NH^+ -based fertilizers that were highly correlated 4 with the quantity of aluminum (Al) (μg/g DW) in the foliage. Recently, Al toxicity was shown to be highly correlated to the type of N supplied in the fertilizer. In the presence of nitrate-nitrogen (NO" "N), 3 Al slightly decreased root elongation; but, when NH^+ "N was present, the highly 4 deleterious responses were correlated with magnesium (Mg^{2+}) deficiency and resulted in root impairment.

Sorghum cultivars varied in their responses to Al. Since the CF supplies a low concentration of Mg^{2+} and utilizes, partially, a NH+ form of N, it is possible that the addition of extra Mg^{2+} might reverse 4 these problems. B. Methods and Materials Ten sorghum (cv GP-10) seeds were planted 1 cm deep in "white quartz flintshot" sand contained in 10-oz nestable plastic cups (9-cm-diam top, 13 cm deep). The pots were treated with 100 mL/pot Benlate DF (600 mg/L) weekly.

Weekly commercial fertilizer applications (500 mg/L) of 100 mL/pot were made. Water status was maintained at field capacity daily using deionized water. Magnesium sulfate (100 mL of 0, 10, 20, 40, 80, 160, or 320 mg/L) was added weekly. After 4 weeks of growth at 32æ% C, plants were harvested for root fresh weight (FW) (g/plant), shoot length (cm), and shoot FW (g/plant). Mineral contents were analyzed by published procedures utilizing perchloric acid digestion and atomic absorption spectrometry. Five replications were utilized and data were subjected to analysis of variance on a randomized complete block design. Means were separated by standard errors. C. Results Addition of MgSO4 (20 mg/L) induced significantly increased growth of plants exposed to excessive Benlate DF to growth levels equivalent to the untreated control pots (Figs. 7, 8, and 9). Addition of MgSO4 >20 mg/L induced progressively decreased growth.

Root mineral ion content increased (i.e., S, P, Mn, Mg, and Cu) as the concentration of Mg mg/L increased when Benlate DF was absent. In the presence of excessive rates of Benlate DF, S, Fe, and Mg mineral ion contents increased as Mg fertilization increased. In shoots, Mg induced significantly increased mineral ion contents (± Benlate DF in S, P, Zn, Mn, Fe, Mg, Al, and Cu). Calcium (Ca) content decreased (± DF). D. Discussion Growth at 32æ% C without $MgSO_4$ and in the presence of Benlate DF was equivalent to similar treatments published previously. Influence of excessive application rates of Benlate DF in the presence of an acid soil stress–inducing incomplete mineral ion fertilization regime is shown by the decreased root FW (g/plant), shoot length (cm), and shoot FW (g/plant). Reversal of the postulated Benlate DF influence by the addition of 20 mL/L indicates an influence of the fungicide on either (a) ion uptake by roots, (b) modification of the low CF Mg^{2+} content to a more balanced fertilizer ratio, or (c) deactivation of the NH^+ influence on acid soil stress. Addition of $MgSO_4$ to the soil solution altered the root ion content. This is in accordance with previously published data showing that roots absorb whatever is available in the soil solution. But variations occur. Calcium contents (± DF) decreased. Therefore, the addition of $MgSO_4$ (± Benlate DF) decreased Ca uptake. Since (a) Ca concentration in the CF was very low initially, (b) Ca concentration plays an important metabolic role as a cytosolic secondary messenger with normal concentrations near 10"6 μM on a DW basis, and (c) the Ca concentrations are a bit high so that internal metabolism would be disrupted, a decrease in Ca content would be expected to be beneficial.

Similar responses were observed in shoots except that Al contents were significantly increased as Mg concentration increased and ± Benlate DF did not alter this response. These data, then, demonstrate a growth-inhibitory response of plants to a CF that was reversed by the addition of 20 mg/L $MgSO_4$. This is indicative of mineral fertilizer imbalance as well as the imposition of acid soil stress onto the plants. Aluminum hexahydrate ($Al[OH]^{3+}$ hereafter called Al^{3+}) solubility is very 6 low at cytosolic pH (i.e., <"pH 6.0). But Al^{3+} attaches to enzymes that normally utilize Mg^{2+} as a cofactor and the Al^{3+} dissociates from those enzymes so slowly that 1 μM Al^{3+} effectively competes for action sites with value is the average of five replications at 4 weeks after planting and growth at 32æ% C. b +, Benlate DF treatment weekly; ", 0 Benlate DF. c Values within an element followed by the same letter are not significantly different as determined by the mean standard errors.

10 mM Mg2^{+}. These include the energy producing systems (i.e., MgATPase) as well as sterol synthesis and other enzyme systems utilize Mg^{2+} as a cofactor. Sterols are requisite for membrane function and membranes become leaky when the sterol quantity is deficient. Thus, Al^{3+} produces deleterious results with Mg^{2+} -containing enzymes and/or any oxygen rich (i.e., PO_4) containing component. Al^{3+} solubility is increased very markedly in soil solutions pH d"5.0. Therefore, application of fertilizers at pH d"5.0 is equivalent to the application of an extremely toxic Al3+ solution. Recently, acid soils (i.e., pH <4.5) have been shown to develop when $NH^{+\ 4}$ is used as a N-fertilizer. This results in Al^{3+} toxicity, which induces Mg^{2+}

deficiency. The CF utilized herein contains 3.96% NH^{+} "N, 5.61% NO" "N, and 10.43% urea-N. The NH^{+} "N, per se, influences soil pH and 3 4 induces $Al3^{+}$ toxicity and Mg^{2+} deficiency. The urea degrades (1 urea '! 2 NH^{+} + CO_2) and further exacerbates the acid soil problem. Additionally, urea, per se, is tolerated by plant leaves at <5 to 15 lb urea/100 gal water. Application of the CF to foliage at 1000 mg/L water was equivalent to <"0.83 lb urea/100 gal water.

But growers often utilize much higher fertilizer rates, and this may induce deleterious results on the foliage due to the urea before it decomposes to NH+ "N and induces acid soil stress problems. Thus, the deleterious responses of plants postulated to implicate Benlate DF have been shown to be a multistress syndrome which includes (a) high temperature, (b) low adsorptive surface within the treated root region, (c) imbalanced mineral nutrition (herein), and (d) acid soil stress. Since (a) cytosolic Ca^{2+} concentration is tightly controlled, (b) Mg^{2+} is requisite for chlorophyll and sterol synthesis, (c) Mn^{2+} is requisite for carotenoid and gibberellin (GA) synthesis, and (d) Zn^{+} is requisite to indoleacetic acid (IAA) synthesis, the data contained herein explain the postulated Benlate DF influence as a multistress syndrome that can be alleviated by removal of any of the individual stresses, most notably Mg^{2+} deficiency. It is still possible that Benlate DF may influence mineral ion uptake. If so, this factor might further confound the condition. But the chloroticnecrotic leaves, stunting, curled leaves, and blackened roots are all symptomatic of plant growth under acid soil stress plus imbalanced fertilizer application. And addition of $MgSO_4$ (20 mg/L) reversed the syndrome.

INFLUENCE OF METHYL-BENZIMIDAZOL-CARBAMATE (MBC), BENOMYL, AND BENLATE DF FORMULATE ON PLANT GROWTH

Benomyl ([methyl-1-butylcarbamoyl]-2-benzimidazole-carbamate) is a systemic fungicide that degrades, T1/2 = 7 hr, to methyl-1H-benzimidazolecarbamate (MBC). However, benomyl water solubility is only 3.8 μg/L, so that excessive applications of benomyl could result in exposure to benomyl per se for extended periods of time. Benlate DF (dry flowable) is a 50% a.i. formulation of benomyl and was shown to be an insignificant factor in deleterious plant responses to a multistress syndrome that included the influence to high temperature, imbalanced fertilizers including absence of calcium and deficient levels of magnesium, and lack of adsorbent material in the rooting medium. The Benlate DF factor was reversed by the addition of 20 mg Mg+ /L into the fertilizer. Since Benlate DF is composed of equal portions of benomyl and a complex formulate, either portion might be the cause of the minor growth responses documented to occur when massively excess applications of Benlate DF were applied. Thus, a question remaining was the response of plants to the long-lived degradation product (MBC) of benomyl, benomyl per se, and the Benlate DF Formulate.

Methods and Materials

1. MBC Concentrations

Ten Sorghum bicolor (L.) Moench. cv GP-10 seeds were planted 1 cm deep in "white quartz flintshot" sand contained in 10 oz nestable plastic cups (9-cm diam top, 13 cm deep), and the plants were grown for 4 weeks at 32æ% C. Weekly fertilization was 100 mL of Hoagland-and-Arnon complete mineral nutrient solution (H&A). Initial chemical treatments were MBC (0, 4.75, 9.5, 19.0, and 38.0 mg/L). At 4 weeks after planting (WAP), the plants were harvested for root fresh weight (FW) (g/plant), shoot length (cm), and shoot FW (g/plant). Five replications were utilized. Data were subjected to analysis of variance on a randomized complete block design. Means were separated by standard errors.

2. Benomyl Concentrations

In sand culture at 32æ% C (see above) sorghum (GP-10) was grown for 4 weeks with weekly applications of H&A (100 mL/pot/ week) + initial applications of benomyl (0, 4.5, 9, 18, 36, or 72 mg/ L). Five replications were utilized and data were subjected to statistical analysis as described above.

3. Formulate Concentration

As in benomyl concentration study.

C. Results

1. MBC Concentrations: Root FW (g/plant) was not significantly decreased at any level of MBC concentration. Root FW was significantly increased at 38 mg/L MBC. Shoot length (cm) was not significantly influenced by MBC. Shoot FW (g/plant) was significantly increased by all MBC treatments.
2. Benomyl Concentrations: Massively excessive benomyl concentrations (72 mg/L) decreased shoot length (cm) by 15%, shoot fresh weight (g/plant) by 22%, and root fresh weight (g/plant) by 20%.
3. Formulate Concentrations: Massively excessive applications (72 mg/L) of the formulate in Benlate DF did not induce statistically significant changes in shoot length (cm) or root evaluation of the active ingredient, benomyl, and the Benlate DF Formulate and plant growth did not reveal any consistent deleterious responses except for a 15% decrease in shoot length in the presence of 72 mg/L benomyl and a 19% decrease in shoot FW (g/plant) at 72 mg/L Formulate. These decreases in plant growth are relatively minor in comparison to the major differences in growth that occurred between complete and incomplete mineral fertilizers or when organic adsorptive material was present in the rooting medium. Thus, in the multistress syndrome symptoms associated with the putative "Benlate DF problem," the causative factors have been shown to be (a) application of nutritionally imbalanced fertilizers, (b) low pH, (c) pots without sufficient potting mix adsorptive surfaces, and (d) high temperature. Excessive applications of Benlate DF can be marginally deleterious in the absence of any potting mix adsorptive surface. But, this limited problem is more a response to temperature, adsorptive surface, and pH than to the fungicide. The major benomyl degradation product,

MBC, did not induce consistent plant growth reductions.

Decreased growth induced by Benlate DF was observed at >35.84 kg/ha (32 lb/A) or the equivalent of 20× the legally registered Benlate DF application rate. Influence of Benlate DF on plant growth. In plants fertilized with CF, shoot length (cm), shoot FW (g/plant), and root FW (g/plant) were increased by Benlate DF (2.24 kg/ha) (2 lb/A). Addition of Mg^{2+} to CF did not further increase growth (Figs. 10 to 12) over that shown in the presence of Benlate DF (2.24 kg/ha) (2 lb/A). The influence of Mg^{2+} availability in the fertilizer. There was a significant linear increase of shoot length with Mg^{2+} application. The CF pH was <3.5 and is composed of NH^+ "N (3.96%) and urea 4 (10.43%). Urea decomposes to 2 NH^+ + CO_2.

Therefore, the CF created a 4 severe acid-soil-stress syndrome around the roots. This was alleviated by the addition of Mg^{2+} or the addition of Benlate DF (<17.92 kg/ha) (16 lb/A). These Benlate DF–induced growth increases were in sterile sand (initially) or in sufficient Benlate DF to prevent the establishment of pathogens. Therefore, there is some totally unexplained response of the plants to Benlate DF that strongly resembles an influence on mineral nutrient uptake. Most likely candidates to explain this response are either Ca^{2+}, Mg^{2+}, or an interaction between the two mineral elements. Magnesium (1 mM) induced a decreased 45 Ca^{2+} absorption by sorghum root tips (1 cm) while NH^+ induced 4 an increased 45 Ca^{2+} absorption.

Similarly, Benlate DF (2 ppmw) induced a decreased Ca^{2+} absorption by sorghum root tips (1 cm) (unpublished data). Since Ca2+ acts as a second messenger in controlling cytoplasmic metabolism, any modification of Ca^{2+} influx through the root plasma membrane (PM) would create problems to the root. Roots normally absorb far more Ca^{2+} than is requisite, and Ca^{2+} efflux through the PM is effected by the PM Ca^{2+} ATPases. Alteration of that system would result in excess Ca^{2+} in the roots and induce major metabolic problems.

Roots of plants grown in CF (0 Benlate DF) were approximately 4 cm long (severely stunted) and dark brown. Shoots from those plants were stunted, chlorotic, and necrotic. Addition of Mg^{2+} resulted in white healthy roots and nonchlorotic shoots. But these CF + Mg^{2+} (0 Benlate DF) plants were intermediate to the plants treated with H&A (0 Benlate) whose roots were white and had grown to the bottom of the pot and then formed a mat. Since (a) low pH and Al^{3+} inhibit root elongation and Ca^{2+} absorption, (b) the putative Benlate DF damage morphological symptoms have been duplicated in cultures without Benlate DF, (c) the CF produces acid soil stress problems, (d) these problems are reversed by Mg^{2+} which fits the acid-soil-stress syndrome, and (e) Benlate DF (1.12–17.92 kg/ha) (lb/A) has been shown to partially reverse the symptoms of the acid soil stress syndrome, the putative damage by Benlate DF has been completely explained by an acid soil stress imposed on the plants by the utilization of a mineral ion incomplete fertilizer which imposes a deleterious pH (<4.0) onto the plants.

This situation is further exacerbated by the presence of NH^+ and urea in the CF 4 which induces even lower pH in the soil with associated increased acid soil stress problems. Finally, what is the influence of quantity of CF applied to plants? Using H&A as a standard, CF at 1000, 2000, 3000, and 4000 mg/L were planted (10 seeds/pot) (five replications). After 3 weeks, numbers of emerged plants were greatest in the H&A and decreased in CF at any level. Numbers of emerged plants remaining alive after 3 weeks was substantially decreased by CF and was essentially zero (0) at CF >2000 mg/L. Shoot length was essentially a pattern of growth. In H&A complete mineral nutrient solution, the plants thrived. In CF 1000 mg/L, the plants were chlorotic and necrotic and did not thrive. At CF >2000 mg/L, the plants were chlorotic and necrotic and did not thrive. At CF >2000 mg/L, the plants (when alive) were at the size that could be supported by the nutrients in the seed. Then they died.

This is a typical pattern of acid soil stress. GP-10 is a sorghum selection that has high tolerance to acid soil stress and grows fairly well at soil pH >4.2. Below that soil pH, the GP-10 fails to thrive. In other studies with the sorghum cultivar TAM428, at pH <4.8 this cultivar germinates and grows to about 7 cm, then becomes static, and subsequently dies. This pattern has been shown to be a response to another characteristic of acid soil stress [i.e., excess manganese (Mn^{2+})], in that isoprenoid biosynthesis is inhibited by excess Mn^{2+} in TAM but not in cultivars tolerant to acid soil stress. Since acid soils present excess H^+, Mn^{2+}, and Al^{3+} to plants, complete isolation of causes of deleterious plant responses to the syndrome of acid soil stress cannot be absolutely certain. But in the responses of GP-10 sorghum to CF and/or Benlate DF, two major factors are evident. First, the responses of these plants were very typical of responses to $Al3^+$ toxicity–induced Mg^{2+} deficiencies and were reversed by the addition of Mg^{2+}. Second, with Benlate DF <10×, the legal registered application rate was not deleterious to plant growth and the responses to CF without added Mg^{2+} were reversed.

INFLUENCE OF BENOMYL, BENLATE DF, AND BENLATE WP ON THE CALCIUM (45 CA^{2+}) UPTAKE BY ROOTS OF SORGHUM AND MAIZE SEEDLINGS

Benomyl [(methyl-1 butylcarbamoyl)-2-benzimidazolecarbamate] is a systemic fungicide that has been reported to induce various plant-growth regulatory responses. The water solubility of benomyl is approximately 3.8 mg/L at 20æ% C. Yet, a drench application utilizes 2 pt/ft2 of a 1 lb/100 gal solution. Since 1 lb = 453.6 g, 1 gal = 3.785 L; 1 qt = 946.25 mL: 1 gal 453.6 g 1 lb Benlate DF 0.5 a.i. benomyl × × × 100 gal H2 O 1 Benlate 3.7851 L lb = 599.2 mg benomyl L H2O

If 2 pt are applied per square foot, 0.94625 L lb 0.5992 g 1 qt 43560 ft 2 × 2× × × L acre qt 453.6 g ft 54.46 lb benomyl acre The original 1 lb/100 gal water is 600 mg/L benomyl. Obviously, this concentration of benomyl far exceeds the water solubility of benomyl. Thus, an undissolved reservoir of benomyl is present in the system. Since benomyl T1/2 in water exceeds 7 hr, a drench application results in the adsorption of benomyl to any surface available. As the benomyl in the soil solution is absorbed into the plant or degraded, the benomyl coneentration will be maintained at saturation by benomyl desorption from the potting media and/or root surface into the soil solution and become available to the plant. Thus, a single benomyl drench application of 600 mg/L would be sufficient to maintain a constant benomyl-saturated soil solution for >6 days.

Benomyl degrades to NBC + BIC (methyl-2-benzimidazolecarbamate + n-butyl isocyanate). The latter degradation product further degrades to nbutylamine and carbon dioxide with a T1/2 of 7 min. But, BIC is an alkyl isocyanate and n-alkyl isocyanates are powerful active-site directors of serine proteases (i.e., trypsin and chymotrypsin).

Thus BIC will react instantaneously and irreversibly with the -OH group of serine, or fatty alcohol. Serine and threonine are requisite protein components (i.e., DNA, RNA, enzymes), and BIC has been reported to be a strong cutinase inhibitor, which was suggested as a possible protective mode of action of the fungicide benomyl because fungi that have a cutinase and penetrate into the host through the cuticle had a decreased infestation in benomyl-treated leaves.

Phosphatidylserine (PS) is a requisite membrane lipid, has a serine functional group, and is a constituent with a negative charge. Neutralization of the membrane negative charge by the positive charges on ruthenium red resulted in decreased 45 Ca^{2+} absorption by sorghum roots, which was explicable as an inhibition of H^+ -ATPase, Ca^{2+} -ATPase, and cation channels. Therefore, because BIC binds to serine and has a strong cationic charge, benomyl (and/or degradation products) might modify Ca^{2+} uptake by roots.

Calcium is a major metabolic "second messenger" in plants whose cytosolic concentration is very closely regulated. Modification of Ca^{2+} influx or efflux could have major implications to plant growth. Therefore, the influence of benomyl, two formulated benomyl products (i.e., DF and WP formulations), and the combined formulate for Benlate DF were evaluated for their influence on root absorption of 45 Ca^{2+} in sorghum and maize. B. Methods and Materials Untreated sorghum (GP-10, Funk G522DR) or maize (B73 × LH132) seeds (25/pot) were planted in sterile white quartz flintshot sand in 8 × 8 × 8 cm pots and watered with deionized water.

After 3 or 4 days, when the roots had elongated to about 6 cm, plants were washed from the sand. Ten seedlings were taped to a 1.25-cm diameter rigid plastic pipe and 1-cm root tips were immersed in 1N ammonium chloride (NH_4Cl) for 5 min to dissolve the root cap mucigel. The plants were transferred to 10 × 10 cm polyethylene refrigerator cartons containing 100 mL of 0.01M sodium acetate (NaAc) (pH 5.5) plus 0.1 μCi 45 Ca2+ (11.16 mCi/mg $Ca2^{+}$) plus the fungicide treatments (benomyl, inert formulation of Benlate DF, Benlate DF, or Benlate WP).

After 1 hr, the roots were removed from the treatment solution, the 1-cm tips were excised and washed with 0.01M ethylenediaminetetracetic acid (EDTA) and inserted into scintillation vials. After the addition of scintillation fluid (Scintiverse BD, Fisher Chemical Co., Pittsburgh, PA), the vials were placed in the dark (>4 hr) to allow fluorescence to decay, and the Ca^{2+} was assayed by liquid scintillation spectrometer (Beckman LS 5801) for 20 min or 1% accuracy.

Background counts/min (CPM) were subtracted from each assay and actual disintegrations/min (DPM) were calculated by dividing DPM by the LS counter efficiency. Because it is impossible to deliver exactly the same Ca^{2+} DPM in the treatment solutions, a 1-mL aliquot was taken of each treatment solution, and the DPM in the roots was adjusted to the equivalent of a 106 DPM exposure. Data from each set of treatments were subjected to analysis of variance and standard errors were calculated.

Fungicides and Benlate DF formulate concentrations were 0, 0.2, 2, 20, or 200 mg/L. C. Results and Discussion Benomyl induced a slight, nonsignificant increase in 45 Ca^{2+} absorption at **benomyl** concentrations below the water-solubility level of 3.8 mg/L. At concentrations greater than its water solubility, benomyl induced slight but statistically significant decreased 45 Ca^{2+} absorption by root tips of both sorghum and maize.

Many organic pesticides are rather insoluble in water, but the delivery system of choice utilizes water as a diluent. Therefore, various surfactants are added to the mixture to hold the active compound dissolved or suspended in the diluent during application.

The complex Benlate DF formulate (2 and 20 mg/L) induced significantly decreased Ca^{2+} uptake in root tips of sorghum and maize. But at 200 mg/L formulate, 45 Ca^{2+} uptake was significantly increased in both sorghum cultivars. The treatment solutions contained <“2×106 DPM/mL. If these surfactants functioned by PM disruption, the roots would have contained 45 Ca^{2+} in concentrations equivalent to those of the treatment solution.

These root tips contained <1% of the 45 Ca^{2+} DPM of equivalent volume treatment solution (<“3000 DPM). Therefore, this response cannot be due to membrane disruption. Rather, these data may be explicable as a partial influence on Ca^{2+} efflux. Differential responses by sorghum root PM of sorghum cultivars have been reported previously.

In Funk G522DR, Benlate DF (0.2, 2, and 20 mg/L) induced nonsignificantly increased Ca^{2+} adsorption but in all three cultivars the highest concentration (200 mg/L Benlate DF) induced significant increased accumulations of Ca^{2+}. These accumulations are explicable as an influence of Benlate DF on the external surface of the PM, where Ca^{2+} -ATPase mediated Ca^{2+} efflux was decreased. Benlate WP (0.2, 2, and 20 mg/L) significantly inhibited 45 Ca2+ accumulation in sorghum root tips, but 200 mg/L Benlate WP induced significantly increased accumulations of Ca^{2+} in both sorghum cultivars and maize.

These differences in response between maize and sorghum are similar to genetically determined differences between sorghum cultivars reported previously. Membranes have different enzymes and capacities to move substances through the membrane. One type of H^+ -ATPase is prevalent on tonoplasts while a second type is prevalent on plasma membranes, but both types are present in both membranes. Movement of ions (Ca^{2+}) through the plasma membrane is determined by the quantity of enzymes (or channels) present, and this is genetically determined.

These data show two basically different responses. At concentrations less than the water solubility, benomyl does not influence Ca^{2+} absorption. Nonsolubilized benomyl is highly adsorptive, and the only surface in these high concentrations available for benomyl to become attached to was the root. Therefore, adsorbed benomyl apparently induced Ca^{2+} accumulation. These evaluations were conducted without any other adsorptive surface in the system.

7

Irrigation of Turf with Effluent Water

INTRODUCTION

Water is a limited natural resource in many arid and semiarid regions of the southwestern United States as well as other parts of the nation. In populated metropolitan areas, large quantities of sewage effluent are available for irrigation of turf, and interest in this option grows annually.

In some municipalities, such as Tucson, Arizona, all new golf courses must use reclaimed water for irrigation. Given that underground aquifer water table levels are decreasing, with a concomitant increase in pumping costs, the use of effluent for turf irrigation is an attractive alternative to potable water supplies. Additionally, ever since PL 92-500 restricted discharge of wastewater, several studies have shown that land application is the lowest-cost alternative for improving water quality.

At the same time, land application of effluent reduces point source pollution that occurs when large quantities of effluent are dumped into dry riverbeds. The source of sewage effluent is sewage, which is processed at wastewater treatment plants through primary, secondary, or tertiary treatment levels. Primary treatment of raw sewage is a screening and settling process that removes organic and inorganic solids. These processes remove large debris, such as rags or sticks, and dense materials, such as sand or small stones. Other undissolved suspended material is normally removed in a second settling tank called a primary clarifier. Here, suspended material gradually settles out into "raw sludge," which is removed and processed further. The remaining liquid in the settling tank is called primary effluent, which still contains large amounts of dissolved organic materials. Such organic compounds can be removed by secondary treatment, which is normally an aerobic digestion process. This digestion is accomplished by bacteria that degrade the organics into less complex organics and, ultimately, to carbon dioxide.

Secondary treatment can remove up to 90% of the organic matter in the primary effluent. Secondary effluent usually has not met health criteria established for open access irrigation. Secondary treated effluent can undergo further treatment, which might include additional filtration and chlorination for disinfection purposes, and it is then called reclaimed water.

Most reclaimed water for irrigation meets health criteria established for open-access irrigation. Many studies in the United States and throughout the world have evaluated the use of municipal effluents as an irrigation source. Effluent has been used in the southwestern United States for irrigation of small grains, sorghum (Sorghum bicolor L.), wheat (Triticum aestivum L.), and cotton (Gossypium hirsutum L.). Municipal effluent is ideally suited for turf irrigation, however, particularly in arid climates:

1. Many arid climates permit continuous growth of turf, which permits year-round utilization of wastewater, which is also produced year round.
2. The high shoot and root density of turf grasses enables large volumes of wastewater to be renovated with respect to removal of potential groundwater pollutants.
3. Large volumes of irrigation water are necessary for the growth of turf, which further increases the volume of effluent that can be renovated.
4. Plant nutrients, routinely found in wastewater, reduce the turf need for commercial fertilizer.

5. Most expanses of irrigated turf are located adjacent to cities, where effluent is produced, thereby minimizing transportation costs.
6. Potential health problems associated with the use of effluent on turf are less than when effluent is used for irrigation of food crops.

Secondary effluents typically contain such elements as nitrogen (N), phosphorus (P), potassium (K), and other essential plant nutrients. Along with beneficial nutrients, other potentially hazardous elements are present, which can be deleterious to turf growth and soil quality and pose a potential threat to the water quality of underground aquifers. In this chapter we evaluate the benefits and hazards of effluent irrigation as well as public perceptions and acceptance of effluent use on turf; we then describe management protocols that optimize effluent use on turf.

PUBLIC ACCEPTANCE

Early Wastewater Reuse

Disposal of waste materials, including wastewaters, on soil has been practiced for centuries. One of the earliest documented land disposal systems was initiated in 1531 at Bunzland, Germany, where a sewage irrigation system continued in operation for over 300 years. Many systems since that time have been in operation throughout the world to utilize wastewater as a source of irrigation water and plant nutrients. During the late 1800s, George Rafter of the U.S. Geological Survey studied and produced comprehensive reviews of wastewater disposal in the United States and Europe. The majority of the sewage treatments facilities studied were land treatment systems at that time. Rafter concluded that wastewater could be purified by percolation through soil and plant material given that the area's climate is sufficiently warm. He also stated that wastewater could be used on crops if special management practices were employed. Land treatment of wastewaters became less popular in the United States during the early 1900s. As interest again increased in the 1970s, it was met with controversy and resistance. Jewell and Seabrook identified some of the factors for the decline of land treatment of wastes as pressure for alternative land uses, resource overloading because of an incomplete technical understanding, and the development of the germ theory (which mistakenly concluded that the use of chlorine could be an effective disinfectant, allowing the "safe" discharge of partially treated sewage into clean waterways). As populations became more centralized in towns and cities, safe disposal of wastes became a more technical problem. This discharge of wastes into waterways during the 1970s produced unacceptable pollution levels in many fresh waters of the United States. Federal legislation and "cleanup funds" for polluted waters were established, beginning with the Clean Water Act of 1972 (P192-500). This act proposed a "zero discharge" of wastes into waterways and encouraged a reuse and recovery philosophy. One way to satisfy all the goals was to revitalize the concept and use of land application of wastes with present-day technology.

Extent of Effluent Use on Turf

Effluent irrigation of turf, in particular golf courses, is now widely practiced in many areas of the United States. It is especially prevalent in the southwestern United States. As an example, the Arizona Department of Water Resources (1999) reports that over 50% of the irrigation water used by turf-related facilities (golf courses, parks, schools, and cemeteries) in the Tucson metropolitan area comes from wastewater. Groundwater is the primary water source and Tucson's central groundwater well-field falls at a rate of about 1 m yr"1 . The use of wastewater irrigation on turf facilities is a means in which Tucson can reduce groundwater depletion. Of the 7995 ha-m of effluent produced in the Tucson area, only 17% or 1.353 ha-m was reused for turf or agricultural purposes. About 6500 ha-m of wastewater is released into dry riverbeds. Therefore, much more wastewater is available for irrigation.

Seventy-one turf facilities in the Tucson area used a total of about 2448 ha-m of water in 1995. Golf courses accounted for 22%

of this total. Effluent use was about 701 ha-m for golf courses in 1995, 127 ha-m for parks, and 11 ha-m for cemeteries. Schoolyards, on the other hand, used no effluent; they irrigated with 90 ha-m of groundwater, using no wastewater at all. Approximately 62 km north of Tucson is the Phoenix metropolitan area. Here, turf-related facilities account for over 50% of all industrial water use, and golf courses account for two-thirds of this amount. Only 6.8% of turf-related irrigation water comes from effluent, with the balance coming from groundwater (50.2%), surface water (35.7%), and Colorado River water (6.1%). For the Phoenix area, turf-related water use has ranged from a total of 9779 ha-m in 1992 to 11,931 ha-m in 1989. Golf course use peaked in 1994 at 8096 ha-m.

Since effluent is now being disposed of on high-use recreational areas, it is clear that public involvement and attitudes must be considered in the decision-making process. In recent years, the public has become increasingly aware of water pollution and environmental concerns. It is important to inform the public that land application of wastewater should decrease potable water demands and reduce water pollution after application through a soil-turf filter. A 1979 survey of 140 California residents indicated that more than 90% of the respondents had favorable attitudes toward the use of reclaimed water for irrigation of golf courses, parks, schoolyards, and common areas around residential buildings. The study included resident recommendations regarding future uses for reclaimed water at Irvine.

Approximately 56% of the respondents recommended continuation of existing uses of the reclaimed water, and 5% recommended expansion of the existing uses. Only 5% recommended eliminating existing uses, and 25% recommended adding new types of uses. This survey was conducted in a community that utilized wastewater and had a relatively high level of public awareness of successful application. Other surveys conducted to determine public attitudes toward reclaimed water use indicated that participant response is increasingly negative as the proposed use of reclaimed water is more closely associated with personal contact. Younger, more affluent, more highly educated respondents who had personally considered the use of reclaimed water had the most favorable attitudes. Acceptance of effluent use was related to respondents who believed that there was a water supply shortage, that modern technology was capable of successfully treating wastewater, that public health officials would approve certain uses of reclaimed water, and that using reclaimed water would benefit the economy. Variables that correlated with rejection of wastewater use were aversion to uncleanliness, aversion to human waste, odors associated with application and storage, and concern with potential health hazards. In addition, many golf course superintendents are concerned over their perceived specialized management needs for turf irrigated with effluent.

BENEFITS OF EFFLUENT

Water Source

Since it is 99% water, one of the major benefits of effluent is that it is a relatively low-cost water source that reduces the use of potable water for irrigation of turf. Its utility as a water source for irrigation of turf in the Southwest has been well documented. As well as water, effluent also contains many beneficial plant nutrients that are essential for the growth of turf.

Nutrients

Effluent routinely contains plant available nitrogen (N), phosphorus (P), potassium (K), calcium (Ca), and magnesium (Mg) and lower concentrations of micronutrients. Nitrogen, as ammonium or nitrate, is often found at concentrations of 20 to 30 mg L”1 and available phosphorus at levels of 6 to 25 mg L”1. Potassium can be found at variable levels in effluent, with typical values of 10 to 15 mg L”1. At the time of that study, the secondary wastewater in Tucson delivered 163 kg N ha”1 , 163 kg P, and 195 kg K in each ha-m. The water was shown to supply bermudagrass turf with an ample supply of nutrients during the summer months, when irrigation requirements were high. All the preceding nutrients are beneficial to turf. Additionally, effluent also contains dissolved organic carbon which can serve as a substrate for heterotrophic soil bacteria.

HAZARDS OF EFFLUENT

Salinity

As with any other irrigation source, the salinity and sodicity hazards of wastewater effluent can vary considerably. The degree of these hazards in wastewater effluent depends primarily upon the quality of the influent. Wastewater reclamation results in increased salt concentrations (usually by about 200 to 400 mg l”1) through evaporative losses in holding tanks and the addition of water softeners. Because wastewater treatment processes are designed to remove bacteria and organic waste materials and not salts, the turf manager should have a chemical analysis performed to determine the wastewater characteristics as defined by the U.S. Salinity Laboratory classification.

This information, combined with information on the turf species (salinity tolerance and rooting depth) to be irrigated and the soil (textural class, bulk density, and infiltration rate) will determine whether this water source is usable and, if so, whether special management practices are required to use it. Harivandi reported that the effluent quality of six wastewater treatment facilities in California had electrical conductivity (EC) values ranging from 1.02 to 1.44 dS m”1 and sodium adsorption ratios (SAR) of 3.4 to 5.7. These waters could all be classified as having high salinity hazards but low sodicity hazards. Gelt stated that at the present time, Tucson and Phoenix treatment plants are producing wastewaters containing acceptable levels of salts for all uses. Effluent waters, such as those utilized in Hawaii and Tucson, have EC values <1 dS m”1 , Na levels up to about 94 mg L”1 , and SAR values of 3.2 to 4.1. These characteristics make them safe for use even on sensitive crops. In addition, the turfgrasses that are normally used are fairly tolerant of salts and Na. Work initiated by Hayes et al. and continued by Mancino and Pepper found a Tucson effluent source to increase turfgrass soil EC from 0.7 to about 1.5 dS m”1 after 3.5 years.

Similarly irrigated turf plots receiving potable water had a final EC of 1.3 dS m"1 . Therefore, the change in EC resulting from the use of effluent was small. Once Tucson begins utilizing Colorado River water, salinity levels of effluent will increase to about 1000 mg L"1 (EC = 1.6). This water will probably still be suitable for turf provided that good soil drainage exists, but it will be less suitable for salt-sensitive landscape plants such as Acacia longifolia, Cotoneaster horizontalis, Pinus halapensis, and Nandina domestica. Colorado River water might actually improve the quality of effluent wastewater in areas of Maricopa and Pinal County because it is better than existing potable water sources. Table 4 shows the range in chemical constituents of a potable water and secondary effluent available for turf irrigation in Chandler, Arizona. A study was conducted to investigate the influence of these waters on turf and soil quality when precipitation rates are varied using a line-source irrigation system.

This irrigation system had a high precipitation rate near the irrigation line which then decreased linearly as one moved away from the line. Two lines were established, one for wastewater and one for potable water. Turf nearest the lines received 0.74 ha-m H2 O y"1 and turf growing 15 m away received no water. After 2 years of irrigation and regardless of water source, soil EC levels range from 2 dS m"1 at the line to 6 dS m"1 where 0.12 ha-m y"1 of irrigation was applied. The breakoff point for acceptable turf quality occurred where 0.43 ha-m y"1 effluent and 0.49 ha-m yr"1 of potable water is applied. Soil salinity was about equal at both locations, with EC = 3 dS m"1 . Soil Na+ levels differed, however, with the potable and effluent irrigated soils approaching 500 and 1000 mg Na+ kg"1 at the breakoff points, respectively. Although "Midiron" bermudagrass appeared to be tolerating these salinity and sodium levels in the soil, other grasses may not. Therefore it would be necessary for a turf manager to select turfgrasses tolerant of saline conditions. The salt tolerance of many turfgrasses has been improved over the last two decades. Table 5 lists the estimated salinity tolerances of commonly used turfgrasses. The turfgrass manager would be better served to select grasses more tolerant of the expected soil salinity conditions to ensure turf of acceptable quality under conditions of mechanical and foot traffic, low mowing heights, pests, heat, drought, and cold stress. In addition to proper turfgrass selection, the turf manager must also estimate the amount of additional irrigation water that must be applied to maintain acceptable soil salinity levels by moving salts beyond the root zone of the turf. The determination of this leaching requirement (LR) (22) can be calculated as:

LR = ECw 5(ECe) " ECw

where ECw is the salinity level in dS m"1 of the irrigation water and ECe is the average soil salinity (saturated paste extract) that is tolerated by the crop. For example, perennial ryegrass, which is moderately salt tolerant, can tolerate soil salinities of 6 dS m"1. If a wastewater of 1.5 dS m"1 is used for irrigation, then the leaching requirement is: 1.5 = 0.05 5(6) " 1.5 Thus an additional 5% of irrigation water would be applied to prevent the accumulation of salts in the root zone that would be beyond the tolerance of the ryegrass. Because leaching requirements of greater than 15 to 20% can be impractical, consideration should be given to the selection of more tolerant grasses and/or the use of this irrigation water on more permeable soils. Regardless of water quality and soil type, internal soil drainage must be adequate for desirable turf.

Osmotic Effects, Nutrient Imbalances, and Specific Ion Toxicities

A great deal of work has been done on the effects of saline water on turf growth and physiology. This work was summarized recently by Harivandi et al., and it could be expected that as salinity levels increased, there would be an increase in the osmotic stress placed upon the plant, with a concomitant increase in the salt ion accumulation of the turf tissue. This would result in a decrease in turf growth (particularly in the shoots), an increased root–shoot ratio, a potential for nutrient imbalances (increased tissue levels of Na^+ , Ca^{2+} , Cl" , and SO_2" , and 4 decreased K+ , Mg^{2+} , and NO_3"), and a reduction in seedling survival. However, the salinity of effluent water often meets the standards set for irrigation waters used even for sensitive crops (<700 mg L"1 of total dissolved solids, EC <1 dS m"1 , <175 mg Cl" L"1). As a result, many reports have discussed the possible detriments of using effluent water to irrigate turf, but the data presented in the scientific literature have shown effluent to be an excellent source of irrigation water for turf. As with any irrigation water, the primary concerns with specific toxicities relate mainly to the ions Na^+, B, and Cl".

All of these ions may be present in higher concentrations in effluent than in the original water source because of the use of water softeners, detergents, and bleaches. The effects of sodium salts on turf growth have been studied in turfgrasses growing under laboratory and greenhouse conditions, and differences in NaCl tolerance have been shown to exist between species and also between cultivars. In actuality it is difficult to find documentation of direct Na^+ toxicity occurring to turf under field conditions because high Na+ levels are almost always associated with high saline and poor soil conditions. It is generally assumed that the inability to grow good turf in soils containing high levels of Na^+ results not from the direct toxicity of Na+ to the plant but rather from its negative impact on the soil itself. Tests of high tolerances of plant species to Na+ are usually conducted after first stabilizing soil structure.

Such grasses as bermudagrass, crested and fairway wheatgrass, tall fescue, annual ryegrass, alkaligrass, saltgrass, Paspalum, and red fescue can tolerate the presence of Na+ in the soil at levels exceeding 15 ESP (exchangeable sodium percentage). The influence of Na+ on soil structure occurs when enough Na^+ is present in the soil to displace the cations Ca^{2+} and Mg^{2+} from soil and organic matter cation exchange sites. Sodium causes clay and organic matter aggregates to deflocculate, resulting in a reduction of the number of soil macropores. The soil then becomes impermeable to water and air. Plant growth is thus reduced. Soils containing higher percentages of clay, particularly montmorillinite, and organic matter are very susceptible to this problem. These soils generally show signs of deterioration at ESP values of 10 to 20%; sandier soils may not decline in physical quality until ESP > 30%. The concentration of Na^+ in an irrigation water must be related to the concentration of divalent cations contained in that water, particularly Ca^{2+} and Mg^{2+}, before its influence on soil structure can be determined. Divalent cations are more strongly attracted to cation exchange sites in the soil than monovalent cations.

Therefore irrigation waters high in Na^+, but also high in Ca^{2+} and Mg^{2+}, may have no negative impact on soil quality. As a result, it is necessary to determine the sodium adsorption ratio (SAR) of a water to access the potential impact of Na^+ on the soil. Like Na^+, B can be higher in effluent water than potable water because of the use of B (boron)-containing detergents. Also like Na+ , B toxicity has not been documented to occur on turf unless grown under experimental conditions. Oertli et al. found that "Seaside" creeping bentgrass, "Highland" colonial bentgrass, and "Alta" tall fescue were quite tolerant of B, even during establishment. They also observed differences in B accumulation by turf grasses: bermudagrass < zoysiagrass < Kentucky bluegrass < tall fescue < perennial ryegrass < creeping bentgrass. Boron accumulation was highest in leaf tips, which would be removed during routine mowing. In another study, the application of B at 1.68 or 8.4 kg ha"1 had little if any effect on "Merion" Kentucky bluegrass turf grown in greenhouse pots and under low-maintenance conditions (no N, P, or K applied).

In fact, B at the lower rate produced sod with improved color and more root production. Boron injury was observed at the higher B application rate, where plants were receiving 28 kg ha"1 10N6P-4K fertilizer every 3 months. Leaf tips were found to die between mowings. In 1976, because of drought conditions, it was necessary for the Calistoga Golf Course in Calistoga, California, to use a sewage effluent water for irrigation that contains high levels of B (4 mg L"1). This level of B in the water would require it to be applied only to tolerant (4.0 to 6.0 mg L"1) or very tolerant (6.0 to 15 mg L"1) crops. The B originated from swimming pools and spas receiving their water from natural hot mineral springs.

Concentrations of B in the loam soil of "Seaside" creeping bentgrass putting greens reached 7.8 mg kg”1 and levels in plant tissue accumulated to 78.2 mg kg”1 . This was not enough to cause injury to the turf, and a deterioration in putting green quality was not reported. It is reported that crop toxicity symptoms occur when B reaches levels of 250 to 300 mg kg”1 (dry wt) in leaf tissue. Under such field conditions, the removal of leaf tips through more frequent mowing and the reduction of fertility levels could help to reduce the accumulation of B in the leaves. Chloride toxicity is the most common toxicity occurring from irrigation water because it moves readily in the transpirational stream of plants. Toxicity can also occur when chlorides are absorbed directly through the leaves. Crop sensitivity may occur when Cl” levels in soil solution exceed 5 or 3.3 meq L”1 in irrigation water, but turfgrasses have been classified as being relatively tolerant to Cl” even though grasses readily accumulate Cl”. Chloride accumulation in turfgrasses appears to be higher than SO_2" , accumulation, re4 gardless of the cation (Na+ , K+ , Ca2+ , or Mg^{2+}). Chloride uptake by turf is also reduced at higher pH values.

Cordukes also reported that total germination of "Fylking" Kentucky bluegrass was not affected by Cl” , but time to total germination was extended by about 5 days on premoistened filter paper. Harivandi reported that some effluent irrigation waters in California contained from 2.8 to 5.2 meq Cl” L”1 . However, effluent used for irrigation in Chandler, Arizona, contains up to 14.3 meq L”1. Chloride levels in plant tissue approached 1.5% on a dry-weight basis with no apparent injury. Under greenhouse conditions, Cordukes and Parupes showed several turfgrasses to accumulate Cl” in response to Cl” level and time, with tissue levels reaching up to 2.2% on a dry-weight basis, yet little impact occurred in terms of total dry-weight production. Therefore Cl” probably has more impact upon trees and shrubs planted in the landscape than on the turf itself. The use of waters with alkaline pH values may also help to offset Cl” uptake by the turf.

Nitrates

Although nitrates are a beneficial source of N for plant growth, excess nitrates in soil pore water can pose a threat to human health. Specifically, high nitrates can cause methemoglobinemia in newborn infants, a condition commonly referred to as blue-baby syndrome, which can be fatal. Current U.S. Environmental Protection Agency (EPA) standards restrict concentrations of nitrate N to 10 mg L”1 in water or leachate entering potable water systems. Effluent usually contains 20 to 30 mg L”1 of N as the ammonium or nitrate ion. Regardless of its initial form, once applied to turf and soil, all N is found as the nitrate ion, as a result of nitrification, within a matter of days. The potential fate of such nitrates is uptake by turf, gaseous loss via denitrification, or loss in solution via nitrate leaching. Anderson et al. applied effluent to turf growing on pure sand or on sand plus an organic amendment, referred to as a “mix.” They found, on average, that the sand removed 33% of the effluent N by soil processes and 19% by turf uptake. The mix, with a slightly higher cation exchange capacity, removed 37% by soil processes and 27% by turf uptake.

These data show that soil and turf can remove substantial amounts of effluent N and that this removal increases with the increasing cation exchange capacity of the soil. Regardless of soil type, however, significant amounts of effluent nitrate are always available for leaching. Leachate nitrate concentrations increased with increased rate of effluent application and were lower from the “mix” soil than from the sand. The data also show that at normal consumptive use rates of effluent application of 7.2 cm week”1 , leachate nitrate concentrations met federal standards. Thus most “normal” soils, which contain some silt and clay constituents, maintain nitrate concentrations in leachate at acceptable levels with respect to human health. Concern about nitrate leachate would be most warranted on sand-based putting greens and athletic fields. However, these turf surfaces are small relative to areas of turf on native soils. Leaching losses of nitrate N from sand-based putting greens have been shown to be small.

Nitrous Oxide Emissions from a Desert Region Turf Soil Irrigated with Wastewater

In summer 1991, Guilbault measured nitrous oxide (N_2O) emissions from an effluent-irrigated turf and the surrounding unirrigated desert soil at the Arthur Pack regional golf course in Tucson, Arizona. Both sites were made up of a loamy sand. The average N_2O-N emission from three fairway sites was estimated to be 40.2 ng m”2 s”1 over a 10-week measurement period. The mean flux from the unirrigated Upland Sonoran desert location was 2.4 ng m”2 s”1 . Periods of large emissions from the turf were correlated with above-average soil moisture levels, total organic carbon, and high soil temperatures. However, it is not possible to say how much of the irrigated turf emission was due to wastewater irrigation, because potable irrigated sites were not part of the study. Mancino et al. found denitrification losses from Kentucky bluegrass sod, based on average N_2O-N emissions, to be highest in warm, wet soils receiving potable water. Mancino and Torello also found turf soils to normally contain large populations of denitrifying microbes. At the same golf facility used by Guilbault, Mancino and Pepper found no differences in the total aerobic bacterial populations under wastewater or potable water irrigated turf. They also found nitrate- and nitrite-reducing populations to be similar in the soil, regardless of irrigation source (unpublished data).

Pathogens

Raw effluent almost always contains large numbers of bacterial and viral pathogens, including Salmonella, Shigella, enteroviruses, and hepatitis A virus. Normally, primary and secondary treatment and chlorination reduce the numbers of pathogens dramatically, but most treated effluents are still likely to contain some pathogens. Survival of pathogens decreases with increased temperatures and exposure to ultraviolet (UV) radiation supplied via sunlight. Recently it was demonstrated that a 99% inactivation of effluent-applied viruses on turf required 16 to 24 h exposure to the environment in the winter and only 8 to 10 h in the summer, presumably as a result of the higher temperatures and increased UV radiation. Similar effects on the survival of bacterial pathogens have been observed. Thus, although most pathogen populations decrease rapidly after application of effluent to turf, there is always a small potential for disease transmission. This potential can be reduced by avoiding direct human contact with effluent and ensuring the use of chlorinated effluents for turf irrigation, particularly in areas with uncontrolled public access. Overall, despite extensive use of effluent for turf irrigation over periods of many years, there are remarkably few reports documenting illness or cause-and-effect cases of disease transmission from the use of effluent.

Despite this, it is still important for turf managers to reduce the likelihood of direct contact of effluent with the public. For example, irrigation should occur at such times of day as to preclude direct contact of the spray with facility users, irrigation spray should not reach privately owned premises or drinking foundations, hose bibs should be posted with signs reading "Reclaimed Water, Do Not Drink," hose bibs discharging reclaimed water should be secured to prevent use by the public, signs reading "Irrigation with Reclaimed Water" should be prominently displayed on the premises, and irrigation pipe should be color-coded or otherwise marked to indicate nonpotable water.

Heavy Metals

Effluents usually contain trace amounts of micronutrients and heavy metals. Normally the metal content of effluents is lower than that of sewage sludges and tends to be beneficial to turf growth. Elements of concern include Cu, Zn, Ni, and Cd, but most treated effluents have low concentrations of these metals and do not pose a threat to growth. The demand for using wastewater to irrigate amenity areas is an international issue. For example, in Oman, about 10 million cubic meters of wastewater is used annually to primarily irrigate amenity roadsides containing shrubs and fruit trees. The fruit is often eaten by the passersby. Therefore, strict international guidelines are being followed to ensure that human and soil health are protected. Soil and water samples collected from different sites in Oman that had been irrigated for 4 to 8 years with industrial and domestic treated effluent or potable groundwater showed no hazardous levels of Cu, Ni, lead (Pb), or Zn. The authors attributed these findings to the stringent implementation of regulations for wastewater reuse and discharge. The effects of rangegrass irrigation with in situ uranium processing wastewater from the Highland Uranium Project (Wyoming) was studied by Levy and Kearney.

Irrigation water was evaluated using guidelines from the U.S. Salinity Laboratory, and selenium (Se), B, uranium (U), and radium (Ra) were monitored for 6 years in the irrigated soil and rangegrasses. Salt accumulation in the soil did not occur because of adequate managed leaching from the root zone.

Metal and anion concentrations in the grasses remained within naturally occurring levels. Soil EC, pH, and SAR increased over time but did not pose a serious plant and soil-management problem because adequate leaching was maintained. Soil B and Ra also did not change. Although soil Se and U accumulation did occur, phytotoxicity was not observed, and plant levels were not considered to pose a threat to grazing animals.

MANAGEMENT OF TURF UNDER EFFLUENT IRRIGATION

Water Use Requirements

Beard and Kneebone et al. reviewed the water requirements of cool and warm-season turf grasses. In general, water use and irrigation requirements vary depending on the quality of turf desired, maintenance practices (i.e., mowing height and frequency and fertilization practices), and the availability of water to the plant. Irrigation water use requirements also depend upon the quality of the irrigation water. When water quality is not an issue, the minimum water requirements of warm-season grasses under arid conditions appear to be about 60% of reference evapotranspiration (ETo) as derived from the modified Penman equation.

Data for cool-season grasses is lacking. The data available are derived mainly from arid and semiarid regions where evaporative demand is high and/or outside of the normal regions of cool-season turf adaptation. It appears that under such conditions, cool-season grasses may require 80% or more of ETo to remain vigorous and esthetically appealing. These arid and semiarid areas are also the most likely to utilize effluent water for irrigation. Cool-season turf use, in particular perennial ryegrass, in arid regions is predominately for the purpose of winter overseeding of dormant warm-season grasses. Winter overseeding usually occurs in mid-October and provides a green turf through the winter months. The cool-season turf usually succumbs to heat stress in late spring and early summer, as the warm-season turf resumes growth. Ryegrass water use in southern Arizona can range from 1.4 mm d"1 in February to 16.5 mm d"1 in May and totals about 686 mm water under nonlimiting conditions.

Bermudagrass turf growing from mid-April into winter dormancy requires water in the amount of about 860 to 1105 mm y"1. Therefore, year-round turf in the Southwest can require up to 1550 mm of water. It is this practice of overseeding that allows effluent to be used for irrigation purposes for 12 months of the year. As mentioned previously, additional water must be applied to ensure adequate leaching of the salts beyond the root zone of the turf. It is recommended that saline irrigation waters be applied in frequent and shallow applications to ensure the downward movement of salts through the soil profile and to minimize the concentration of salts in the upper soil as water is lost through evapotranspiration. Turfgrasses have been shown to use more water under nonlimiting conditions than is biologically necessary. This "luxury" consumption of water by turf was first described by Kneebone and Pepper.

Therefore, from a practical standpoint, turf irrigated with effluent could use more water than it requires because of the way the water is applied. It is generally recommended that deep, infrequent irrigations be applied to turf to conserve irrigation water, promote deeper rooting, lose less irrigation water to evaporation, and to reduce luxury water consumption. Whether or not constituents contained in effluent increase or decrease turf water use is yet to be determined. The routine application of N from fertilizers, in combination with N from effluent, could increase the water use of the turf. It has been shown that a primary factor contributing to turf ET is vertical leaf extension rate.

A well-fertilized turf would have a rapid leaf extension rate, which promotes loss of water to the atmosphere by lowering canopy resistance. B. Fertilizer Requirements Because of macro- and micronutrients present in effluent, turf irrigated with wastewater requires less inorganic fertilizer for high-quality turf growth. For example, actively growing bermudagrass (Cynodon dactylon L. Pers.) during the summer requires 25 to 73 kg N ha"1 , whereas perennial ryegrass (Lolium perenne L.) requires 25 to 49 kg N ha"1 when used to overseed bermudagrass during the fall. At an effluent application rate of 0.6 ha-m y"1 , an average wastewater could supply approximately 50% of the suggested N requirement for this turf. The ability of effluent to supply turf with additional N, which illustrates the nitrate content of soil fertilized at four rates of N and irrigated with either potable water or effluent. The data indicate that the effluent significantly increased the nitrate content of the soil relative to the potable water source.

In this study, soil P levels increased 20 mg kg"1 in effluent-irrigated turf soil. The P levels of the same soil irrigated with potable water decreased 13.7 mg kg"1 . These data suggest that effluent water contains P in excess of plant requirements. Similar results were reported by Pell and Nyberg (52). Note, however, that high soil P can lead to the production of insoluble compounds with Cu, Mg, Fe, and Zn and render these elements less available for plant use. Effluent also contains other plant nutrients, including K and micronutrients, but the concentration of these elements are low relative to N and P. Overall, the nutrients contained in effluent results in reduced fertilizer requirements for good-quality turf. During the summer months, when irrigation rates are high, no additional N or P may be necessary for areas of low-intensity management, such as home lawns, playgrounds, and parks. High-intensity managed turf, such as golf greens, may require small additional increments of N. Similarly, during the winter months, when irrigation rates are decreased, additional N may be needed to increase the winter quality of cool-season turf.

Soil Amendment Requirement

The over accumulation of Na^+ in the soil from effluent irrigation is probably the primary concern of turf managers, particularly when the amount of water available for irrigation may be limiting due to budgetary constraints or governmentinduced water restrictions. Hayes et al. and Mancino and Pepper found that the Na+ levels in a turf soil irrigated with effluent reached about 350 mg kg"1 after 3.3 years of irrigation. This was with about a 15% leaching fraction. In another study in Chandler, Arizona, effluent-irrigated turf plots accumulated upward of 1000 mg kg"1 of Na^+ in the top 30 cm of soil when leaching was essentially absent. Under such conditions, it is imperative that amendments be applied to the soil to reduce Na^+ levels. Calcium sulfate (gypsum) and other sulfur-bearing (S) compounds are useful in reducing the Na^+ content of agronomic soils even when saline irrigation water is used. For agronomic crops, gypsum and S can be tilled into the soil or dissolved in the irrigation water and flooded onto the soil. Sodium can also be leached before planting every year with heavy applications of water and amendment. Permanent turf swards, as the name implies, are permanent and cannot be disrupted by plowing. The flooding of large turf areas has essentially been replaced by sprinkler irrigation. Therefore, it is recommended that finely ground gypsum and sulfur materials be applied to the turf surface and sprinkler irrigated into the soil.

Gypsum and S, because of their low cost, are usually the amendments of choice for reclaiming soils high in Na^+. Before applying amendments, it is necessary for the turf manager first to have the soil analyzed for the exchangeable Na^+ percentage (ESP). The amount of amendment to apply to the soil can then be applied based upon the meq Na^+ 100 g"1 soil to be removed. It is desirable to lower ESP levels to 10 or less in heavier soils, but higher levels may be acceptable in sandier soils. Either gypsum or S can be used on soils containing alkaline-earth carbonates, and gypsum is most often recommended on soils free of these carbonates. Mancino and Kopec found that gypsum applied at 4480 and 8960 kg ha"1 y"1 reduced the Na^+ content of an effluent irrigated turf soil (gravelly sandy loam) by 150 mg kg"1 3 months after application. After 12 months, soil Na+ levels had fallen by 250 mg kg"1 . This represented a decrease in ESP from 10 to 5.1. In comparison, a gypsum application rate of 2240 kg ha"1 year"1 reduced the soil ESP level to 7.4. However, the lower rate became as effective as the higher rate in reducing soil Na^+ levels six months following a second annual application.

Overall Turf Quality

To ensure acceptable turf quality (i.e., good color, density, and groundcover, freedom from pests, and good recuperative potential following environmental stress and injury), the turf manager must have a thorough understanding of the irrigation water and soil being dealt with. In addition, the proper turf species must be selected for the region. As water quality decreases, more careful attention must be paid to irrigation efficiency, frequency, and duration. Soil conditions must also be closely monitored, particularly on heavier soils, and drainage must be adequate. Without careful attention to these details, turf failure is almost guaranteed. Work to date with wastewater irrigation of turf has shown turf quality to be adequate.

This research can be confirmed by the increased use of this water source on what one might consider prestigious golf course facilities. The quality of effluent-irrigated turf may even be considered better compared to potable water-irrigated turf of similar salinity. For example, the research done at Chandler, Arizona, indicated that an acceptable quality of turf can be produced on about 0.47 ha-m y"1 , but potable water–irrigated turf (of the same salinity) required 0.59 ha-m y"1 for the same quality. This is probably a result of the additional macro- and micronutrients delivered by the effluent.

Turf quality can suffer during certain times of year because of effluent irrigation. Iron chlorosis has been shown to occur more frequently with this water source. Kneebone and Pepper reported high pH–induced Fe chlorosis on effluent-irrigated giant and common bermudagrass.

Hayes et al. reported similar findings but attributed them to N-induced Fe chlorosis with N-induced plant growth exceeding the ability of the roots to take up Fe. It is also possible that high P-containing effluents could precipitate Fe from the soil solution as Fe phosphate compounds. Applications of ferrous sulfate or chelated Fe amendments could be used to correct this condition. Hayes et al. also reported a rapid decline in ryegrass quality in effluent-irrigated plots when additional N was applied as fertilizer. This decline occurred in early summer as a result of heat stress. The N from fertilizer, even at a low rate of 16.3 kg N ha"1 , in combination with the N delivered in the effluent, made new ryegrass growth susceptible to high-temperature injury.

Therefore, there is a great potential for overfertilization of overseeded ryegrass during the transition period from rye back to bermudagrass. It may be advisable for the turf manager to discontinue N applications from fertilizer 2 or 3 months before high-temperature stress periods. Salinity can reduce turf seed germination. The saline conditions of effluent water can also have the same effect. Hayes et al. reported that the emergence of common bermudagrass was lowered by effluent irrigation. They suggested that a higher quality water be used during turf establishment if available, or that seeding rates be increased to compensate for lower seedling survival. However, those seedlings that survive can have more rapid establishment than seedlings receiving potable water and N fertilizer.

INFLUENCE OF EFFLUENT IRRIGATION ON WATER QUALITY

Irrigation of turf always results in leachate percolating through the soil profile to the vadose zone and ultimately entering the groundwater. Thus, continuous use of effluent has the potential to alter the quality of potable water in the groundwater. The main constituents of concern in effluent are pathogens, salts, and nitrates. Fortunately, soil acts as an effective filter in removing bacterial and viral pathogens, and thus pathogens are not highly mobile in soil leachate. Also, the life expectancy of pathogens on the turf leaf surfaces appears to be low. However, effluent leachate usually contains higher concentrations of salts than leachate from potable irrigation sources. This increased salt content results in increased EC values, but these increases are normally modest, do not exceed EPA maximum levels for drinking water, and are not injurious to turf growth. If effluent contains large amounts of salts, then additional irrigation water should be applied in excess of plant needs to keep salts out of the root zone. By far the greatest potential hazard to water quality is nitrates.

Despite the high nitrate content, turf and soil combine to form an effective filter that removes large amounts of nitrates. Anderson et al. showed that very high rates of effluent, in excess of consumptive use rates of turf, could be applied and still yield leachates that meet federal standards with respect to nitrates. Even on a pure sand soil, 12.7 and 13.6 cm week"1 of effluent water could be safely applied in summer and winter periods, respectively. This corresponds to approximately three times consumptive use rates. The same study showed that slightly increasing the cation-exchange capacity of the sand by the addition of organic matter significantly increased the ability of the soil filter to remove nitrates. Therefore, use of "real" soil rather than sand, in conjunction with turf, should have a great capacity to renovate leachate with respect to N. A. Modeling Computer modeling may provide some insight into the offsite impacts of turfgrass irrigation with reclaimed water. Wade and Balogh used a computer simulation model, EPIC (Environmental Policy Integrated Climate model), to try to predict the fate of NO" -N and two commonly used turfgrass pesticides, 3 fenamiphos and monosodium methylarsenate (MSMA).

Fenamiphos is a highly toxic and mobile nematicide. MSMA is a moderately toxic, low-mobility postemergent herbicide. Simulated management practices used in the model included different fertilizer, pesticide, and irrigation strategies. The fairway soil modeled was an Austin silty clay (fine-silty, carbonatic, thermic Udorthentic Haplustoll). The putting green soil was a United States Golf Association sand : peat rootzone mix. Both sides had bermudagrass (Cynodon dactylon L. Pers.) and the greens were winter overseeded with ryegrass (Lolium perenne L.). Greens received only one level of irrigation, in which watering occurred when soil moisture dropped to 85% of available water-holding capacity (AWC). The reduced management treatment for the fairway also had a 75% AWC trigger point. On the putting green, the model showed that type of irrigation water (reclaimed or potable) had no effect on turf/soil water balance, fenamiphos fate, or surface loss of NO" -N. Leaching of NO" -N from the green was highest from the reclaimed water/normal fertilizer management treatment (RWNM) but was lowest with the reclaimed water/reduced fertilizer management treatment (RWRM).

Therefore, NO" -N in the reclaimed water could pose a risk for off3 site fertilizer transport from a sand : peat putting green, but the risk can be overcome by reducing the amount of fertilizer used. Hayes et al. showed that municipal wastewater in Tucson could supply most of the N required by bermudagrass turf. On the modeled fairway site, water source had no effect on MSMA surface runoff. The RWRM treatment was predicted to have less NO" -N_3 in surface runoff than the RWNM treatment, the potable water/normal irrigation and fertilizer treatment (PWNM), and the potable water/reduced irrigation and fertilizer treatment (NWRM). Lechate NO" -N was lowest for the RWRM 3 treatment, while that for the RWNM treatment was lower than that for PWNM treatment.

CONCLUSIONS

The reality that water is a dwindling natural resource in many parts of the world has resulted in the increased use of sewage effluent for irrigation of turf. The benefits of using effluent as a water resource and also as a source of nutrients for turf growth far outweigh the potential hazards of its use. Potential hazards to human health include excess nitrates and bacterial pathogens; but the use of chlorinated, secondarily treated effluent applied at turf at consumptive water-use rates minimizes these hazards. Potential hazards to turf include increased salts, particularly sodium. Once again, because of the rather modest increases of these constituents with most effluents and also due to the resilient nature of turfgrasses, these hazards do not appear to be particularly injurious to turf growth. Hazards to turf can be minimized by appropriate management systems.

These include application of effluent at consumptive turf use rates or slightly above, reduced N and P commercial fertilizer applications, and applications of gypsum or S to replace Na^+ on cation exchange sites. Currently in some areas of the United States, particularly the Southwest, use of effluent for turf irrigation is widely practiced and increasing in scope. This is an appropriate use of a valuable resource, particularly since turfgrasses are well suited to this type of irrigation. However, large volumes of effluent remain unused in many municipalities, and there is a need for public education to further increase the use of effluent for turf and amenity irrigation.

8

Waterlogging Responses and Interaction with Temperature, Salinity, and Nutrients

INTRODUCTION

Waterlogging has a major impact on both natural vegetation and agricultural crops. Soil waterlogging occurs when over-irrigation and excessive rainfall combine with poor drainage resulting from soil compaction or poor soil quality, as in the case of heavy fine-textured or layered soils. Waterlogging alters soil properties, such as increasing acidity and reducing oxygen diffusion rate or availability, which can inhibit plant growth and productivity. The most detrimental effect of waterlogging is oxygen deficiency in the soil, because roots are particularly sensitive to anaerobic conditions, which can severely affect nutrient relations of the soil. In waterlogged soils, air spaces filled with water delay diffusion of gases between atmosphere and the rhizosphere, leading to oxygen deficiency.

Soil waterlogging reduces shoot and root growth, dry matter accumulation, and final yield. It affects many physiological processes, including water relations, carbohydrate metabolism, nutrition, and hormone synthesis. The severity of waterlogging injury varies with species, plant age, and physiological conditions and also depends on soil conditions such as temperature, salinity, and nutrient availability. Mechanisms of plant adaptation to waterlogging have been reviewed extensively. This chapter focuses on the discussion of physiological responses of plants to waterlogging and its interaction with temperature, salinity, and nutrient availability.

PLANT RESPONSES TO WATERLOGGING

Root and Shoot Growth

Common effects of waterlogging include reductions in root and shoot growth and decreased plant density, persistence, and early seedling vigor. Huang et al. reported that root growth was reduced earlier than shoot growth and root-to-shoot dry weight ratio was reduced by low-oxygen stress in wheat (Triticum aestivum) seedlings, suggesting that the root system was more sensitive to waterlogging than was the shoot. Mian et al. reported that waterlogging for 21 days did not affect shoot fresh weight and number of tillers but decreased root fresh weight of wheat seedlings. Topa and Cheeseman also reported that root growth was affected more than shoot growth by low oxygen stress in 10-week-old pond pine (Pinus serotina Michx.). Root elongation is very sensitive to low-oxygen stress.

The threshold oxygen concentration at which root extension begins to decrease is commonly about half that of air (0.2 atm). Kramer suggested that in general, an oxygen diffusion rate of 0.2 µg cm"2 min"1 or less was limiting to root growth in most plants, whereas values greater than 0.4 µg cm"2 min"1 were adequate for root growth; but the adequacy of values in the range between 0.2 and 0.4 µg depended on temperature. Latey reported that an oxygen diffusion rate above 0.2 µg cm"2 min"1 was critical for root growth of "Newport" Kentucky bluegrass (Poa pratensis) and common bermudagrass (Cynodon dactylon). The ability of roots to survive continuously anaerobic conditions is of short duration, ranging from 0.5 to 3 hr for cotton (Gossypium hirsutum) tap roots to 96 to 120 h for rice (Oryza sativa) seminal root. Root elongation ceased and did not resume after reaeration when the period of anoxia exceeded 6 hr for peas (Pisum sativum) and 12 hr for pumpkin (Cucurbita maxima), which was attributed to lower carbohydrate reserves in root tips under anoxic conditions. Elongation is substantially more sensitive to low oxygen stress seminal roots of wheat than in the crown roots, which is related to the variation in the extent of porosity in the two types.

Crown root porosity increases, whereas the porosity of seminal roots is less affected under low-oxygen stress. Waterlogging induces the formation of intercellular gas spaces in root cortex (aerenchyma) in many species. The ability to form aerenchyma in roots is evident in both nonwetland and wetland plant species, but the fraction of root volume that becomes aerenchymatous generally is more pronounced in wetland species. The extent of aerenchyma in roots also varies among species and cultivars within nonwetland species. For example, Huang et al. found that waterlogging-tolerant wheat cultivars had significantly higher root porosity than waterlogging-sensitive cultivars under waterlogged conditions.

The presence of aerenchyma in roots is clearly conducive to the survival of the plants under low-oxygen conditions and has been considered as an important adaptive response. For the plant species surveyed by Justin and Armstrong, the extent of aerenchyma development was related to waterlogging tolerance. The functional significance of aerenchyma can be deduced from several aspects of aerenchymatous root characteristics. In many species, aerenchyma may provide most or all of the oxygen requirements of the roots as well as some of the requirements of the surrounding rhizosphere. Increases in root porosity significantly enhance the internal oxygen transport and shoot growth, along with the continued growth of roots in anaerobic conditions.

Elongation is greater for roots with elevated root porosity than for roots with less aerenchyma. Additionally, aerenchymatous roots in maize have higher values of ATP content, adenylate energy charge, and ATP/ADP ratios than nonaerenchymatous roots when transferred to anoxic conditions. Finally, in aerenchymatous Senecio roots, the activity of the cytochrome path is not inhibited when the roots are transferred to an anoxic solution. The number of adventitious roots increases under low-oxygen conditions in many species. Adventitious roots tend to emerge from the stem base close to the surface of flooded soils.

The formation of adventitious roots near the more oxygenized soil surface could facilitate oxygen uptake from the aerobic root/soil interface and may replace oxygen losses from the damaged functioning of original roots, which occurs under low oxygen conditions. Adventitious roots originating from waterlogged conditions generally are more aerenchymatous than primary roots, which enhances plant aeration, especially when the adventitious roots become a larger portion of the entire root system. Stimulation of development of adventitious roots under waterlogged conditions has been related to accumulation of ethylene and auxin. In wheat plants grown under well-aerated conditions, increases in the concentration of ethylene applied to the rooting medium enhanced production of adventitious roots.

Waterlogging enhances production of large-diameter roots. The increased diameter of both adventitious roots and primary roots for two wetland species, Rumex palustris and Rumex hydrolapathum, indicates a high resistance of these roots to low soil-oxygen status. Increasing root diameter decreases the relative radial oxygen loss to the rhizosphere and thereby enhances oxygen diffusion to the root tip. Leaf growth and development are affected adversely by waterlogging. An 83% reduction in leaf area in wheat has been reported and is attributed primarily to nutrient deficiency. Huang et al. demonstrated that the reduction in leaf area during waterlogging was more severe for a waterlogging-sensitive cultivar than a tolerant cultivar in wheat.

Waterlogging often causes leaf chlorosis and premature senescence, which may be related to reduced cytokinin and gibberellin or increased abscisic acid (ABA) and ethylene. Reduced cytokinin and gibberellin levels may promote deterioration of membranes, affecting a range of leaf metabolism including synthesis of chlorophyll and protein. Limited capacity of nitrogen uptake has been considered a dominant factor in induction of leaf senescence in barley (Hordeum vulgare) and wheat. The inhibitory effects of waterlogging on root and shoot growth can be attributed to its effects on various physiological processes, including water relations, carbohydrate metabolism, nutrient uptake, and hormone synthesis. Responses of their processes are discussed below.

Root Water Uptake and Leaf–Water Relations

Waterlogging reduces water uptake and transport in various species, which could be related to its inhibitory effects on root permeability and hydraulic conductivity. The reduction of root hydraulic conductivity has been attributed to an occlusion of xylem vessels by debris of the rotting root system and restricted axial water movement through roots under waterlogged conditions. Huang et al. observed that the diameters of central metaxylem and protoxylem vessels were reduced significantly by waterlogging in both waterlogging-tolerant and -sensitive cultivars of wheat, which could lead to a reduction in axial conductance for water movement. Kramer attributed the reduced root hydraulic conductance to the toxic effect of high carbon dioxide concentration in flooded soils, but Hunt et al. attributed it to accumulation of ethylene in the soil and the plant.

Decreased hydraulic conductivity of roots under waterlogged conditions may induce stomatal closure, resulting in reduced rates of transpiration and photosynthesis. Stomatal closure and reduced transpiration rate of leaves generally are among the early responses of plants to soil waterlogging and have been reported in many plant species, including important crops such as tomato (Lycopersicon esculentum), wheat, pepper (Capsicum annuum), and bean (Phaseolus vicia). The effects of waterlogging on leaf water status and stomatal conductance vary with species or cultivars differing in waterlogging tolerance. For example, Huang et al. reported significant reduction in leaf water potential and stomatal conductance in a waterlogging-sensitive cultivar of wheat but not in a tolerant cultivar. In some cases, stomata of waterlogging-tolerant plants may reopen following prolonged waterlogging, because of formation of new adventitious roots that allows resumption of water uptake.

Stomatal closure can be caused by water deficits resulting from reduced water uptake and supply from roots to shoots. Reduction in leaf water content along with stomatal closure and transpiration rate have been observed in many studies. In some cases, stomatal closure occurs without significant reduction in leaf water status. Thus, factors other than water deficit may inhibit stomatal conductance and leaf growth during waterlogging. Several studies suggested that roots in flooded soil may transmit a stress signal to leaves, causing stomatal closure and inhibiting leaf growth. Zhang and Davies suggested that root-sourced ABA is mainly responsible for the early stomatal closure following waterlogging. Jackson and Hall, however, showed that roots could not be the source of ABA in flooded pea plants. An effect of ABA on stomatal closure during prolonged periods of waterlogging is doubtful, because most roots collapse rapidly and die within a few days of flooding. A decline in shoot supplies of potassium ions and cytokinin also may contribute to stomatal closure in flooded plants.

Carbohydrate Metabolism

Carbohydrates serve as energy reserves and are often associated with stress tolerance. Carbohydrate metabolism, including photosynthesis and respiration, plays an important role in plant tolerance to waterlogging. Photosynthesis of waterlogging-sensitive plants decreases rapidly following waterlogging. Huang et al. reported that photosynthetic rate started to decline to values lower than those of well-aerated plants 3 days after waterlogging in wheat; the reduction was more severe in a waterlogging-sensitive cultivar than in a tolerant cultivar. Pezeshki and Chambers reported that photosynthesis in Quercus falcata seedlings decreased to zero after 3 days of waterlogging. The decline in photosynthetic rate can be caused by stomatal closure or/and changes in metabolic (nonstomatal) processes, such as chlorophyll degradation and reduced activity of photosynthetic enzymes in waterlogged plants. Changes in carbohydrate translocation and accumulation of inhibitory plant hormones such as ethylene and ABA also may be responsible for photosynthesis inhibition during waterlogging. Reduced rates of assimilate translocation to roots have been reported in plants grown under low oxygen conditions.

The latter authors reported that the translocation of carbon to anoxic roots was less than 50% of that to aerated roots in two genotypes of dry beans (Phaseolus vulgaris); Also, most of the newly photosynthesized carbon translocated to roots grown under anoxic conditions was excluded from respiratory metabolism and was an order of magnitude less than that in the aerated controls. Restricted carbon translocation to roots may lead to low carbohydrate availability in roots. Shortage of sugars has been observed in root apices, which are most likely to suffer more injury than mature roots under low-oxygen stress. In most experiments, however, sugar content remained constant or increased in entire root systems under low oxygen conditions. Sugar accumulation in roots has been regarded as an adaptive change, facilitating ion uptake via a supply of energy. Limpinuntana and Greenway and Benjamin and Greenway, however, suggested that sugar accumulation in roots is a consequence of reduced root growth rather than adaptation to waterlogging. Sugar may accumulate at low oxygen concentration because the synthesis of polysaccharides is restricted or the lycholysis of cell water constituents is accelerated.

Increased sugar levels also may be related to nutrient deficiency. The importance of carbohydrate status of roots in low oxygen tolerance has been confirmed by experiments that supplied exogenous sugars to roots grown under low oxygen conditions. Supplies of carbohydrates to roots strongly influences the ability of roots to survive low-oxygen stress. Glucose supply prolongs the retention of root elongation potential under anoxia. Webb and Armstrong reported that adventitious roots of rice seedlings survived only 4 hr of anoxia, but this time was extended to 44 hr with exogenous application of glucose. The addition of glucose to the rooting medium improves the anoxia tolerance of 2-day-old seedlings of maize (Zea mays) by increasing the ATP content of the root tips. Root ultrastructural injury under low oxygen conditions is prevented after feeding the roots with glucose, demonstrating positive effects of both exogenous sugar and endogenous reserves of carbohydrates in survival of plants under low-oxygen stress.

Reduction in aerobic respiration rate of roots is the most immediate effect of waterlogging, but the severity of respiration inhibition varies with plant species and cultivars. McKee observed that root respiration rate was maintained in Rhizophora mangle, whereas it was decreased by 31 and 53% in Avicennia germinans and Laguncularia racemosa, respectively, during a 12-week hypoxia. Huang and Johnson reported that the reduction in root respiration rate was more dramatic for waterlogging-sensitive cultivars of wheat seedlings than the tolerant cultivars. Similar results have been reported in apples and grapevines. The ability of plants to minimize the reduction in root respiration seems to be associated with their ability to tolerate waterlogging stress. Roots of some species switch to anaerobic respiration when oxygen is deficient in the rooting medium, which produces insufficient ATP for growth and cell maintenance. For each glucose molecule that enters aerobic respiration, ATP molecules can be produced, whereas anaerobic respiration produces only 2 ATP molecules per glucose. Anaerobic respiration of roots does not completely oxidize glucose to carbon dioxide and water, as does aerobic respiration. It produces toxic substances such as acetaldehyde and ethanol, which can lead to cell death and leaf chlorosis.

Nutrient Accumulation and Uptake

Uptake of nutrients such as nitrogen (N), potassium (K), and phosphorus (P) often is inhibited under waterlogged conditions, which reduces nutrient supply to shoots. Drew and Sisworo reported that in barley, the concentrations (μmol g"1 dw) of total levels of N, P, K in leaves declined, respectively, to 75, 69, and 77% of the levels in aerated controls in just 48 hr; At 6 days, the corresponding figures were 37, 34, and 43%.

Hocking and coworkers reported reduction in N nutrition after brief periods of waterlogging or excessive irrigation in cotton.

Orchard and coworkers found that P levels in sorghum (Sorghum bicolor) and sunflower (Helianthus annuus) were depressed following 9 days of waterlogging. In wheat seedlings grown in flooded soil, Huang et al. observed reductions in N, P, K, Mg, and Zn in leaves and stems but increases in the root system. Consequences of reduced nutrient levels in leaves are numerous, including a reduction in leaf chlorophyll content and photosynthetic capacity and induction of premature leaf senescence. The inhibition of nutrient uptake induced by waterlogging may be due to restriction of root growth, the inefficiency of anaerobic respiration in providing adequate energy for active ion uptake, and increased permeability of cell membranes in roots. Limited N uptake may also be due to denitrification and leaching and the dilution of ions in waterlogged soil.

Waterlogging creates reduced acidic anaerobic conditions in the soil, which affect the availability of some nutrient elements. In waterlogged soils, nitrate abundance is low and soil N is dominated by ammonium. The availability of phosphate is also reduced in acidic soils. In anaerobic soils, the ferric form of Fe and the manganic form of Mn are converted to the more reduced and soluble ferrous and manganous forms, which are taken up readily by roots and can lead to the accumulation of these elements in plants. Waterlogging increases Fe and Mn accumulation in shoots, which can cause toxicity.

Huang et al. found that increased Fe and Mn in shoots occurred only in a waterlogging-sensitive wheat cultivar. The lack of increases in Fe and Mn in the tolerant cultivar could have been related to the formation of extensive aerenchyma (intercellular gas spaces) in its root cortex. The well-advanced development of aerenchyma improves radial oxygen leakage to the rhizosphere for tolerant plants, which helps to oxidize ferrous Fe and manganous Mn and thus to reduce their availability. Iron deposition resulting from oxidation of Fe^{2+} to Fe^{3+} has been observed around roots.

Waterlogging also inhibits translocation of nutrients between plant parts. Huang et al. reported an increased proportion of N in the root system in a waterlogging-sensitive cultivar of wheat, while shoot N was reduced. They also found that roots had much larger quantities of Fe than shoots under well-aerated conditions, but the proportion of Fe in leaves and stems increased in waterlogged plants, especially in a waterlogging-sensitive cultivar. McKee et al. found that P accumulated in roots and was reduced in shoots in loblolly pine during flooding, suggesting that waterlogging restricted P translocation. The reduction in nutrient transport from roots to shoots could be related to reduced water transport.

Hormone Synthesis

Low oxygen supply to roots in waterlogged soils inhibits synthesis of auxins, gibberellins, and cytokinin. Also, low oxygen concentration reduces cytokinin flux in xylem sap of roots and blocks the supply of cytokinin and gibberellins from roots to shoots. Production of ABA and ethylene in roots and translocation of these hormones from root to leaves, however, increase under waterlogged conditions. An ethylene precursor (ACC, 1-aminocyclopropane-1carboxylic acid) is synthesized in roots at an accelerated rate under conditions of oxygen deficiency. The general inhibitions of shoot growth and leaf senescence have been attributed to reduction of auxins, gibberellins, and cytokinin and to the accumulation of ethylene and ABA. Spraying of leaves with synthetic cytokinins or with mixtures of cytokinins and gibberellic acid partially restored growth and leaf chlorophyll, and application of benzyladenine to the foliage delayed or prevented chlorosis in waterlogged plants.

Susceptibility of Plants to Diseases

In addition to the effects already discussed, anaerobic soils can increase the attacks of fungi and bacteria on roots, because a number of species of pathogenic fungi and bacteria thrive in poorly aerated soils and reduced root vigor increases susceptibility to infection. For example, waterlogging induced infection of maize roots by Pseudomonas putidaa, tomato roots by Pythium, and pine roots by Phytophthora cinnamomi. Pythium spp. and Phytophthora are among the most common pathogens damaging roots in poorly drained soils.

FACTORS INFLUENCING WATERLOGGING INJURY

Growth Stage and Physiological Conditions

The degree of damage incurred from waterlogging varies with plant growth stage or age. Letey et al. concluded that waterlogging was most detrimental to cotton, green beans, and sunflowers during early stages of vegetative growth. Cannell et al. examined the responses of winter wheat to waterlogging at different stages of growth and found that it was most sensitive after germination but before emergence. At this stage, 16 days of waterlogging killed all seedlings, and 6 days of waterlogging depressed plant density to 12% of the control in clay soil and 38% in sandy loam soil. Teutsch and Sulc reported that young seedlings of alfalfa (Medicago sativa) were more sensitive to waterlogging than more vegetatively advanced seedlings. In contrast, Fick et al. reported that sensitivity of alfalfa to waterlogging increased up to 6 weeks of age.

VanToai et al. found that when maize seedlings 2 to 7 days old were exposed to anoxic stress, 3-day-old seedlings had much lower sensitivity than 2-dayold seedlings. Waterlogging during the flowering stage can cause severe yield reduction. For example, Cannell et al. reported that waterlogging for only 24 hr at flowering reduced the yield of peas. Waterlogging generally is much less injurious to dormant plants than to actively growing plants. Turfgrasses that are dormant or semidormant can tolerate a longer duration of waterlogging than actively growing plants. Dormant buffalograss (Buchloe dactyloides) has survived 19 months of continuous waterlogging. This is explained by the fact that the oxygen requirement of dormant plants is much less than that of growing plants because of their low respiration rate. Waterlogging injury in actively growing plants usually occurs to tissues that are in the process of development at the time of waterlogging.

Temperature

The prevailing temperatures at the time of waterlogging can have a major influence on plant responses and the degree of injury.

Waterlogging injury typically increases as temperature increases. In temperate climates, plant tolerance to waterlogging generally is greater during winter and cool springs than in warmer spring or summer temperatures. Soil temperature has a greater impact on waterlogging tolerance than air temperature. Beard reported that red fescue (Festuca rubra) can be killed in 1 day from waterlogging at a high water temperature (30°C) and creeping bentgrass (Agrostis palustris) can survive waterlogging durations of more than 60 days at a low water temperature (10°C).

Huang et al. reported that turf quality, leaf chlorophyll content, photosynthetic rate, and root viability of creeping bentgrass were reduced under waterlogging conditions, and increasing temperature during waterlogging caused more damage to both shoots and roots. Canopy respiration rate, however, increased under waterlogging and high-temperature conditions, which may have been due to an increase in maintenance respiration with increasing temperatures.

Heinrichs reported interactions of waterlogging, soil temperature, and species. Sainfoin (Onobrychis vicaefolia) and alfalfa, which had low and moderate waterlogging tolerances, could withstand longer periods of waterlogging as the root-zone temperatures were decreased from warm (25°C) to cool (19°C) to cold (13°C); roots died faster at high period temperatures. Birdsfoot trefoil (Lotus corniculatus), which was very tolerant to waterlogging, survived equally well at all root-zone temperatures.

The greater tolerance to waterlogging at the lower temperatures may have reflected the plant's improved ability to adapt in some way to oxygen deficiency and/or the diminished growth rate of the plant or the slowing of root metabolism.

Temperature affects the concentrations of dissolved carbon dioxide, ethylene, nitrous oxide, nitrate, calcium, and potassium in waterlogged soils. The effects of increasing temperature on plant responses to waterlogging have been attributed mainly to increased demand for and rapid depletion of oxygen at high temperatures. Root respiration rates increase with increasing temperatures. Trought and Drew suggested that temperature modification of wheat responses to waterlogging was due mainly to its direct effects on shoot and root growth. Leaf damage from waterlogging at high air temperatures could result from internal heat stress caused by stomatal closure.

Salinity

Waterlogging and salinity can occur simultaneously in over-irrigated saline soils or in heavy soils irrigated with saline water. These conditions exist in many intensively irrigated fields. Simultaneous occurrence of salinity and waterlogging is also common in coastal swamps and marshes and in low-lying land subject to primary or secondary salinization.

Waterlogging in combination with high salinity can cause greater depression in growth and photosynthesis capacity than would occur with either stress alone. Plants exposed to waterlogging and salinity exhibit yellow-colored leaves with burning. The mechanisms involved in the interactive effects of salinity and waterlogging are not well understood. Among the major factors that may cause inhibitory growth in saline, waterlogged soils are water deficits and excess ion accumulation (Na^+, Cl^-).

The salinity of the water affects plant–water relations. Saline water can induce osmotic-drought stress in plants grown in waterlogged soils. However, Galloway and Davidson and Huang et al. failed to observe interactive effects of salinity and waterlogging on water relations. Galloway and Davidson suggested that large fluxes of Na^+ and Cl^- dominated the interactive effects of salinity and waterlogging. Under saline waterlogged conditions, uptakes of Na^+ and Cl^- increase in many plants species, which may lead to shoot senescence and adverse effects on growth.

Anaerobiosis caused by waterlogging, in turn, is likely to interfere with the mechanisms of salt tolerance that normally operate in aerobic conditions. Many salt-sensitive species tolerate moderate salinity by the root's ability to exclude ions from the xylem sap through energy-dependent processes. In waterlogged plants, the energy available for the ion pumps involved in excluding salts from the roots is reduced; as a result, appreciable amounts of sodium (Na^+) enter the leaves.

Nutrient Availability

As discussed above, waterlogging can lead to nutrient deficiency, particularly of N, K, and P, in various plant species. Therefore, nutrient supply and availability in the soil may have significant impacts on waterlogging tolerance of plants.

Garcia-Novo and Crawford reported that plants were more resistant to anaerobic stress when the nonaerated growing solution was supplied with ample nitrate. Foliar feeding of urea as a relatively nontoxic nitrogen source to the leaves of wheat during low-oxygen stress delayed leaf senescence.

Nitrate fertilizer application to waterlogged soil alleviated symptoms of waterlogging damage in cereals. With barley, three daily additions of calcium nitrate to the surface of the flooded soil compensated for the ability of the oxygen-deficient roots to grow deeper in the soil, and no symptoms of waterlogging injury were observed.

Doubling the concentrations of all major and minor nutrient elements in waterlogged soil slowed the rates of decline in photosynthesis and chlorophyll content and improved shoot nutrient status and growth in wheat. Application of P fertilizer to flooded soil increased growth of loblolly pine.

Trought and Drew reported that by supplying of a full-strength nutrient solution to a single seminal root in wheat, it was possible to alleviate waterlogging injury, whereas leaves quickly showed typical symptoms of waterlogging injury without that nutrient supply. The mechanisms involved in effects of various nutrients on waterlogging tolerance remain unclear. Studies have suggested that under anaerobic conditions, nitrate may act as an alternative electron acceptor to free oxygen for anaerobic soil micro-organisms, retarding a fall in redox potential in the soil and thereby slowing the accumulation of reduced, potentially toxic solutes to concentrations harmful to plants. Nitrate may also act as an alternative electron acceptor to free oxygen in roots, thus enabling root respiration and root functions to continue. Nitrate may serve as an inorganic N source for metabolism of roots or offset nitrate lost by microbial denitrification. Root nutrient status also can affect aerenchyma formation.

The presence of nitrate, ammonium, or phosphate in aerated solutions strongly reduces aerenchyma formation. This could occur because nitrate or ammonium supports the protein synthesis relevant to the integrity of the tonoplast membrane, so that rupture of this membrane and cell collapse are prevented. Nitrate may also positively affect the phospholipid composition of membranes, thus influencing aerenchyma formation. The inhibitory effect of phosphate on aerenchyma formation is less than that of nitrate. Phosphate may promote membrane integrity by positively affecting phospholipid metabolism.

SUMMARY

The effects of waterlogging on plant growth are complex, including damage to various plant physiological processes. Research reviewed herein provides substantial evidence, ranging from whole-plant to biochemical responses, that the sensitivity of plants to waterlogging varies with species and cultivars and plant processes. Reduced root respiration and stomatal closure appear to be among the earliest responses to waterlogging.

Waterlogging-tolerant plants have the ability to develop extensive aerenchyma in root cortex and adventitious roots close to the surface soil during waterlogging, which facilitates oxygen transport and utilization. The ability to maintain energy balance is also paramount in the survival of roots in anaerobic soils.

Therefore, waterlogging tolerance could be improved by incorporating various morphological, anatomical, and physiological adaptive mechanisms in waterlogging-sensitive plants using conventional breeding or molecular biology techniques. This literature overview also provides evidence for possible practical solutions to enhance root and shoot growth under waterlogged conditions, particularly supplementing plant nutrients.

Most waterlogging research to date has concentrated largely on seedlings grown under controlled environmental conditions. There is a great need for research examining responses of plants in different growth stages under field conditions, because, as we have mentioned, damage incurred from waterlogging varies with plant growth stages and can be affected by many environmental factors. Understanding the mechanisms of the interactive effects of waterlogging and other environmental factors such as temperature, salinity, and nutrient status in the soil remains an important challenge.

9

Role of Heat-shock Proteins in Creeping Bentgrass

INTRODUCTION

Animals are able to move in response to environmental stresses, whereas most higher plants are sessile and have developed mechanisms for coping with stresses while remaining fixed in their environment. Plant metabolic activities affected by stresses include a wide array of reactions and processes that can be characterized according to enzymatic and biochemical pathways, diffusion processes, and photochemical reactions. All of these processes are temperature-sensitive. The level of sensitivity depends on species, predisposing habitats, and nutritional status. Tissue temperatures above or below optimum cause some degree of plant stress.

As plants evolved, the mechanisms used to cope with environmental stress have become genetically fixed. Heat stress limits plant productivity and survival. Certain morphological characteristics, such as leaf shape, may help plants to avoid heat stress. Or plants may tolerate high-temperature stress by altering physiological processes. In many cases, heat stress causes reversible damage to cellular and subcellular structures and functions. Plants that rapidly repair this damage and resume normal metabolic functions are more heat-tolerant than those that cannot. They have a competitive advantage because they resume normal cellular functions, such as photosynthesis, sooner than nontolerant plants.

THERMAL ENERGY BALANCE

All plants, except for a few rare exceptions, are unable to elevate their own tissue temperature to stimulate their metabolic activity. Therefore, plants must rely on absorbed radiation to increase their internal temperature. This dependence on solar radiation has resulted in the adoption by plants of an energy-balance strategy based on plant adaptations that influence absorption and emission of solar radiation. When radiation absorption significantly exceeds emissions, tissue temperatures rise and may exceed the optimum, causing plants to experience heat stress. Heat stress affects plants differently, depending on many factors. Generally, high-temperature stress is most detrimental to enzymatic reactions and biochemical pathways, moderately damaging to diffusion processes, and least detrimental to photochemical reactions. However, many photochemical reactions are enzymatically based, and heat stress is evident in these systems. Photosystem II is reported to be more sensitive to high-temperature stress than the Calvin cycle enzymes. The deleterious effects of heat stress on enzymatic reactions and biochemical pathways are manifested in the energy levels of substrates and thermal stability of enzymes. If heat stress is excessive in duration or level, it may result in plant death.

THERMAL TOLERANCE

Plants have evolved varied and multiple mechanisms that allow them to survive heat stress. These include limiting or avoiding direct absorption of solar radiation, dissipation of excess radiation absorbed, and physiological mechanisms that counteract the effects of heat stress on metabolism. All three strategies of tolerance are equally important for survival. These strategies of tolerance have arisen through the evolution of specific developments in plant morphology, anatomy, and physiology. The discussion and research presented in this chapter address some of the physiological dimensions of thermal tolerance. The physiology discussed herein centers on the heat-shock response (HSR), which results in the synthesis of a special set of proteins known as heat-shock proteins (HSPs). These proteins function to counteract the negative effects of heat stress on plant metabolism.

SPECIES USED TO STUDY

HSPS Studies of the HSR have been conducted in many plant species. However, selecting the appropriate genotypes within a species to study is critical to avoid misinterpretation of results that may be due to genotype variability. The research conducted in our laboratory used unique creeping bentgrass (Agrostis stoloniferia var. palustris) genotypes to study the HSR. Creeping bentgrass is a common cool-season grass adapted and grown widely in temperate regions. It is classified as a C_3 plant type and has economic importance as a turfgrass. Cultivars of this species are commonly grown outside their zone of adaptation (e.g., subtropical tropic regions) as a preferred putting green turf. In 1984, cell culture techniques were initiated with heat as a selection pressure to recover elite genotypes of bentgrass having superior heat tolerance. During the course of this research, two uniquely similar but different phenotypes were recovered.

One was a heat-tolerant bentgrass genotype (SB) and the other a non–heat tolerant bentgrass genotype (NSB). The original source of plant material was a single seed of "Penncross" (creeping bentgrass), a synthetic cultivar resulting from the open pollination of three selected vegetative clones of creeping bentgrass. To obtain SB and NSB, callus was initiated from a single seed (genotype) of Penncross. After being subjected to high-temperature stress at 40°C for 10 days, plants were regenerated from the surviving callus. One of the heat-tolerant variants isolated was SB. NSB was regenerated from the same starting callus as SB, but this callus was not subjected to high temperatures and was later found to lack thermal tolerance. Other heat-tolerant variants were isolated during this process, which suggests that increased tolerance was due to the selection and not loss of tolerance in NSB. Karyotyping indicated that both NSB and SB have 14 pairs of chromosomes.

Therefore, phenotypic differences are probably not due to alterations in chromosome number that occurred during tissue culture.

Clonally propagated SB has been grown in the field for at least 10 years and has retained its thermal tolerance. We think that SB and NSB provide an ideal model system for studying a mechanism of heat tolerance in higher plants. Because SB and NSB originated from the same seed, we expect fewer genetic differences than would be observed between different cultivars or ecotypes. Consequently, physiological, biochemical, and molecular differences between these two variants may be related to heat tolerance. Increased knowledge about thermal tolerance in this species could provide a better understanding of heat tolerance in other grasses such as wheat, barley, and rye. It has been demonstrated that the members of the grass family—including corn, sorghum, rice, and wheat—have similar gene composition and map collinearity. If genes related to thermal tolerance are found in bentgrass, it may be possible to place them on genetic maps of other grass species.

DISCOVERY AND ROLE OF HSPS IN PLANTS

Studies with a number of organisms, including higher plants, indicate that brief exposure to moderately high temperatures improves the ability of an organism to survive subsequent exposures to potentially lethal temperatures. This is known as acquired thermal tolerance. Sublethal doses of heat stress induce the HSR, which protects cells and organisms from severe damage, allows resumption of normal cellular and physiological activities, and leads to a higher level of thermal tolerance. The postulated mechanisms for acquisition of this increased thermal tolerance is synthesis of a set of special proteins, known as HSPs, that occurs during exposure to sublethal temperatures. In general, HSP synthesis is induced when the temperature increases approximately 10°C above the optimal growing temperature for the organism. HSPs are believed to protect the cell's proteins, membranes, and organelles during heat stress by acting as molecular chaperones.

Molecular chaperones are proteins that prevent "improper associations" among proteins. They prevent protein aggregation, help denatured proteins refold, and assist in the folding of nascent proteins. HSP synthesis is usually accompanied by a "shutdown" or reduction in the synthesis of "normal" cellular proteins. The accumulation of HSPs and inhibition of normal protein synthesis is termed the heat-shock response (HSR). Plant tissues that do not have a HSR are more sensitive to high temperatures. The synthesis of HSPs by cotton, soybean, and other legumes grown in the field suggests that their synthesis is a normal occurrence that may protect plants from daily exposure to high temperatures in some environments. Studies in corn have indicated that the synthesis of HSPs is influenced by nitrogen (N) nutrition and the stage of plant development.

These studies also suggested that there is a N cost for HSP synthesis. The N needed for HSP synthesis maybe the result of hydrolysis of the soluble photosynthetic enzymes such as ribulose-bis-phosphate carboxylase oxygenase and phosphoenolpyruvate (PEP) carboxylase. There is increasing evidence that plants develop "cross tolerance" to environmental stresses, including heat stress. Salt stress increases thermostability of photosystem II in sorghum, and water deficit improves heat tolerance in geranium. Cross-protection between HSPs and other stresses has been reported, but there does not appear to be a common mechanism underlying these interactions.

Recently it has been demonstrated that drought (under high light), ultraviolet A (UV-A), exogenous abscisic acid treatment, and oxidative stress will induce HSP synthesis in Chenopodium and Lycopersicum. More research is needed to elucidate the complex interactions among HSPs and other stress-induced proteins. HSPs are generally divided into two classes: high-molecular-weight (HMW) (60 to 110 kDa) and low-molecular-weight (LMW) (15 to 30 kDa).

There are four HMW-HSP families that contain HSPs with approximate molecular mass of 104, 83, 70, and 60 kDa. HSP104 is essential for heat tolerance in yeast. Genes encoding HSP104 from either soybean or Arabidopsis can complement a yeast mutant lacking this gene. In addition to responding to several abiotic stresses,

HSP104 accumulates in embryos of developing rice seeds. In animals, HSP83 maintains steroid hormone receptors in proper conformation. Homologous forms of HSP83 have been found in plants.

In rice, they are expressed during seed development in vascular bundles and procambrial cells. In tobacco cells, HSP90, an analog of HSP83, is associated with microtubules. HSP83 synthesis is induced in response to cold and heat stress and by pathogen infection. In Drosophila, members of the HSP90 family interact with proteins involved in signal transduction pathways. Insects with mutations in HSP90 have abnormal morphological characteristics. When HSP90 function is compromised (e.g., by temperature), cryptic morphological forms of Drosophila result and selection leads to continued expression of these traits even when functional HSP90 is restored. The authors speculate that HSP90 responds to environmental conditions linked to signal transduction pathways and hence acts as a capacitor for morphological evolution. This hypothesis has not been tested in plants. The HSP70 family is ubiquitous, and homologous forms of this HSP have been found in most organisms. Some members of the HSP70 family are always present in the cell, whereas others are synthesized only in response to heat stress.

The main function of the HSP70 family is to assist in protein folding and assembly. A member of the HSP60 family is constitutively synthesized and present in the chloroplast, where it assists in the assembly of the large and small subunits of ribulose-bis-phosphate carboxylase oxygenase. Another HSP60 interacts with proteins in the mitochondria. The LMW-HSPs are more abundant in plants than in other organisms. It is believed that the diversification of the LMW-HSPs is the result of gene duplication and occurred after the split of plant and animal lineages. There are two general size classes with approximate molecular mass of either 25 or 18 kDa. They are encoded by five nuclear gene families. These classes include HSPs that are found in the cytoplasm (type I and II), endoplasmic reticulum (type IV), mitochondria, and chloroplast. The LMW-HSP are similar in structure to á-crystallins found in the vertebrate eye lens. The á-crystallins, murine HSP25, human HSP27, and plant HSP18.1 and

17.7 have chaperone activity and assist in the folding of "model substrates." Chloroplast LMW-HSPs form high-molecular-weight aggregates in vivo and in vitro.

It has been demonstrated that the rate of synthesis and accumulation of the LMW-HSP corresponds with acquired thermal tolerance in soybean. In addition, constitutive expression of members of the HSP18 family improved thermal tolerance in Arabidopsis. All of the LMW-HSPs contains two regions of conserved amino acid sequences in the carboxyl terminal. These are designated heat shock domains I and II. Because the accumulation of HSPs of both size classes has been correlated with increased heat tolerance in a number of organisms, we were interested in studying the HSR in two somoclonal variants of creeping bentgrass (cv. Penncross) derived from the same seed that differ in thermal tolerance. A better understanding of the HSR in this turfgrass will provide basic information that may potentially be applied to turf management.

HEAT-SHOCK RESPONSE IN CREEPING BENTGRASS

The following summarizes our research on bentgrass thermal tolerance. It focuses on the areas we have studied most extensively: whole-plant performance, physiological assays, identification and role of HSPs, and genetic analysis.

WHOLE PLANT PERFORMANCE

Initially, heat tolerance and turf quality of SB and other clones derived from the Penncross callus were visually assessed in the field. SB ranked better than Penncross in visual turf quality and percent cover. In one field experiment, irrigation was interrupted for 72 hr, resulting in turf surface temperatures ranging from 37 to 52°C. SB was one of the variants that survived this stress, but NSB did not. When these plots were reevaluated 4 months later, the SB plug had doubled in diameter, whereas the other variants remained the same size. Tests were conducted to evaluate the ability of bentgrass to recover from varying environmental conditions by measuring dry-matter accumulation. From late June through December, samples were collected monthly from field plots in Starkville, MS. The total dry weight that accumulated over an 8-week period following each collection date was determined.

SB accumulated significantly more dry weight than NSB during the hot summer months, when the average air and sod temperatures were approximately 28 and 30æ% C, respectively. There were no differences between SB and NSB in regrowth during the more temperate fall and winter months. Dry weight that accumulated following the sampling date was determined at 2-week intervals. The rate of dry-weight accumulation was greater for SB than NSB in July, but there were no differences between the variants in October. Although SB and NSB are morphologically indistinguishable at normal temperatures (approximately 22°C), there is an observable difference between SB and NSB following high-temperature stress. After a growth-chamber malfunction when the temperature exceeded 37æ% C for 24 hr, leaves of SB where relatively undamaged, whereas those of NSB were severely withered.

An experiment conducted in a growth chamber indicated that both SB and NSB survived a day/night temperature regime of 40/38°C. However, after being maintained at 40–42°C for 3 days, 50% of SB and no NSB plants were capable of regrowth (DM Ford, Southeast Missouri State University, personal communication). Thermal tolerance was quantified for SB and NSB by growing plants hydroponically at 40°C for 3, 6, and 9 days and rating the leaf damage. Damage was assessed by scoring brown necrotic regions on each leaf blade. A high score was indicative of greater damage. NSB incurred more damage at each sampling date, and NSB damage scores were significantly greater at 9 days (7.37 ± 3.06) than those of SB (1.55 ± 0.53).

PHYSIOLOGICAL ASSAYS

Additional experimental techniques were used to determine if SB was more thermotolerant than NSB. The tetrazolium reduction assay, which tests for cell viability, indicated that SB could withstand higher temperatures than NSB (data not shown). Electrolyte leakage assays have been used to measure membrane thermostability in response to high-temperature stress. The premise of this technique is that membranes become more fragile at high temperatures. Consequently, the damage that occurs during heat stress results in "leaky" membranes. To determine the amount of electrolyte leakage, leaf blades were exposed to increasing temperatures for various times. The amount of electrolyte released into the solution surrounding the tissue was measured and then compared to that of leaf blades that were "killed" by a freeze/thaw cycle (100% electrolyte leakage).

The ratio (Le) of conductivity after heat treatment to conductivity following killing is an indication of the relative injury caused by the stress and membrane thermostability. The larger the ratio, the more damage occurred during the stress. When Le was measured at 25 and 35æ% C, there were no differences between SB and NSB at any of the time intervals. However, the Le was less for SB than NSB when leaf blades were exposed to 40°C for 180 to 270 min. When incubated at 40°C for this length of time, SB had greater membrane stability than NSB. The Le of SB and NSB was high and similar at 45°C, which suggested that the "critical temperature" for both variants had been attained and that plant death was occurring. The critical temperature depends on the length of the incubation time and temperature.

When the Le is 50% or greater, the critical temperature has been reached. The critical temperatures for NSB ranged from 52.4°C at 30 min to 39.8°C at 300 min. They were 52.7 and 42.0°C for SB at the same time points. On average, the critical temperature for SB was 2.1°C greater than that for NSB, which indicated that it had greater membrane stability at high temperatures. All of these assessments, field trials, regrowth experiments, tetrazolium reduction, electrolyte leakage assays, and evaluation of damage during hydroponic heat stress confirm that SB is more heat-tolerant than NSB. The next focus of our research was to determine why SB is more heat tolerant than NSB.

HSP IDENTIFICATION AND LOCALIZATION

Since the HSR and the synthesis of HSPs has been implicated in acquisition of thermal tolerance in a number of organisms, differences in the HSR between SB and NSB may provide information regarding the greater heat tolerance of SB. First, HSP synthesis in the two variants was evaluated. Leaf blade segments were incubated in buffer containing radioactive amino acids. The proteins synthesized during this in vivo labeling process were analyzed by one-dimensional (1D) gel electrophoresis (SDS-PAGE) followed by fluorography, which allows detection of the radiolabeled proteins. After 1 hr at 40æ% C, both SB and NSB synthesized the HMW-HSPs of 97, 83, and 70 kDa and LMW-HSPs of 27 and 18 kDa. Unfortunately, there were no obvious differences in the pattern of HSPs synthesized when they were analyzed by 1D electrophoresis. Because there were no apparent differences in the pattern of HSPs synthesized by SB and NSB when analyzed by 1D electrophoresis, two additional aspects of the HSR were determined: the temperature and time required to induce HSP synthesis.

If SB initiates HSP synthesis at a lower temperature or after a short time period, it may account for the better thermal tolerance of SB. Because the bentgrass used in these experiment was grown at 22°C (day temperature) and 16°C (night temperature), one would expect HSP synthesis to be induced at approximately 32°C (10°C above the optimal temperature). For both SB and NSB, synthesis of the HMW-HSPs and HSP25 was induced between 30 and 32°C, whereas HSP18 synthesis was induced at 32 to 34°C. Maximal HSP production was between 36 and 40°C. At 45°C, all protein synthesis was inhibited, suggesting that this temperature was lethal to both SB and NSB. As is the case for other plants, the synthesis of many normal proteins decreased as the temperature increased. In addition to measuring the temperature at which HSP synthesis was induced, we also measured the length of time required for HSP synthesis to begin. At 40°C, synthesis of the HMW-HSPs began within 5 min and the LMW-HSPs within 15 min. Again, there were no major differences between the two variants in the length of time required to induce HSP synthesis. Since we were unable to detect differences between SB and NSB in the time or temperature required to induce the HSR, we analyzed the pattern of HSPs synthesized using an alternate technique. 2D gel electrophoresis, which separates proteins according to their size and charge, was used to determine if HSP variants were present that were not detected when proteins were analyzed by 1D electrophoresis. Each spot on the 2D gel represents a unique protein synthesized during the labeling period. Figure 5 shows the pattern of HSPs from SB and NSB. Several variants of the HMW HSP97, 83, and 70 were synthesized by SB and NSB. Because of the abundance and complexity of HSPs in this region of the gel, it was difficult to determine if there were differences between SB and NSB in the HMW-HSPs.

However, differences between SB and NSB in the LMW-HSPs were apparent. In the HSP18 family, there were at least 17 polypeptides distributed in the pH range of 5.7 to 7.5. Two of these polypeptides with isoelectric points of approximately 6.5 and 6.8 were present in NSB and not SB. In the HSP25 family, approximately three polypeptides were found in the acidic region of the gel. These proteins were distributed in the pH range of 5.4 to 5, had an apparent molecular mass of approximately 27 kDa, and were synthesized by both SB and NSB. However, in SB, there were two to three additional polypeptides in this group. These HSPs were smaller (with an apparent molecular mass of 25 kDa) and slightly more basic than the HSP27 polypeptides found in both SB and NSB.

The smaller HSP25 polypeptides were found only in SB, and in this chapter they are designated as the HSP25 isoforms. The synthesis of the HSP25 isoforms in SB is one factor distinguishing SB from NSB in the heat-shock response. Since the HSP25 isoforms were synthesized by the heat-tolerant SB, it is possible that they may be correlated with its superior thermal tolerance. Several other heat-tolerant variants, derived from Penncross in a different series of selections, were also tested to determine whether the HSP25s were present.

All of the heat-tolerant variants tested synthesized the HSP25s. LMW-HSPs are found throughout the plant cell. They are localized in the cytoplasm, ER, mitochondria, and chloroplasts. There is evidence that some members of the HSP25 family are present in the chloroplast of a number of plant species. Since the genes encoding these HSPs are in the nucleus, the plastid HSPs must be synthesized in the cytoplasm and posttranslationally transported into the chloroplast. To determine if members of the bentgrass HSP25 family were localized in the chloroplast, they were isolated from in vivo labeled leaf blades and analyzed by 2D electrophoresis. The results indicated that one or two members of the HSP27 family were present in the chloroplasts of both SB and NSB and that at least one of the HSP25 isoforms was present in chloroplasts isolated from SB.

The LMW chloroplast HSPs are characterized by three consensus or conserved regions. Sequences I and II, found in the carboxyl-terminal region, are homologous to the á-crystallin domain of other LMW HSPs. Consensus region III is a methionine-rich region that is common to chloroplast-localized HSPs. This region forms an amphipatic á-helix that has methionine and other hydrophobic amino acids on one side and hydrophilic amino acids on the other. Antibody (Abmet) has been made to a 28 amino acid peptide derived from the consensus sequence of this region. This antibody recognized LMW chloroplast HSPs in plants from six divergent Anthophyta species, including C3, C4, CAM, monocot, and dicot species. Immunoblot analysis indicated that Abmet recognized HSP27 in heat-shocked leaf blades from both SB and NSB. It also recognized the HSP25 isoforms found in SB. In addition, this experiment indicated that members of the HSP25 family could be detected by Western blot within 1 hr of heat shock at 40°C. Access to Abmet " has simplified much of our research, because it is no longer necessary to label leaf blades in vivo with radioactive amino acid prior to electrophoresis. Leaf blades can be detached from intact plants that have been subjected to high temperatures in the growth chamber and immediately assayed for the presence of

HSP27 and HSP25. For example, during hydroponic heat stress at 40°C, members of the HSP25 family were present in the leaf blades of both SB and NSB throughout a 11-day hydroponic stress period at 40°C.

After 1 day of hydroponic heat stress at 40æ% C, roots from NSB and SB contained HSP27, and SB contained the HSP25 isoforms. This indicates that the HSP25 family is also synthesized in the root, but we do not know if they are localized in the plastids. The root HSPs were not present after 11 days of heat stress. A more detailed time course must be done to determine when HSP25 synthesis ceases in this organ. However, if HSP25 synthesis in the root does not persist for long periods of time, it may account for the observation that roots of turfgrass are more susceptible to heat stress than leaf blades. We used Abmet to show that the synthesis of the HSP25 family in bentgrass occurs in the cytoplasm and not the chloroplast. Leaf blades were incubated with either cyclohexamide, which inhibits cytoplasmic protein synthesis, or chloramphenicol, which inhibits chloroplast protein synthesis. Synthesis of the HSP25 family continued in the presence of chloramphenicol but was inhibited by cyclohexamide.

This suggests that the HSP25 genes in bentgrass are nuclear and that the HSP25 polypeptides must be posttranslationally transported into the chloroplast. If temperature increases too rapidly, import into the chloroplast is impaired. The availability of Abmet has been used for research regarding the role of LMW chloroplast HSPs. When the antibody was used to survey an evolutionarily diverse group of plants by immunoblot analysis, there was a general correlation between the amount of chloroplast LMW-HSP and thermal tolerance of the species. For example, Ferocactus, one of the most thermotolerant plants known, produced more of the chloroplast HSPs than plants that grow in more temperate climates. The presence of LMW-HSPs that cross react with Abmet in a wide array of species indicates that the methionine-rich sequence is highly conserved and that these HSPs may be essential for survival. Photosystem II (PSII) and the oxygen-evolving complex (OEC) of

PSII are especially sensitive to heat and oxidative stress. When tomato plants were grown at 25/18°C and photosynthetic electron transport measured at 47°C, there was a 80% drop in whole chain electron transport due to inhibition of PSII.

However, if plants were allowed to acclimate (pre–heat stress) at 43°C prior to the measurement at 47°C, there was only a 20% drop in photosynthetic electron transport. Presumably this occurred because chloroplastlocalized HSPs were synthesized during the pre–heat stress period and protected PSII during the subsequent 47°C treatment. The addition of ABmet , which preferentially associates with the chloroplast HSPs and prevents them from interacting with endogenous chloroplast proteins, eliminated the protection of PSII. Neither preimmune serum nor bovine serum albumin alleviated the heat-induced inhibition of electron transport. Furthermore, addition of purified chloroplast HSP25s protected PSII during heat stress at 47°C.

But, addition of exogenous HSP25 could not reactivate PSII that was already heat-denatured. Oxidative stress, UV light, drought, and abscisic acid also induced the synthesis of the LMW chloroplast HSPs in tomato and Chenopodium album. The induction of these HSPs by a variety of abiotic stresses results in tolerance that enables the plant to survive several types of adverse conditions. Subsequent research demonstrated that chloroplasts of Chenopodium album contained HSPs of 25 and 22 kDa. Fractionation of chloroplasts indicated that HSP25 was located in the stroma and the smaller HSP22 within the thylakoid. Immunoblot analysis indicated that HSP22 was associated with OEC proteins of 32, 23, and 16 kDa. As the temperature increased, HSP25 became less soluble and appeared to aggregate with the thylakoids. Recent experiments (Dr. S. Heckathorn, Syracuse University, personal communication) indicate that the HSP25 isoforms found in SB but not NSB are localized within the thylakoids. Preliminary results suggest that the HSP25 isoforms are associated with OEC33. The larger HSP27 isoforms are present in the stroma of both SB and NSB.

The results presented in Figure 10 (Dr. S. Heckathorn, unpublished data) indicate that PSII electron transport measured at both 26 and 41æ% C was protected to a greater extent in SB than NSB following a 6-hr period of preheat stress. These data suggest that SB is more heat-tolerant than NSB because it is capable of synthesizing the smaller, thylakoid-localized HSPs that protect the OEC during heat shock. Figure 11 summarizes our proposed model for induction, synthesis, and localization of the HSP25 family in SB. After sensing high temperature, the transcription of genes encoding HSP27 and HSP25 occurs. These mRNAs move from the nucleus into the cytoplasm, where they are translated into the "pre"protein form. The transit peptide on the preprotein targets the HSPs to the chloroplast. Following movement into the plastid, the "pre" sequence is removed and HSP27 and HSP25 are localized to the stroma and thylakoid lumen, respectively (Dr. S. Heckathorn, unpublished data). In the lumen, HSP25 associates with the OEC and protects this complex from high-temperature stress. In NSB, the HSP25 isoforms are absent and OEC is afforded less protection.

THERMAL TOLERANCE AND RECOVERY FROM HEAT STRESS

As mentioned above, a typical aspect of the HSR in most organisms is a dramatic decrease in synthesis of normal proteins during heat shock. In bentgrass, this was demonstrated as decreased incorporation of radioactive amino acids into protein during in vivo labeling experiments at high temperatures. When leaf blades were returned to near optimum temperature, incorporation of amino acids increased, which suggested that synthesis of normal cellular proteins had resumed. Our research indicated that the synthesis of normal proteins increased 4 hr after heat shock in SB and 6 hr thereafter in NSB. This was not due to increased amino acid availability in SB, nor were there differences between SB and NSB in the abundance of mRNAs encoding the general population of normal cellular proteins. However, more of these "normal" mRNAs were associated with polysomes (and hence being translated into proteins) in SB than in NSB at 4 hr postrecovery. 2D electrophoresis indicated that more normal proteins were being synthesized at 4 hr in SB than in NSB. In addition, the synthesis of the HSP18 and HSP70 families decreased faster in SB than in NSB during recovery. The synthesis of the HSP27 family continued throughout the 8-hr recovery period in both NSB and SB. The recovery of normal protein synthesis 2 hr earlier in SB than NSB may account for its increased dry-weight accumulation during recovery from hightemperature stress. According to Howarth, the ability to resume normal protein synthesis following heat shock is a characteristic of heat-tolerant plants. In corn, decreases in the amounts of OEC33, 23, and 16 following heat shock correlated with a decline in net photosynthesis, and subsequent recovery depended on the replacement of these proteins. If these OEC proteins are afforded greater protection during heat shock by the HSP25 isoforms found in SB and if SB can replace damaged ones more rapidly than NSB, this could ultimately result in the increased dry-weight accumulation observed in SB.

GENETIC ANALYSIS

Two LMW HSP genes have been isolated from the SB heat-shock cDNA library and sequenced. The derived amino acid sequences for ApHsp16.5 and ApHsp26.1. Both HSPs contain the conserved heatshock domains I and II that are typical of LMW-HSPs found in plants and other organisms. Sequence alignment comparing the amino acid sequences of the two bentgrass HSPs with members of each class of soybean HSPs. A phylogenetic comparison of the bentgrass and soybean HSPs indicates that ApHsp16.5 is most closely related to soybean class I HSP. The phylogenetic tree also indicates that ApHsp26.1 is more similar to the chloroplast-localized HSP from soybean than to the other classes of soybean HSPs. Therefore it is likely that ApHsp26.1 codes for a HSP that is localized in the plastid. ApHsp16.5 codes for a putative 16.5 kDa HSP. Sequence comparison indicates that it is a member of the cytoplasmic class I LMW-HSP family and it has greatest homology with LMW-HSP from wheat and barley (data not shown).

Northern blot analysis demonstrated that it was transcribed in response to heat shock and hybridized to a single 0.8-kb mRNA in both variants.

Southern analysis indicated that ApHsp16.5 belongs to a relatively large multigene family. This was expected, because there are approximately 18 distinct HSP18 polypeptides on the 2D gel. There are several polymorphisms in the hybridization patterns between SB and NSB, which confirms that gene structure and/or organization is different between the two variants. We also know that there are at least two additional members of the HSP18 family that are synthesized by NSB and not SB. The derived amino acid sequence for ApHsp26.1, which codes for a putative chloroplast-localized HSP, is compared with those of other chloroplast LMW-HSPs from several different plant species.

The N-terminal sequence of ApHsp26.1 (from positions 1 to 59) is characteristic of transit sequences found in proteins that are transported into the chloroplast and homologous to those found in several other chloroplast HSPs. Transit sequences have a high serine content, are rich in basic amino acids, and lack acidic amino acids. When the putative transit sequence is removed during movement into the chloroplast, the resulting HSP has a molecular mass of approximately 22 kDa.

This is slightly less than the molecular mass determined by SDS-PAGE; however, it is not unusual for estimates from SDS-PAGE and derived amino acid sequences to disagree. In addition to the transit sequence, the putative protein also contains methionine-rich region and conserved heat-shock domains I and II. The presence of a putative transit sequence, the methionine-rich region, and its general homology with other chloroplast HSPs in the data base suggest that ApHsp26.1 encodes a chloroplast-localized HSP. In addition, ApHsp26.1 has the five–amino acid sequence EVKMR at positions 162 to 166 just before heat-shock domain II. This sequence is present in chloroplast localized LMW-HSPs from wheat, barley, and maize. The related sequence EIKMR is found in HSP25 from pea, petunia, and soybean. Phylogenetic analysis indicates that ApHsp26.1 has the greatest homology (approximately 64%) with chloroplast HSPs from wheat and barley. It has less homology with the dicot LMW-HSP. Because the antibody raised against the methionine-rich peptide cross-reacts with several proteins ranging from 25 to 27 kDa in SB and NSB, genes encoding these proteins must be present in the bentgrass genome and remain to be identified and isolated.

Northern blot analysis indicated that ApHsp26.1 hybridized to a single mRNA species of approximately 1 kb in NSB and 0.8 kb in SB. The smaller size of the hybridizing mRNA in SB suggested that ApHsp26.1 may code for one of the smaller HSPs found in this variant, but this has not been confirmed. Southern analysis indicated ApHsp26.1 hybridized to two bands in both SB and NSB, suggesting that there may be two genes encoding this protein. There were no polymorphisms between SB and NSB with the three restriction enzymes used for the digestion. This indicates that genes encoding ApHsp26.1 may have similar or identical sequences in both variants. The differences in transcript size between SB and NSB may occur because only one of the two genes is transcribed in each variant. ApHsp26.1 maps to chromosome 1 (bin 1.03) on the maize genome, which is the same site as a cDNA for a chloroplast-localized HSP from maize. After it was observed that SB and NSB had different patterns of LMW HSP synthesis, we wanted to determine if this change in gene expression was genetically stable and if it correlated with the improved thermal tolerance of SB.

Due to the high level of self-incompatibility, it was difficult to obtain progeny from NSB × SB (and the reciprocal cross), but 20 were obtained. Of these progeny, 13 synthesized the HSP25 isoforms and 7 did not. This suggested the presence of HSP was inherited as a heterozygous dominant trait ($X2 = 1.8$, $p = 0.18$) in SB. Hydroponic heat-stress experiments demonstrated that the presence of HSP25s was correlated with increased thermal tolerance in the F1 progeny ($X2 = 22.45$, $p < 0.001$). To the best of our knowledge, this was the first genetic evidence demonstrating a correlation between the synthesis of a particular HSP and heat tolerance in a higher plant.

Subsequently, others have shown that increased heat tolerance is genetically associated with the production of HSP25 in wheat. To extend the genetic analysis, progeny from the NSB × SB cross ("F1 ") that demonstrated the highest (progeny 4 and 20) and lowest (progeny 7) levels of heat tolerance (47) were crossed and several backcrosses were also made. Using Abmet , the progeny from these crosses were examined for the presence of the HSP25 isoforms. Although we previously postulated that the ability to synthesize the HSP25 isoforms was inherited as a heterozygous dominant trait, data from these analyses suggest that two genes, A and B, may be involved.

Our model predicts that SB is heterozygous dominant for A and B, with A having a greater effect on the trait than B. When A, or both A and B, are present, the plants synthesize the HSP25 isoforms. The X2 values obtained appear to confirm this model. Progeny (28 individuals, 5 replicates) from one of the second-generation crosses (4 ×20) were analyzed for thermotolerance. All of the progeny lacking the HSP25 isoforms were in the highly damaged class. These data also indicate that the presence of the HSP25 isoforms is correlated with increased heat tolerance. When these data are considered along with the data indicating that the HSP25 isoforms are localized in the thylakoid lumen and probably associated with OEC (Dr. S. Heckathorn, personal communication), there is strong evidence that the presence of the HSP25 isoforms in SB are a major factor contributing to its enhanced heat tolerance.

SUMMARY AND CONCLUSIONS

Heat stress in plants occurs when the absorption of solar radiation significantly exceeds emission and tissue temperatures are above their optimum for normal metabolism. If heat stress occurs at extreme levels or duration, metabolic activity may be irreversibly impaired and the plant will die. All plants have evolved strategies of heat tolerance using adaptation of morphology, anatomy, or physiology. A physiological strategy of heat tolerance used by plants is the synthesis of HSPs triggered by heat stress and other abiotic stresses. Starting in 1985, we initiated a series of studies to elucidate the HSR in SB and NSB. These studies were based on determining the presence and role of HSPs in these two distinct variants of creeping bentgrass.

These bentgrass plants were somaclonal variants consisting of an apparent heat-tolerant genotype (SB) and the non-heat-tolerant genotype (NSB). Because SB and NSB were derived from the same seed and share many of the same genes, we felt that these two plant types would be an ideal model system to study HSP synthesis and the role of HSPs in bentgrass heat tolerance. In addition, the close genomic relationship of grass species, in general, and the economic importance of grasses in agriculture further justified our selection of bentgrass as an attractive model system. A number of different physiological analyses confirmed that SB was more heat-tolerant than SB. Although there were no differences in the time or temperature required for NSB and SB to initiate HSP synthesis, SB synthesized two to three HSP25 isoforms not synthesized by NSB. Work conducted by Heckathorn (unpublished data) indicates that the presence of the HSP isoforms found in SB protects photosystem II during heat stress. In addition, his work suggests that these isoforms (which are not present in NSB) are localized within the thylakoids, where they probably protect the OEC of photosystem II.

These findings mesh with those of Bjorkman et al., who reported that photosystem II activity was most closely associated with the thermal tolerance in Atriplex sabulosa and Tidestromia oblongifolia. SB was also found to recover from heat stress faster than NSB in both the field and the laboratory. SB recovers its ability to accumulate dry weight faster, which may be due to its ability to protect photosystem II during heat stress. It also recovers normal levels of protein synthesis earlier than NSB. Although SB appears to recruit more normal mRNAs onto polyribosomes faster than NSB, the precise mechanism for this is presently unknown. There are still many questions regarding the difference in the thermal tolerance between SB and NSB and the function of the HSP25 isoforms. Why does SB synthesize the HSP25 isoforms? It seems unlikely that these extra genes were added to SB during the cell culture process. Some event must have occurred that allowed genes already present in the bentgrass genome to be switched on in SB and not in NSB.

This may be due to a change in the promoter region of the HSP25 genes, possible demethylation of HSP25 genes, or synthesis of altered heat-shock transcription factors. The possibility of posttranscriptional regulation of HSP25 expression cannot be ruled out. The putative mutation may have pleotropic affects that alter the entire heat-shock response pathway. If we could understand the molecular switch resulting in the synthesis of the HSP isoforms, we might be able to trigger it in other species. It may also be possible to genetically modify other species with these unique HSP25 genes and produce more heat-tolerant plants.

The knowledge of temperature levels and duration of these temperature levels needed to trigger the HSR in SB may also be useful in predicting the deterimental effects following the onset of heat stress in bentgrass. Adjusting cultural practices in response to this prediction may allow practitioners to better manage creeping bentgrass as a putting-green turf in the field.

10

Cold Response and Freezing Tolerance in Plants

INTRODUCTION

Plants show a great variability with regard to their tolerance to low temperatures and are thus capable of occupying a wide range of climatic regions in the world. Plant species of tropical origin are mostly sensitive to chilling (temperatures between 0 and 12æ% C) and do not typically tolerate subzero temperatures and the presence of ice in their tissues, while plants from temperate regions are generally resistant to chilling.

The chilling-resistant plants typically tolerate subzero temperatures and freezing of their tissue water. They also exhibit a wide range of tolerance to subzero temperatures, from slight frost to below “196æ% C when fully acclimated. While many temperate woody conifer and deciduous plant species could survive extreme low temperatures, most herbaceous plants tend to be much less cold-tolerant. Cold stress, often referred to as freezing stress, is distinctly different from chilling stress with regard to the stress imposed on plants, the subsequent plant response, and perhaps even the mechanisms of tolerance.

Cold stress in plants, unlike chilling stress, always involves the following: (a) the freezing of tissue water, which entails ice growth, cell dehydration, osmotic concentration, and a complex freeze-induced cell-volume changes, and (b) the subzero temperatures. Furthermore, it is important to recognize that the lethal freezing injury, unlike chilling injury, occurs at a well-defined "killing temperature," with little or no dependence on the time of exposure at this temperature. Also, supercooled cells and tissues (no tissue water freezing) can remain without apparent injury symptoms for fairly extended periods, suggesting that freezing of tissue water and consequent events must have a specific role in causing the characteristic well-defined killing temperatures.

However, this is not to rule out the possibility that subzero temperatures per se, like chilling temperatures in chilling-sensitive plants, can inflict chronic disorders and injury over a longer periods of time. Thus, clearly, the freezing of cellular water and its consequent effects on the cell would make cold tolerance and injury unique in plants. The varying ability of plants to tolerate low temperatures is determined largely by the genetic factors. A wide variation in freezing tolerance does exist not only among plants, as mentioned above, but also within a plant, among the various plant parts. For instance, roots, which are guarded from the extremes of midwinter air temperatures, tend to be much less freezing-tolerant than the shoots in most plant species. Other factors such as age, nutrition, and abiotic and biotic stresses can significantly affect the freezing tolerance of plants as well. Furthermore, most temperate plant species show a characteristic seasonal fluctuation in their freezing tolerance. Actively growing plants have little ability to tolerate cold, but they acquire the ability to survive much lower temperatures in autumn, as they become dormant.

Thus, hardy plants that may be killed by slight frost while actively growing could survive freezing below "196°C without injury in midwinter. They subsequently lose all their acquired freezing tolerance rapidly as they break dormancy and begin growth in spring. We are far from clearly understanding this remarkable transformation that takes place in plants and the specific factors or processes that enable plants to survive low temperatures in autumn. Nonetheless, it is clear that the ability of plants to tolerate cold is an inducible one and can be triggered by specific environmental stimuli, as will be discussed below. This complex plant response to the environmental cues at the molecular, cellular, and whole-plant levels has long been the subject of numerous studies. As a result, we have gained some insights into freezing behavior in plant tissues, cold acclimation changes, the nature and mechanism of freezing injury, genetic control, and the regulation of freezing tolerance.

This has enhanced our understanding in various areas of plant survival against cold, including but not limited to the aspects of the molecular basis of freezing tolerance and freezing characteristic of plant tissue water. The new advances, though preliminary in nature, may provide a basis for the development of some strategies and methods that may have potential in improving the freezing tolerance of plants. In this section, a brief overview of plants response to cold, the mechanisms of freezing tolerance, and possible approaches to developing plants with enhanced freezing tolerance is presented.

FREEZING BEHAVIOR IN PLANTS

Under natural conditions of slow cooling, ice initiation in plant tissues occurs primarily in xylem and vascular elements and grows in the extracellular spaces. In most plant tissues, ice grows in the extracellular spaces at the expense of cellular water. As temperature drops, the cellular water migrates to the extracellular ice, which lowers the melting point (freezing point) of cellular water in the cells and thus prevents the formation of ice within the cells. Thus, extracellular freezing involves cell dehydration and the consequent concentration of solutes.

Plants can tolerate extracellular freezing, with its associated cell dehydration and osmotic concentration, to varying degrees. Tender herbaceous tissues may tolerate only slight freeze-induced dehydration, while cells of hardy woody tissues can dehydrate completely, losing all their freezable water to extracellular ice. Generally, most of the freezable water is lost from the cells by about "50°C; the fact that many hardy tissues can survive below "196°C suggests that dehydration may not be critical for survival in these plants.

However, in a number of plant species that are moderately or slightly freezing-tolerant, dehydration may contribute to freezing injury. Plants that tolerate ice within them can do so only if ice is excluded from the cells in the intercellular spaces; otherwise ice crystals formed within the cells can cause damage to cell membranes and other organelles. During extracellular freezing, if cells are unable to dehydrate fast enough to keep up with the decreasing water potential of extracellular ice, as can be expected, the intracellular ice formation occurs.

This scenario may occur because of (a) rapid cooling rates, which can lead to an increasing disequilibrium in water potentials between the extracellular ice and supercooled unfrozen cellular water—one way the equilibrium is reached is by allowing the ice formation to occur within the cells, and (b) the limited water permeability of the plasma membrane at subzero temperatures, which again may contribute to disequilibrium between the cellular water and the extracellular ice. Evidently, the above factors are likely to become more significant in hydrated tissues than in less hydrated ones. Generally, unhardened plant tissues, typically with high levels of hydration, have a higher propensity for intracellular freezing than unhardened tissues.

Also, depending on the extent of supercooling, supercooled tissues that freeze are prone to intracellular ice formation resulting in lethal injury.

Plant Supercooling

Very rarely, tissue water does not freeze at its actual freezing point (melting point) but rather supercools to varying degrees before it freezes. This phase change is facilitated by a nucleation process, and thus the extent of supercooling varies and is dependent on the efficiency of either the intrinsic ice nucleators in the tissue or the extraneous ice nucleators on the plant surface or its surroundings. As intrinsic ice nucleators in plants are usually not very efficient, plants tend to supercool to varying degrees, often limited by the efficacy of extraneous sources of ice nucleation. Indeed, some biological sources such as resident epiphytic bacteria—Pseudomonas syringae and Erwinia herbicola—are very good ice nucleators and can limit the extent of supercooling in plants. Generally, freezing in tender plants or plant parts such as flower buds and blossoms can lead to freezing injury. As a matter of fact, most plants would be prone to frost injury in early or late spring, when plants are beginning to lose their freezing tolerance. As long as these plants remain supercooled and avoid ice in their tissues, there is likely to be no injury.

Hence, various strategies to reduce the ice-nucleation bacterial population by chemicals and by competing populations of inactive strains have been used to provide protection against frost injury. This approach is aimed at keeping plants supercooled only to a few degrees (perhaps 2 or 3°C) and for a limited length of time, because as the temperature decreases or if plants or plant parts remain supercooled for a long time, other ice nucleators, including the intrinsic ones, are likely to become active, causing ice formation. As discussed above, supercooling followed by freezing in tissues can lead to intracellular ice formation and thus to lethal injury. However, most plant tissues and the bulk of tissue water typically do not supercool below "10°C, and ice nucleation eventually occurs by either extraneous or intrinsic sources (heterogeneous ice nucleation). However, there are many specific tissues—such as stem xylem-ray parenchyma, flower-bud primordia, and partially hydrated seeds—that may avoid ice formation completely until they reach their homogeneous nucleation temperature (approximately "40°C), which is the empirical limit of supercooling for water. This phenomenon is sometimes referred to as deep supercooling.

This is distinct from the small degree of supercooling observed in most tissues, which typically freeze by heterogeneous nucleation. At the homogeneous nucleation temperature, water may self-nucleate, causing instant and rapid intracellular ice formation. Thus, as indicated above, as long as the tissues remain supercooled, no apparent injury is observed, but subsequent freezing invariably results in lethal injury. An overwhelming number of woody plants—including many native temperate species and most of economically important crops like apple, pear, many species of Prunus, and grapes—show supercooling characteristics in their dormant stems, flower buds, or both. Since these plant tissues remain supercooled, avoiding ice and injury, the deep supercooling characteristic has been regarded as a winter survival mechanism.

However, as their winter survival is strictly limited by the homogeneous nucleation temperature, the supercooling plant species typically do not tolerate temperatures below approximately 40°C. Thus, supercooling can limit the survival of many native and cultivated temperate plants and has a remarkable impact on the geographic distribution of native woody plants.

George et al. showed that most deciduous North American woody plants that show supercooling in their stem tissues were found in regions where midwinter temperatures did not drop below 40°C, while the nonsupercooling species extended to much colder northern regions. Similarly, the supercooling characteristic has been shown to have a remarkable impact on the distribution of native flora of the Rocky Mountains of Colorado and may explain the occurrence of treeline in these mountains. A majority of the upright trees (both conifers and deciduous species) show the supercooling characteristic in stem tissues and grow up to elevations corresponding to midwinter 40°C isotherm.

This gives rise to the characteristic treeline observed in these mountains, while the species found above the treeline do not show the supercooling characteristic. Furthermore, as most horticulturally important perennial plants also show supercooling, either in their stem tissues or flower-bud primordia, their commercial cultivation is likely to be limited to regions where midwinter temperatures do not drop below 40°C on a regular basis. Thus, the supercooling characteristic appears to determine not only the geographical distribution of native flora in temperate regions and but also the successful cultivation of many perennial fruit and landscape plants. Therefore, one could conclude that the supercooling characteristic is an undesirable trait and plants that survive extreme cold avoid the supercooling characteristic and appear to have developed specific mechanisms to tolerate cell dehydration during freezing.

Cell Tension and Cavitation

The freezing behavior of plants is complex and, like the supercooling characteristic, extracellular freezing can clearly have a significant impact on plant survival. As mentioned above, extracellular freezing in plant tissues is associated with cell dehydration. Cells need to shrink or deform as water migrates to the extracellular space during extracellular freezing. Any resistance to cell-volume change can lead to reduction or even cessation of water efflux, resulting in the development of negative pressures within the cell. As plant cells are often bound by rigid cell walls, one can expect to have cell resistance to volume changes during freezing. In fact, most herbaceous and woody plant tissues offer varying degrees of resistance to cell deformation during extracellular freezing, which can reduce cell dehydration and lead to the development of cell tension. Obviously, woody, rigid tissues are likely to offer more resistance to cell deformation and can develop higher tensions than softer herbaceous tissues. Also, the cold acclimation of plants can lead to significant changes in physical properties and composition of cell walls.

Among these changes in the cell walls, an increase in their thickness and rigidity coupled with the decreasing cell wall pore sizes are significant in relation to the freezing behavior of cells. It is reasonable expect that these changes can alter the freezing behavior of cells, making them more resistant to cell-volume changes during extracellular freezing. This is supported by the fact that the cold hardened cells typically develop higher cell tensions than their unhardened counterparts. A good example of a dramatic change in the freezing behavior resulting from cold acclimation is the acquisition of deep supercooling characteristics in stem tissues. It is indeed remarkable that supercooling stem tissues such as stem xylem-ray parenchyma do not largely dehydrate, although these cells are surrounded by ice in the adjacent tissues and xylem vessels. Assuming that these cells are in equilibrium with the ice at a water potential as low as 46 MPa at 40°C, it is surprising that they can resist cell dehydration and cell deformation. Thus, these cells are expected to develop remarkably high cell tension, in the neighborhood of 46 MPa.

This raises the obvious question as to whether water is actually physically stable at such high tensions. Green et al. estimated that aqueous solutions, as in cell sap, are likely have higher stability under tension than pure water and that it can withstand approximately a tension of 240 MPa. In fact, one can expect even higher stability in viscous water. Zheng et al. proposed that it could be on the order of gigapascals at the glass transformation temperatures. Thus, viscous proptoplasm in cold-hardened cells at low temperatures can remain stable at cell tensions likely to occur in deep supercooled plant cells. As cell dehydration is inseparably tied to changes in cell volume, one can actually predict the extent of cell dehydration during extracellular freezing for varying levels of cell rigidity.

Cells that are very rigid and resist cell deformation and dehydration are prone to exhibit the deep supercooling characteristic, which, as discussed before, can predispose cells to homogeneous nucleation and the resulting lethal injury. In cases where supercooling cells could dehydrate slightly, as they do during long cold winters, the cell osmolality increases, which can actually depress the homogeneous nucleation temperature well below 40°C. Such observations have been made in many supercooling woody species grown in the northern latitudes.

On the other hand, very resilient to moderately rigid cells that can allow for cell dehydration to occur during extracellular freezing can prevent homogeneous nucleation in cellular water. In fact, plant tissues that survive extreme low temperatures fall into this group. Thus, typically nonrigid or soft tissues can avoid supercooling. It is significant to note that the cell rigidity enables cells to supercool to varying degrees provided that heterogeneous nucleation of cellular water does not occur and therefore could be implicated as the primary cause of supercooling in woody tissues. Furthermore, as the freezing behavior of cell water is modulated by cell rigidity, the amount of unfrozen water cannot be predicted solely by osmotic concentration of cell sap in most plants, as once thought.

This is because the rigid cells can restrict the efflux of water and therefore the extent of extracellular freezing. Thus, on the basis of osmotic considerations alone, one can expect to underestimate the unfrozen water during freezing. In fact, recent studies show that the freezing of tissue water is very different from the ideal freezing behavior of dilute aqueous solution. However, it can approach the ideal behavior only if either cells do not offer any resistance to cell-volume changes during extracellular freezing or intracellular freezing.

Indeed, tissue water in soft herbaceous tissues of some species (e.g., potato and spinach) may show nearly an ideal freezing behavior and develop no cell tension during extracellular freezing. Also, intracellular freezing, which typically does not involve significant cell deformation, does not lead to cell tension. As freezing progresses in the extracellular spaces of rigid tissues, cell tension increases until it reaches the limit of the tensile strength of water. At this point cellular water ruptures, which is often referred to as cavitation, leading to a loss of cell tension. Thus, declining cell tension is a good indicator of cavitation events in a tissue. Even small tensions in stem xylem or in osmotic cell have been shown to result in cavitation.

The stretched water (under tension) ruptures to give rise to cavities of water vapor, which are typically associated with acoustic emissions. Acoustic emissions have been detected during freezing in a number of plant tissues. As cell tension is terminated by cavitation, it can often lead to spontaneous ice nucleation within the cells causing lethal injury. Cavitation during freezing can be damaging to cells and has been associated with injury in a number of plants species. Furthermore, cavitation has been associated with the production of reactive oxygen and free radicals, which can also contribute to freezing injury. Our recent studies have shown that freeze-induced cell tension leading to cavitation is associated with free radical formation, which contributes to lethal injury in a number of plant species (unpublished results). In grape stem and boxwood leaves, extracellular freezing gave rise to higher chemiluminescence than did the intracellular freezing, suggesting that cell tension and subsequent cavitation can lead to the production of free radicals. Freezing injury has been linked to oxidative stress in alfalfa, and efforts to genetically engineer plants with higher antioxidant enzyme (superoxide dismutase) activity have resulted in plants with enhanced cold tolerance.

COLD ACCLIMATION

Cold acclimation is an adaptive response in plants inducible by certain environmental conditions and results in enhanced freezing tolerance. Most temperate plants increase their ability to tolerate cold in response to environmental conditions such as low temperatures, short days, and water deficit. Although low nonfreezing temperatures can trigger cold acclimation, some hardy plant species may need slight frost to acquire their full potential of freezing tolerance. Some plants may take only a few days to acclimate to cold such as Arabidopsis plants, in which a substantial increase in freezing tolerance can be induced within 24 to 48 hr, while others, such as winter wheat and many woody plants, may need several weeks to acclimate fully to cold. In response to these environmental cues, plants can acquire freezing tolerance to varying degrees in autumn and can subsequently deacclimate rapidly in response to conditions conducive to active growth in spring. Numerous physical, physiological, and biochemical changes are known to occur during cold acclimation. Some of the common responses associated with cold acclimation include decreased tissue hydration; metabolic changes including increase in levels of soluble sugars, proline, and other osmoprotectants; changes in plasma membrane lipids; increased abscisic acid level; and altered gene expression.

Most of these changes are correlated with freezing tolerance, but only limited direct evidence exists demonstrating that they are actually involved in inducing freezing tolerance in plants during cold acclimation. For the most part, they are regarded as the metabolic adjustment that plants have to make to cope with low temperatures and freezing of tissue water. As plasma membrane is considered the primary target of freezing injury, changes in its composition, structure, and function during cold acclimation have been suggested to directly affect the freezing tolerance of plants.

The lipid composition of plasma membrane most certainly can influence its stability; thus, changes in lipid composition—including the types of lipids and the increase in their fatty acid unsaturation during cold acclimation— have been proposed to augment the membrane stability against freezing stress. Thus, it is reasonable to conclude that membrane stability can play a role in preventing freezing injury. It has therefore been the focus of wide-ranging efforts to improve freezing tolerance in plants. There have been numerous and extensive studies to characterize the role of various traditional osmoprotectants and novel cold-inducible proteins in the freeze protection of membranes, organelles, and whole plants. Even some of the proteins induced during cold acclimation have been shown to be directly involved in providing membrane stability against freezing stress.

Recently, a small hydrophilic protein (7 kDa) was isolated from cold-acclimated cabbage that is effective in protecting thylakoids against freeze-thaw damage. There is now evidence that other proteins are induced during cold acclimation that can help preserve membrane integrity during freezing. Also, our preliminary studies have shown that the approach involving engineering plants to suppress a key phospholipidmetabolizing enzyme involved in membrane degradation (phospholipase D) may help provide protection against freezing injury. Thus, one can expect that the structural changes of plasma membrane play a key role in injury during freezing and any strategies or approaches to increase membrane stability may prove to be promising tools in improving freezing tolerance in plants.

As plants acclimate to cold, one of the typical and well-known changes in cells is a marked increase in solutes, including soluble sugars and other osmolytes. Because of their clearly demonstrable cryoprotective function, osmoprotectants have long been examined extensively to explain their possible role during cold acclimation. There is overwhelming experimental evidence that when used exogenously, these osmoprotectants can protect cell membranes and organelles during freezing; they have thus become valuable additives for cryopreservation of plant tissues.

However, it is unclear whether these compounds accumulate at high enough concentrations to explain the observed increase in freezing tolerance during the natural cold-acclimation process. Nonetheless, it is possible that these osmoprotectants can concentrate during freezing and can have a stabilizing effect on the membranes. In addition to well-known cryoprotectants such as sucrose, raffinose, and proline, recent studies have suggested that glycine betaine may play a key role in providing protection against freezing injury in plants. Glycine betaine, a quarternary ammonium compound generally considered to provide protection against salt and drought stresses, also accumulates in a wide range of plants during cold acclimation. Accumulation of glycine betaine in response to low temperatures has been shown in wheat, rye, barley, spinach, and blackberry. The response is often rapid; for example, a threefold increase in the leaf glycine betaine level occurs within 24 hr of exposure to low temperatures in Arabidopsis. Furthermore, the direct role of glycine betaine in cold acclimation has been established by its exogenous application in a number plant species including strawberry, blackberry, barley, spinach, and Arabidopsis. The results show that glycine betaine consistently increased the freezing tolerance in these plant species. This effect may be attributed to the ability of glycine betaine to protect the structure and function of membranes, enzymes, and proteins at low water activity.

Glycine betaine is also believed to be involved in the osmoregulation in plants. Glycine betaine is considered as a compatible solute. While plants can accumulate considerable amounts of glycine betaine without any apparent deleterious effects, high levels of exogenous glycine betaine have been observed to cause leaf scorching in strawberry plants. Interestingly, abscisic acid (ABA), which plays a major role in cold acclimation of plants, can activate the BADH gene, which encodes for one of the enzymes involved in the synthesis of glycine betaine. Exogenous application of ABA has been shown to result in the accumulation of glycine betaine in the leaves of Arabidopsis and strawberry plants, leading to their increased freezing tolerance. Thus, it is reasonable to conclude that enhanced freezing tolerance induced by ABA in plants is perhaps mediated through the accumulation of glycine betaine in these plants.

Our studies have also shown that exogenous glycine betaine can induce pathogenesis-related proteins such as chitinase and thaumatin-like protein in beans leaves (unpublished results). Pathogenesis-related proteins, such as chitinase, â-1,3-glucanase and thaumatin-like protein, are typically induced in a wide variety of plants in response to pathogen attack and abiotic stresses, including water deficit and high salt levels. Their accumulation is a characteristic response to stress which is considered a defense mechanism, often leading to the development of a resistance against pathogens. However, their role in relation to abiotic stresses is not clearly understood. In response to salt stress, tobacco-cultured cells accumulate a basic protein called osmotin, which shares structural homology with a sweet-tasting protein thaumatin, a pathogenesis-related protein. The gene encoding osmotin has been cloned, and its expression and regulation have been studied extensively in tobacco. Accumulation of osmotin has been proposed to enhance salt tolerance in tobacco cells as well as pathogen defense in transgenic plants. Interestingly, Zhu et al. showed that a gene encoding osmotin-like protein in potato cells was induced by low temperature and ABA.

However, they found that the transgenic potato plants constitutively expressing this protein showed only improved disease resistance but not freezing tolerance. Similar results were noted in Arabidopsis plants, where freezing tolerance was not significantly affected in the transgenic Arabidopsis plants constitutively overexpressing the thaumatinlike proteins. However, recently one of the pathogenesis-related proteins, â1,3-glucanase, which accumulates during cold acclimation in spinach, has been shown to have a cryoprotective role in thylakoids against freeze-thaw injury. These results present the possibility that pathogenesis-related proteins may have a role in freezing tolerance of plants, but our understanding of these proteins in relation to abiotic stresses, especially cold, is too rudimentary to enable us to unequivocally implicate these proteins in the cold acclimation of plants. Undoubtedly, accumulation of these proteins is a complex plant response and the fact that many biotic and abiotic stresses produce a similar response in plants makes it difficult to identify their specific functional involvement in freezing tolerance.

Interestingly, perhaps their similarity to antifreeze proteins may shed some light on their relationship to the cold response. Pathogenesis-related proteins share structural similarity with antifreeze proteins which accumulate in a number of plants including monocots and dicots during cold acclimation. They are not, however, induced in chilling-sensitive plants, such as maize or tobacco. These proteins can bind to the ice crystals in the apoplast and perhaps modify the ice growth. Although pathogenesis-related proteins share structural similarities with the antifreeze proteins, they do not appear to modulate ice growth in plants. Considering the induction of pathogenesis-related proteins under a variety of biotic and abiotic stresses, it is possible that antifreeze proteins are isozymes or perhaps derived from pathogenesis-related proteins. However, to date, not enough is known to indicate the possible role that the antifreeze proteins or pathogenesis-related proteins may play in the cold acclimation of plants.

MOLECULAR BIOLOGY AND GENETIC CONTROL

Signal Transduction

When plants are exposed low temperatures for acclimation, the low-temperature signal obviously must be perceived by the cell and transduced to bring about a series of changes, including the activation of cold-responsive genes. Although the specific pathway of signal transduction is far from clear, certain elements have been proposed to play a role in the activation of these genes. One of the earliest responses to low temperature in plants is perhaps the oxidative burst, which involves a sharp transient increase of hydrogen peroxide in the cells and has been traditionally associated with pathogen attack. The oxidative burst appears to be involved in the development of a defense a mechanism against pathogens. It has also been shown to trigger an accumulation of calcium in the cells, which is considered as a second messenger in low-temperature signal transduction. This may involve influx of calcium from the cell wall to the cytosol by the activation of calcium channels in the plasma membrane.

Clear evidence of the involvement of calcium in signaling the cold response has come from blocking calcium influx in alfalfa cells. The results showed that this prevents the expression of cold-responsive genes and cold acclimation; conversely, by facilitating calcium influx into the cytosol, the cold-responsive genes could be activated. Calcium appears to trigger phosphorylation of preexisting proteins. Thus, the increased levels of phosphorylated proteins are essential for induction of cold acclimation and are believed to mediate the lowtemperature signal, which eventually leads to the activation of cold-responsive genes in alfalfa. Interestingly, the level of phosphorylation of specific protein has been shown to be sensitive to temperatures. The increased protein phosphorylation at low temperatures via suppression of protein phosphatase activity has been proposed as a mechanism for plants to sense the low-temperature signal. ABA is known to accumulate in a wide range of plants during cold acclimation, and exogenous application in a number of plant species can induce freezing tolerance in cell cultures and whole plants.

This seems to demonstrate the possible role of ABA in the cold acclimation of plants. In fact, ABA can substitute low temperatures for acclimation and even sometimes appears to be more effective than the acclimating low temperatures in inducing freezing tolerance. Thus, ABA has been hypothesized to be a part of signal transduction pathway in response to low temperatures, but a number of recent studies indicate that it may share only a part of the cold-transduction pathway. ABA-responsive genes are only some of the genes activated by cold, and it has been suggested that ABA- and cold-responsive genes may be regulated independently. Furthermore, the gene products in response to low temperatures are somewhat similar but not identical to those in response to ABA treatment. ABA has been known to cause plasma membrane depolarization, which allows for increased cytosolic calcium, considered as a part of signaling cascade.

However, it is not clear whether this is the case during low-temperature exposure as well or if it plays a role in signal transduction. In view of the recent evidence ABA may only share in the path of signal transduction for the cold response.

Genetic Regulation and Expression of Cold-Responsive Genes

Since the first proposal about 30 years ago that cold acclimation may be regulated by genes, there has been considerable work in characterizing the genetic expression and regulation of cold-responsive genes in a number of plants, including both monocots and dicots. Detailed and comprehensive overviews of the cold-responsive genes and their role in the freezing tolerance of plants have been presented by Hughes and Dunn and Thomashow. An increasing number of cold-responsive genes have been identified and cloned and their expressions have been characterized in a wide range of plants. Freezing tolerance in plants is a multigene trait; thus, one can expect a number gene products in plants in response to cold acclimation, and is often variable among species. Although a number of diverse proteins have been shown to be induced by low temperatures, many of them share similarities.

Many of the cold-induced proteins belong to a general group called late embryogenesis abundant (LEA) proteins, which typically accumulate in the late stages of seed development. They have been shown to accumulate in plants as well in response to ABA and drought and are, therefore, referred to as dehydrins. Dehydrins have conserved amino acid motifs characterized by a tract of serine residues followed by lysine-rich domains near the C terminus.

However, it should be noted that not all cold-inducible proteins belong to this family of proteins; for example, a number of novel proteins have been identified in response to cold in Arabidopsis.

Nonetheless, an important characteristic of many cold-inducible proteins is that they are hydrophilic, like traditional osmoprotectants, are heat-stable, and remain soluble upon boiling. Therefore, it is reasonable to expect that these proteins can exhibit a cryoprotective effect on membranes and enzymes. In fact, a novel cold-inducible protein (9.4 kD) in Arabidopsis plants has been found to be highly hydrophilic and to confer cold tolerance to chloroplast and protoplasts. The role of cold-inducible proteins in cold acclimation appears to be further substantiated by the observations that a number of cold-responsive genes in many species are also activated by such factors as drought and ABA, which are clearly known to induce freezing tolerance in plants.

However, the challenge still remains in that it is essential to characterize the role or function of many of the cold-inducible proteins in order to understand their relationship to freezing tolerance in plants. Most cold-responsive genes activated by water stress seem to involve ABA during cold acclimation. Studies with ABAinsensitive mutants of Arabidopsis suggest that an ABA-independent pathway may also exist for the expression these genes. In Arabidopsis, the products of cold-responsive genes (COR 15a and COR78) that are hydrophilic proteins are also induced by water stress. Recently, studies have shown the overlapping mechanisms of regulation of these genes by water deficit and low temperatures.

A cis-acting DNA regulatory element responsive to dehydration consisting of 5-bp core of C repeats (CCGAC) has been identified in the promoters of many cold-responsive genes and has been shown to activate transcription of coldresponsive genes upon exposure to low temperatures.

In addition, a 24-kDa protein from Arabidopsis, which binds to this regulatory element and can activate the transcription, has also been identified. When this transcription factor was overexpressed in transgenic Arabidopsis, a number of cold-responsive genes were expressed in unhardened plants, leading to a significant increase in cold tolerance.

This substantial increase in cold tolerance in Arabidopsis plants appears to be due to the activation of multiple cold-responsive genes. However, expression of just one cold-responsive gene (COR 15a) did not have much effect on the freezing tolerance of plants. Undoubtedly the expression of multiple cold-responsive genes is a significant step in providing direct evidence linking cold-responsive genes to the induction of freezing tolerance. This clearly offers a promising prospect for improving freezing tolerance in crop plants. Although the specific cause and mechanism of freezing injury are not clearly understood, there is considerable evidence that impairment of structural or functional integrity of the plasma membrane plays a key role in freezing injury.

Thus, enhanced ability to tolerate freezing in plants during cold acclimation has been attributed to membrane stability arising due to changes in lipid and fatty acid compositions. We have used a method involving the suppression of a major membrane-metabolizing enzyme, phospholipase D (PLD), to improve freezing tolerance in Arabidopsis plants (unpublished results). PLD hydrolyzes phospholipids in the membranes and is one of the first steps in the breakdown of membranes in a number of physiological processes in plants, including senescence, aging, wounding, and pathogen attack. The marked degradation of phospholipids and involvement of PLD have been demonstrated in relation to freezing injury in plants.

Recently, there is evidence that PLD activity may be related to the membrane stability of plants. Higher PLD activity was noted in chilling-sensitive maize than in chilling-tolerant maize, and the enzyme activity in membranes appears to increase due to the chilling injury. PLD has been shown to mediate the degradation of membrane phospholipids during senescence.

Thus, by inhibiting the PLD activity in plants, it was possible to retard the senescence process. Our studies have examined the role of phospholipase D (PLD) in the freezing tolerance of Arabidopsis plants and chilling tolerance of tobacco plants. The PLD activity was suppressed in transgenic tobacco plants with an antisense construct of cDNA of the PLD gene. The results show that transgenic plants with low PLD activity were chilling-tolerant compared to the untransformed plants. On the other hand, the transgenic plants with overexpression of the PLD gene were more chilling-sensitive than the untransformed plants. A similar response was observed in Arabidopsis plants, in which unhardened transgenic plants expressing the antisense PLD gene were more than twice as freezing tolerant as the untransformed plants. In addition, our results show that cold acclimation can induce significantly higher freezing-tolerance levels in transgenic plants with low PLD activity.

Leaves of cold-hardened transgenic Arabidopsis plants with a specific antisense construct (PLD 351) could survive about 13.5°C, while those of from cold-hardened untransformed plant survived 7.5°C. This shows that the suppression of PLD activity can markedly increase the freezing tolerance not only in unhardened plants but also in cold-hardened plants, suggesting that the low PLD activity can actually augment the freezing-tolerance potential in these plants. These results show that the suppression of PLD activity in antisense plants could enhance tolerance to low temperatures in both chilling-sensitive as well as cold-tolerant plants. The above studies also offer promising strategies to engineer crop plants with enhanced freezing tolerance, which would allow not only for their better winter survival but also for the extension of their cultivation to colder regions.

SUMMARY

Cold-tolerant plants are able to tolerate subzero temperatures and tissue water freezing to varying degrees. These plants tolerate only extracellular freezing, which is associated with cell dehydration and cell-volume reduction. When cells offer resistance to cell deformation, as happens in a number of plant species, they can develop negative pressures. Increasing cell tension predisposes cells to cavitation, which is associated with injury. Many woody temperate plants avoid ice formation in certain tissues until 40°C but are killed when supercooling is followed by ice formation. The supercooling characteristic has been shown to have a significant impact on the plant survival and the native geographical distribution of temperate plants.

Temperate plants show wide variation in their ability to survive cold; typically most of the freezing tolerance in plants is acquired as they acclimate in autumn. The fact that this characteristic is inducible by environmental conditions such as low nonfreezing temperatures has allowed researchers to investigate the mechanisms of induction of freezing tolerance in plants. Cold acclimation in plants is a complex response and is mediated by a number events, among which the oxidative burst appears to be one of the early steps in the signaling cascade. The oxidative burst can trigger cytosolic calcium, which is required for the protein phosphorylation and activation of certain cold-responsive genes. Presently, our understanding of low-temperature sensing and signal transduction in plants is, at best, too sketchy to allow us to identify the major elements of the signal-transduction pathway.

Integrity and stability of membranes appear to play a central role in relation to freezing injury and tolerance. Loss of membrane stability and function has been implicated in the freezing injury of plants. Also, major changes during cold acclimation in the membranes, especially in relation to their composition, have been proposed to increase membrane stability, which, in turn, can lead to increased freezing tolerance. Similarly, a number of other changes during cold acclimation in plants have been viewed as contributing to the membrane stability. For example, accumulating sugars, proline, and compatible solutes such as glycine betaine are osmoprotectants and are known to protect membranes, proteins, and organelles against dehydration and freezing. Recent studies have identified cold-inducible proteins that may have cryoprotective effects in plants. Many cold-responsive genes have been identified and their regulation and expression have been characterized in a wide range of plants. A common feature of many of these genes is that they are also activated by drought and ABA, indicating that these factors are involved in the cold response.

Many of the coldinducible proteins belong to the group of LEA proteins or dehydrins, which are highly hydrophilic and heat-resistant and may protect membranes against dehydration and freezing. Another family of proteins that accumulate in response to low temperatures are pathogenesis-related proteins. Although their role in the freezing tolerance of plants is unclear, they share structural similarity with antifreeze proteins. These proteins can modulate ice growth in plant tissues and are known to be synthesized in response to low temperatures. Direct evidence of cold-responsive genes in freezing tolerance comes from studies where many cold-responsive genes were induced by overexpressing a transcriptional factor. This can substitute for the cold-acclimation treatment and lead to the induction of freezing tolerance in plants. The results provide a valuable insight into the regulation and control of the freezing-tolerance trait and may offer a promising approach to improving it.

Another current strategy aimed at improving freezing tolerance is to modulate the membrane-catabolizing enzyme phospholipase D. Suppression of the activity of this enzyme shows significant potential in enhancing freezing tolerance. Preliminary results show that this approach may make it possible to increase freezing tolerance beyond the existing freezing-tolerance potential. Although our understanding of mechanisms of freezing tolerance and injury is limited, recent advances in the molecular biology of cold acclimation, freezing behavior, and injury are significant and are thus likely to expand the scope of future investigations, which can lead to many promising approaches in developing freezing-tolerant crops.

11

Effects of Humidity on Plant Growth

INTRODUCTION

Growth and development are influenced by humidity in and around the plant. Low air humidity creates an environment that enhances the potential for significant plant water loss. At the same time, regulating water loss through stomatal closure causes a reduction in carbon dioxide (CO_2) diffusion that limits growth. High air humidity, on the other hand, promotes environmental conditions favorable for disease development. Humidity refers to the amount of water vapor in the atmosphere. Globally, water vapor levels vary from almost zero in the arctic regions of the world to 4 or 5% of the atmospheric volume in the equatorial regions. The percentage of actual vapor in the atmosphere at any given time in relation to the maximum amount of vapor that can be held is termed relative humidity (RH).

RH = actual vapor pressure saturation vapor pressure

The actual vapor pressure is a measure of the amount of water vapor in a volume of air. As the amount of vapor pressure increases, the actual vapor pressure will increase. Saturation vapor pressure (also referred to as absolute humidity) is established when the number of water molecules evaporating is equal to the number of water molecules condensing. Relative humidity can change from location to location, day to day, and hour to hour. Relative humidity changes through evaporation and temperature. Water evaporation into the atmosphere changes the amount of vapor in the air. This process is slow, because it takes a considerable time for the water vapor to diffuse into the atmosphere. The amount of moisture held in the atmosphere is determined by temperature. As the air temperature rises, the relative humidity will drop.

Conversely, when the air temperature drops, the relative humidity increases, even though no water vapor has been added. During the night, if temperatures fall, relative humidity will increase, reaching 100%. If the temperature continues to fall, then the water vapor begins to condense and form dew. Relative humidity is not a useful measurement when describing plant transpiration. Transpiration is better described when differences in vapor pressure between the leaf and the atmosphere are used. Water vapor is expressed as either (a) the absolute humidity (mol or g mL"3 ; kg m"3), (b) specific humidity (kg kg"1), or (c) as vapor pressure (kPa). Transpiration occurs because a vapor pressure gradient forms between the leaf surface and the surrounding air. The relative humidity within the leaf or near the leaf surface is considered at or near 100%. Even if the canopy temperature is the same as the ambient temperature, rarely is the atmospheric relative humidity at 100%. Thus a vapor pressure gradient forms between the leaf and the atmosphere, which drives transpiration.

PENMAN EQUATION

Penman defined potential evapotranspiration as "the amount of water transpired in unit time by a short green crop, completely shading the ground, of uniform height and never short of water." Using this definition, he developed the following equation for calculating potential evapotranspiration (2,3): Jn î =1+ LE where Jn = net radiation LE = latent heat es = saturation vapor pressure (absolute humidity) at the surface e = vapor pressure of the air above the surface ea = saturated vapor pressure above the surface î = psychrometric constant (relates wet-bulb and dry-bulb thermometers to vapor pressure) = slope of the saturated vapor pressure versus temperature curve.

The potential evapotranspiration is calculated by measuring net radiation, temperature, vapor pressure, and wind velocity above the crop canopy. Monteith modified the Penman equation to take into account vapor transfer from slightly less than saturated surfaces. This modification, and incorporation of a canopy resistance variable to account for canopy resistance vapor transfer, is known as the Penman-Monteith equation. From these equations a vapor pressure gradient between the plant surface and the surrounding atmosphere is calculated. The greater the deficit between the plant surface, which is at or near 100 relative humidity and the atmospheric relative humidity, the greater the transpiration.

STOMATES

The amount of water being driven from the leaf to the atmosphere, as dictated by the vapor pressure deficit, is governed by stomates. Stomates play a dual role, since they are also the port of entry for CO_2. Stomatal openings are governed by the CO_2 concentrations in the intercellular spaces and not at the leaf surface or in the stomatal pore. If CO_2 concentrations in the leaf are low, stomates will open. Conversely, if CO_2 concentrations in the leaf are high, stomates will close. The dual role of stomates leads to interactions between CO_2 and vapor pressure. Stomatal conductance is a measure of CO_2 and water vapor into and out of the leaf via stomates. Conductance is used instead of resistance because conductance is directly proportional to photosynthesis (CO_2 diffusion) or transpiration. Bunce demonstrated, in a series of short-term studies under controlled and field conditions, that C_4 plants were less sensitive to low humidity than C3 plants even at vapor pressure deficits of 4.5 kPa in the field. Due to the greater CO_2 levels found in the leaf tissue of C4 plants, stomatal conductance had little effect on photosynthesis.

The interaction between CO_2 and vapor pressure deficit depends on the situation. For example, stomatal closures in plant species that grow well in arid regions with adequate soil moisture, like date palm (Phoenix dactylifera), are insensitive to vapor pressure deficit. Under desert conditions, CAM plants open their stomates during the night and close them during the day, which is the opposite of the occurrence for most plants. For CAM plants, the advantage of stomatal closure during the day is that it minimizes water loss, and then closure during the less stressful nighttime open to fix CO_2. Stomatal conductance is governed by other factors, such as light and plant water potentials, besides CO_2 and vapor pressure. Vapor pressure interacts with both light and plant water potentials. In the following sections, stomatal governance by light and leaf water potential is discussed, with attention directed toward the interactions with water vapor.

Stomatal Evolution and Structure

The earliest land plants were astomatous, with thick cuticle around their aerial organs. The lack of stomates, along with a thick cuticle minimized any plant water loss. These plants, however, had a low diffusion rate of carbon dioxide (CO_2). The lack of CO_2 diffusion for photosynthesis probably contributed to the slow growth and development in these early plants. Today, there is a diversity of astomatous plants, which are classified into two groups. The first group contains those species that never possessed stomates, like the gametophytes of bryophytes and lichens. The second group contains plants that were stomatous at one time but developed effective astomatous characteristics. In general, these types of plants are aquatic or parasitic in nature. Many aquatic flowering plants are astomatous when submerged, having little need for gaseous diffusion. Some aquatic flowering plants have dysfunctional stomates that remain permanently open. In some instances, parasitic flowering plants have lost their stomates or have dysfunctional ones. For example, in Neottia nidus-avis, the guard cells have fused shut. Early land plants and stomata most likely evolved during periods of high CO_2 concentrations in the atmosphere. Subsequent periods of low atmospheric CO_2 may have driven evolutionary forces toward high stomatal densities in plants like horsetails, ferns, conifers, and angiosperms. Stomates evolved initially for gaseous diffusion, and then as a mechanism to regulate water loss. Structurally, Esau considers the stomatal area of the leaf to include the guard cells and the stomatal pore. The stomatal area generally accounts for 1% of the leaf surface (<"100 stomates per millimeter). The actual number of stomates per given area varies among species. Green and coworkers calculated the number of stomates, both adaxial and abaxial, for 10 different turfgrass species. The stomatal density was greater on the adaxial than the abaxial leaf sides for most of the grasses. Stomates on the adaxial side ranged from 68 stomates per millimeter for tall fescue (Festuca arundinacea) to 203 stomates per millimeter for hard fescue (Festuca longifolia). No stomates were present on the abaxial side of hard fescue, sheep fescue (Festuca ovina spp. vulgaris), chewings fescue (Festuca rubra spp. commutata), or rough bluegrass (Poa trivialis).

No correlation between stomatal density and the evapotranspiration rate of the grass species was found. This would be expected, given the similar boundary layer among the species. Stomatal size varies depending on whether a plant is grown under optimum moisture levels or under moisture stress. Spence and colleagues studied stomatal size and guard-cell turgor of Vicia faba plants watered twice weekly and plants watered once a week. The plants watered twice weekly never showed wilt symptoms, while those watered once weekly showed wilting symptoms before each watering. The well-watered guard cells were either short and wide or long and thin, with the average size of 40.4 and 46.1 μm, respectively. The water-stressed guard cells were significantly smaller, measuring 37.4 μm. The geometry of the water-stressed guard cell allowed the stomatal pore to remain open at lower guard-cell turgor pressures relative to the surrounding epidermal cells.

Effects of Light on Stomates

Light plays an important role in the governance of stomatal opening. Illumination of the guard cells increases the synthesis of malate and uptake of potassium and chlorine, which results in swelling of the guard cells, thus increasing the pore opening. Blue light is more effective than red light in governing stomatal opening. In grasses, blue light elicits an initial rapid increase in transpiration, followed by a second slower increase. Blue light presumably creates an electrical gradient flux of potassium in the guard cell through hydrogen extrusion and ATP-dependent membrane hyperpolarization. Although red light is not as effective as blue light, continuous background red light enhances the blue light affect.

The magnitude of the blue light effect on stomatal opening is sensitive to CO_2 concentration and vapor pressure. Assmann, working with the plants Paphiopedilum harrisianum and Commelina communis, found that a reduction in intercellular CO_2 concentrations enhanced the blue light response. Assmann found in both plants that increasing vapor pressure deficit, from 0.34 to 0.59 kPA, diminished the stomatal response from blue light. The effects of the vapor pressure deficit were greater than those of the corresponding reduction in intercellular CO_2.

Temporary reduction in light influences stomatal conductance in a plant community. Plants that are continually exposed to short-term reductions in light (passing cloud cover) experience a reduction in photosynthesis and in some cases stomatal closure. Knapp and Smith compared herbaceous and woody plants in a subalpine community with regard to photosynthesis and water loss. The herbaceous species had higher photosynthesis and transpiration rates, lower leaf water potentials, and more rapid stomatal closure during shade than did the woody species. This response would indicate that herbaceous species maximized overall water use efficiency while the woody species with weaker stomatal responses maximized carbon gain. In a later study, Fay and Knapp evaluated the stomatal responses of two tallgrass prairie C3 plants, plains wild indigo (Baptisia bracteata) and annual sunflower (Helianthus annuus).

Although both plants would be expected to perform similarly to the herbaceous plants in their previous study, these two plants inhabit the prairie at different times. Plains wild indigo inhabits the prairie during the cool, wet season while the annual sunflower prefers the hot, dryer season. Wild indigo had no stomatal response to shade and lower photosynthetic capacity, stomatal conductance, and transpiration compared to annual sunflower.

This would be expected given that plains wild indigo experiences little water stress during the time it inhabits the prairie. Annual sunflower, however, had rapid stomatal closure during shade as well as higher photosynthetic capacity, stomatal conductance, and transpiration rates—all characteristics of a plant that experiences some period of water stress. Temporal shade reduces carbón gain and water loss in C3 and C4 plants. In a comparison of two row crops, C4 sorghum and C3 soybean, stomatal movement in response to temporary shade was much more apparent in soybean than sorghum, presumably due to the lower water use rate.

In both species the short-term shade (5 min) at 300 to 400 µmol m”2 s”1 photosynthetic photon flux density reduced photosynthesis, leaf temperature stomatal conductance, transpiration, and water use efficiency. Once the plants were reilluminated, photosynthesis was delayed. When Fay and Knapp compared sorghum with a native C4 grass, eastern gamagrass (Tripsacum dactyloides), responses to temporary shade were similar. Thus, domesticated and native plant responses to temporary shade are similar.

DEFICITS IN VAPOR PRESSURE AND XYLEM CAVITATION

In response to large vapor pressure deficits, many plant species close their stomates. The conditions most favorable for closure are low air humidity and high leaf temperature. In a review article, Grange and Hand point out that humidities between 1.0 and 0.2 kPa have little effect on the physiology and development of horticultural crops. Vapor pressure deficits lower than these lead to water stress, while higher values promote biotic problems like disease. In the studies reviewed here, vapor pressure deficits ranged from 0.5 to 6.0 kPa. Idso et al. reported, under nonirrigated conditions, vapor pressure deficits of 2 to 6 kPa. A number of studies reported vapor pressure deficits greater than 3.0 kPa. Given the range of vapor pressure deficits that a plant faces, rapid water loss due to transpiration can occur. In response to vapor pressure deficits, water moves upward under tension through the plant in conduits collectively known as the xylem. The water tension in the xylem increases as soil moisture decreases and transpiration increases. If the tension increases to a point where the water breaks in the xylem vessels and tracheids, water vapor and air begin to enter the xylem.

This process, whereby water continuity is broken, is termed cavitation. As the xylem vessels and tracheids continue to fill with air and the hydraulic conductivity decreases or ceases, embolism occurs. Cavitation and embolism are often associated with tall, woody materials, where water transport through the xylem travels great distances. Embolism is triggered by air aspirated into the xylem vessel through pores in the wall. Once air is in the vessel, it disrupts water flow. As air fills and embolism occurs, the process can spread to other vessels. Generally larger-diameter vessels and tracheids are most vulnerable to embolism. The pressure necessary to induce embolism varies depending on the species.

Most of the reported threshold values for xylem embolism in woody plants fall between "2.0 and "3.0 MPa. Some plants have xylem embolism at greater or lesser pressures. The importance of stomates in CO_2 diffusion is critical, yet due to the catastrophic nature of embolism, the primary purpose of stomatal closure may be to regulate water loss so as to avoid xylem cavitation. From an evolutionary point of view, stomates would have had to appear first since xylem cavitation would limit how tall a plant could grow. Woodward suggested that increased stomatal density enhanced the evolutionary development of plants by preventing xylem cavitation, resulting in longer xylem pathways in taller and more competitive genotypes.

LEAF WATER POTENTIAL

Moisture deficits in the plant elicit a number of detrimental responses. Hsiao outlined the sequence of events that occurs once moisture stress occurs. Cell growth is the most sensitive to a drop in water potential. A slight decrease in the leaf water potential ("0.1 MPa) causes a reduction in cell growth, resulting in a reduction in shoot and root growth. For this reason, numerous plants have been observed to grow mainly at night, when water loss is minimal. As water potentials become more negative, protein synthesis, nitrate reductase level, growth-regulating substances [abcisic acid (ABA) and cytokinin], CO_2 assimilation, respiration, protein accumulation, and proline accumulation are all affected.

Leaf water potentials in some plants may fluctuate during the day based on vapor pressure deficits and soil moisture, while other plants maintain constant leaf water potentials even under limited soil moisture. Anisohydric behavior is a term used to describe plants that have changing leaf water potential over a given period of time. Plants that exhibit anisohydric behavior include the herbaceous species wheat, sunflower, soybean, subterranean clover, barley, and the woody species of almond and peach. Isohydric plant behavior is the ability to maintain leaf water potentials at a constant value in the presence of changing soil moisture and vapor pressure deficits. Plants that exhibit isohydric behavior include the herbaceous species maize, pea, and sugar cane and the woody species poplar and lupin. Tardieu and Simonneau compared sunflower (anisohydric) and maize (isohydric) behavior during flowering under various irrigation regimes. Predawn leaf water potentials of sunflower were dependent on the moisture treatment.

Higher leaf water potentials were found in the plants under full irrigation compared to the leaf water potentials of the mildly water-stressed plants, which had higher leaf water potentials than the severely water-stressed plants. As the day progresses, stomatal conductance decreases following changes in light energy (photosynthetic photon flux density). Thus, stomatal closure provides control against dehydration, but fluctuation in leaf water potential occurred in response soil moisture and evaporative demand. The response patterns to these fluctuations were similar across the moisture stress treatments. When Tardieu and Simonneau looked at maize, leaf water potentials stabilized during midday for the three water-stress treatments even under high evaporative demand and changing soil moisture. The decrease in stomatal conductance was correlated with ABA levels.

No relationship between ABA and stomatal conductance was found with sunflower. Tradieu and Simonneau postulated that isohydric behavior is linked between hydraulic and chemical information (ABA), while anisohydric behavior lacks this interaction. Interestingly, commonly used classifications of species like monocyte versus dicot or C3 versus C4 were not associated with anisohydric and isohydric plants. Although leaf water potential is often used as an indicator of water stress, stomatal conductance is closely correlated with soil water availability. Naor and coworkers correlated stomatal conductance with stem water potential ($r^2 = 0.90$) as a better indicator of water stress than leaf water potential for apple. This study was followed up with additional field studies with apple, nectarine, and grapevine trees under various irrigation treatments and found similar correlation between stem water potential and stomatal conductance.

NUTRIENT DEFICIENCIES

The major plant nutrients except for calcium are not associated with humidity. Calcium-related disorders have been reported for many fruit and vegetable crops. Common calcium disorders include "tipburn" of strawberry, chicory, and lettuce leaves; "blackheart" of cauliflower, celery, and brussel sprouts; and "blossomend rot" of tomato and bell pepper. Calcium depends almost entirely on the xylem for distribution in the plant. If the water supply is reduced or eliminated to sections of the plant, localized calcium deficiencies occur. Humidity levels around and in the plant influence the likelihood of calcium disorders. Enclosed leaves are usually the most susceptible to calcium deficiencies due to low transpiration rates. Root pressure flow appears to be more important than transpiration in supplying calcium to enclosed leaves. Bradfield and Guttridge, working with tipburn of strawberry, found that nontranspiring leaves depend on water flow from root pressure to supply calcium. High relative humidities at night enhance root pressure, providing calcium to needed areas of the plant.

The presence of guttation is a sign of adequate root pressure. After leaf emergence, calcium movement to the leaves is promoted by dry days, thus indicating that calcium is supplied by transpirational flow. In similar studies, high humidity at night and low humidity during the day was confirmed to alleviate calcium disorders of cabbage and cauliflower. The time of year does not appear to be critical to fruit-associated disorders. Cline and Hanson, working on bitter pit of apple, determined that calcium movement to the fruit was largely due to xylem flow regardless of the season.

Calcium disorders are often independent of the calcium levels in the soil or other portions of the plant. Attempts at alleviating calcium disorders through supplemental calcium [$Ca\ (NO_3)_2$] fertilization have had inconsistent results. In greenhouse studies with blossom-end rot of bell peppers, Schon found that calcium sprays decreased the calcium disorder but also decreased yield. Alexander and Clough treated blossom-end rot of bell peppers with calcium and reported a 50% reduction in yield.

Antitranspirants have had little effect on reducing calcium disorders without also reducing yields. Recently, researchers have looked at combinations of calcium sprays or applications with spun-bonded polypropylene row covers. The row covers reduce solar radiation and lower leaf temperature. Alexander and Clough looked at spunbonded row covers and calcium fertilization on bell peppers grown in the field. They found that sunscald and bottom-end rot were reduced with row covers. Calcium in combination with row covers reduced bottom-end rot.

MANAGING WATER LOSS

Vapor-pressure deficits and stomatal regulation are measures for determining drought-tolerant species. Canopy temperatures are used as an indicator of plant water use and yield. Increases in leaf temperature would indicate decreased transpirational cooling from stomatal closure. Chaudhuri et al. evaluated sorghum genotypes and 42 millet genotypes in a line-source irrigation system. By measuring canopy temperature and air temperature and then regressing these data on the observed vapor pressure deficit, Chaudhuri et al. determined the drought tolerance of the genotypes.

Genotypes with a mean temperature greater than the average mean temperature for all genotypes were considered warm. Warm genotypes and genotypes less sensitive to changes in vapor pressure deficits produced viable heads under the more extreme drought treatments. The concept of warm genotypes being more drought tolerant appears to be species-specific. Warm soybean genotypes were found to be no more droughttolerant than cooler genotypes.

The growth stage of certain plants plays an important role in stomatal sensitivity. Sorghum stomates are quite sensitive to changes in leaf water potentials during vegetative growth and are insensitive during reproductive development.

The regulation of stomatal conductance through management or chemical applications could potentially reduce water loss during periods of high vaporpressure deficits. Agronomic practices like row spacing influence stomatal activity.

Peanuts grown in narrow 30-cm-spacing north-south rows lost less water due to evapotranspiration than peanuts grown 90-cm-spacing north-south rows or 30-cm rows planted in an east-west direction. An explanation for this was provided in work done by McCauley and colleagues, who found that water loss was less in narrow north-south rows because of a reduction in net radiation, and the aerodynamic roughness of the plant canopy reduced the prevailing south wind effect.

In later studies, narrow-row plantings of peanuts were observed to close their stomates earlier in the day than wide-row-planted peanuts. Regarding yield, the closer row plantings produced higher yields for peanuts and sorghum.

Early closing of stomates has been attributed to morphological characteristics of the plants growing in the narrow rows (thinner, smaller leaves and longer internodes). Similar morphological features of high shoot density, low leaf area, and narrow leaf texture are associated with C4 turfgrasses with low evapotranspiration rates. Antitranspirants are chemicals that induce stomatal closure to reduce transpiration. It has been argued that there is no need for antitranspirants because plants close their stomata in response to water stress.

However, given the habit of growing plants outside of their native habitat, antitranspirants have been widely tested. The two major types of antitranspirants are the stomata inhibitors and the film-forming compounds. Stomata inhibitors are synthetic substances that induce stomatal closure by directly affecting the stomatal mechanism.

Many of these types of products are plant-growth regulators, herbicides, and fungicides. Film-forming compounds are products that, when applied to the leaf's surface, act as a physical barrier to water vapor. These compounds form a film that obstructs the stomatal pore and reduces transpiration. Film-forming compounds tend to have a selective permeability to water and carbon dioxide, causing a greater reduction in photosynthesis than transpiration and producing a poorer production ratio. Reductions in production yields are associated with limited antitranspirant use in row crops.

HIGH HUMIDITY AND LEAF WETNESS

Studies looking at the effect of high humidity around the plant are few. Generally, high humidity has little positive effect on many horticultural crops. However, there have been reports on tuber crops that high relatively humidity can increase yield. Wheeler et al. grew three potato cultivars at 20°C at two vapor-pressure deficits, 0.40 kPa (85% relative humidity) and 1.15 kPa (51% relative humidity); they measured dry weights of leaf, stem, total plant, and tuber. No difference was found in total dry weight of the plants between humidity treatments, but plants grown under 0.40 kPa produced higher tuber yields.

Similar results have been required with sweet potato. Additional research has reported on field-grown crops of lettuce, wheat, and sugar beet, stating that increasing humidity created positive growth responses. Free moisture on the leaf causes detrimental growth and yield loss by providing conditions favorable for pathogens to infect the host and establish themselves in it. Rainfall, irrigation, and dew are the major sources of free moisture on the leaf.

Dew is of interest here because of its association with water vapor. Dew forms from condensation of water vapor on the leaf and from guttation water forced out of hydathodes by root pressure. The temperature at which moisture condenses on the leaf is referred to as the dew point.

If the dew point is above 0°C, then dew forms; if the temperature is below 0°C, frost forms. The maximum condensation rates for plants growing under soil—and atmospheric— saturated conditions is approximately 0.07 to 0.09 mm h"1. The amount of dew accumulated is linearly related to the duration. Conditions favorable for guttation are high soil moisture levels with corresponding high humidity (low transpiration).

In most row crops and orchards, condensation would be the primary source of dew. However in short, dense canopies with minimal wind movement, guttation could be a significant component of dew. Williams and coworkers reported that on a short cut (19-mm) creeping bentgrass fairway, guttation could account for 33% of the total dew on the plant canopy. Leaf wetness refers to the period of time where free moisture is present on the leaf blade.

Fungal pathogens vary in their dependence on free moisture for infection and sporulation. Oomycetes and chrtridiales are extremely dependent on free moisture for infection and development, while free moisture plays a minor role with the powdery mildews. Most fungal pathogens fall between these two extremes. In general, spore production requires longer periods of leaf wetness than the duration of free moisture needed for infection. The necessary period for wetting varies depending on the pathogen. In a review article by Huber and Gillespie, they reported that the wetting periods required for several foliar pathogens ranged from 0.5 to 140 hr. In general, increasing periods of leaf wetness increase the severity of infection. From a disease-management perspective, minimizing the period of leaf wetness could reduce spore loads and/or disease severity.

The pathogen downy mildew (Bremia lactucae) sporulates at night; spore release begins at sunrise. If the leaf wetness period continues 3 to 4 hr after sunrise, the spores that were released reinfect lettuce tissue.

Reducing the leaf wetness period after sunrise could potentially minimize the severity of downy mildew of lettuce. The concept of reduced disease through a reduction of the leaf wetness period has been demonstrated.

Early-morning dew removal from a creeping bentgrass golf course fairway by mowing reduced the severity of dollar spot (Sclerotinia homoeocarpa). Interrupting the leaf wetness period may also affect the infection cycle of certain diseases. Alternaria linicola is a pathogen of linseed that is sensitive to interruptions in leaf wetness. Dry interruptions of wet periods, whether short (2 hr) or long (12 hr) in duration, occurring sometime between 2 and 6 hr after inoculation stopped conidia germination.

Monitoring the length of leaf wetness is a practical means of timing fungicide applications. Fungicide applications for downy mildew of lettuce were reduced by 67% relative to a standard calendar-based schedule, with no difference in disease intensity, based on the presence of leaf wetness at 1000 hr.

Dainello and Jones made fungicide applications for the control of white rust (Albugo occidentalis) on spinach based on leaf wetness periods. They found that if they made fungicide applications of metalaxyl based on a 12-hr continuous leaf wetness period—as opposed to a 7-day preventative schedule—they required five fewer sprays and still provided the same level of control. On cantaloup, a delay in fungicide applications until leaf wetness periods were of 8 hr duration gave equivalent control, with a one-third reduction in number of applications compared to applications based on crop phenology.

CONCLUSIONS

Balancing CO_2 diffusion and water loss has been an ongoing battle since the first land plants appeared. Rapid water loss through transpiration, driven by vapor pressure deficits, can lead to plant stress. However, by regulating water loss through stomatal closure, plant growth and thus yield is decreased by a lack of photosynthesis. Agronomically, as we continue to try to grow crops in harsher environments of high transpiration and little moisture, further efforts to understand water vapor effects on plant growth and crop yield will be needed in the future.

12

Plant Response to the Wind Environment: Heat and Mass Exchange

INTRODUCTION

Plants are living, synthesizing, growing, respiring, and decaying in a fluid that is generally in a state of motion. This air in motion exchanges momentum, heat, gases, and particulates between canopy elements and/or between the canopy layer and the atmosphere. Physical, biological, and chemical processes that control the rate of turbulent transfer are intimately coupled and atmospheric environmental conditions influence biochemical sources and sinks of H_2O, CO_2, O_2, O_3, terpenes, and isoprenes. In turn, the presence of vegetation in the flow modifies environmental conditions through its influence on turbulence production. Vegetation–atmosphere transfer of momentum and scalar entities (heat, H_2O, CO_2, O_3 and atmospheric pollutants) influences environmental conditions and processes, including the energy and water balance of the surface, vegetation temperatures, the deposition and reentrainment of dust and other particles, and wind damage to forests and crops. Investigations of the deposition of gases and particulates to a crop

or to a forest stand or of the efficiency of a herbicide or pesticide spray operation on forests and crops, for example, demand detailed information concerning the canopy flow and the mechanisms by which the vegetation and the free atmosphere above are coupled.

The present review examines the influence of wind on heat and mass exchange between the canopy layer and the atmosphere at the plant element scale. Specifically, it reviews the influence of the flowfield on the exchange of heat and mass between plant organs, mostly leaves and the atmosphere. To do so, it details the effect of the wind on the leaf boundary layer and on the stomatal resistance for a wide range of environmental conditions, with special consideration given to the effect of wind modification on plant response in opentop chambers.

LBL RESPONSE TO THE WIND ENVIRONMENT

LBL Thickness: Definition and Relevance

One of the most significant effects of the wind on plant response can be attributed to the action of the wind in the immediate local environment of the leaf, the LBL. The crucial importance of the LBL for leaf-atmosphere processes arises from its role as a buffer between the leaf and the atmosphere. Gases, heat, and momentum are exchanged between the atmosphere and the leaf through this layer, with the properties of the layer thus largely dictating the exchange rate of gases and momentum. The leaf boundary layer (LBL) is largely responsible for the leaf wetness duration from both rain water and dew. A thick boundary layer retards the leaf surface water evaporation while a thin boundary layer leads to a short wetness duration, since much of the water droplet height at the onset of the drying cycle protrudes outside a compressed LBL. This local leaf environment—characterized by an abrupt transition of temperature, moisture, and wind conditions between the leaf and the atmosphere—also determines the onset of spore germination and pathogen development. By the same token, this layer acts as a microhabitat to insects, providing a calm, warm, and moist shelter. But just what constitutes the LBL? And how does this influence plant response?

The LBL represents the shallow air layer in direct contact with the leaf. This layer develops from the interaction between the leaf surface and the air flowing above it. Close to the leaf surface, the wind speed is reduced by the friction between the leaf surface and the air, and it is this region that defines the boundary layer thickness. Typically, the LBL includes the region from the surface to that streamline where the wind velocity is 99% of the free stream velocity u. The thickness of the LBL is dictated by a wide variety of factors, including the organ size, shape, pubescence, fluttering, angle of attack between the local wind and the leaf, sheltering from neighboring leaves, position in the canopy layer, and its link with canopy scale turbulent events.

Leaves having a thin LBL are closely coupled with the atmosphere and respond quickly to environmental changes. A thicker LBL has a higher resistance using the analogy to Ohm's law, and this leads to reduced exchanged rates of heat and mass. (Mass in this context designates gases such as carbon dioxide, ozone, terpenes and isoprenes, water vapor and particulates.) Since the boundary layer thickness ä governs the rate of diffusion of heat and mass between the leaf and the surrounding air, it is thus one of the most important variables in dictating the exchange rate between the vegetation and the atmosphere.

Exchange of Gases and Heat Across the LBL: Relationships to Flow Variables

The heat and gaseous exchanges between the leaf and the atmosphere are governed by molecular diffusion through the LBL. For heat or gaseous transport across a laminar BL, the flux rate F equals the diffusion coefficient times the concentration gradient as described by Fick's first law for molecular diffusion. This concept is borrowed from molecular diffusion theory, where the diffusion coefficient is a function of the product of the mean free path between the molecules and their exchange velocity, which is determined by the mean kinetic energy of the molecules. Fick's law is commonly applied in an integrated form to describe the transport to/from leaves—e.g., of heat H and mass Fi : H = ñcp ht (Ts “ Ta) Fi = hi (cis “ ci)

where ñ is the density of air, cp the specific heat capacity of air at constant pressure, and ht and hi are the conductances for heat and for mass respectively. Note that g is sometimes used to designate conductances and is used interchangeably. (Ts “ Ta) and (cis “ ci) represent the temperature and concentration difference between the organ surface and the atmosphere. The conductance, the inverse of the boundary layer resistance rb for a laminar BL, is the ratio of the diffusion coefficient to ä. In addition, the mass transfer rate decreases with increasing BL thickness. This exchange rate is higher for leaves outdoors, since turbulence levels are usually considerably higher than those in wind tunnels, where turbulence levels are often of the order of tens of percent. In addition, leaves inside canopies are subject to turbulence intensities of values as large as several 100%. The flow highturbulence levels present in this natural environment are thought to be responsible for wide discrepancies between direct determination of BL conductances/ resistances with predicted values. For a turbulent BL and in turbulent conditions, the diffusion coefficient is replaced by a turbulent diffusivity, which is typically four to six orders of magnitude greater than its molecular diffusivity counterpart. In turbulent conditions, the leaf is more closely coupled to the atmosphere, since in that case the higher mixing (or lower BL resistance) reduces concentration differences of heat, water vapor, oxygen, ozone, and carbon dioxide between the leaf and the atmosphere.

This often acts, in a daytime scenario, to alleviate the heat load on sunlit leaves. It is sometimes more convenient to refer to resistances instead of conductances, as in cases where resistances are used in series, in analogy to electrical networks. For example, the total resistance to water-vapor exchange through a plant can be naturally expressed as the sum of the stomatal resistance, the LBL resistance, and the aerodynamic resistance. A general relationship between the LBL conductance and wind speed may be estimated using traditional engineering expressions derived for heat transfer between a plate and the overlying laminar free stream. [Several prominent work have detailed, in more or less technical terms, many of the concepts reviewed below.] This convenient approach facilitates comparison of transfer rates between different shapes and sizes of objects by expressing the resistance as function of dimensionless numbers: the Nusselt number Nu and the Sherwood number Sh. The Nusselt and Sherwood numbers are the ratio of the characteristic dimension to the equivalent BL thickness for heat and mass transfer. The conductance/boundary layer resistance to heat and mass transfer may be written in terms of its Nu and Sh as

hH = 1 ê = Nu rH d and hM = 1 d = Sh rM D

where ê is the thermal diffusivity of air, d is the characteristic dimension of the leaf in the direction of flow, and D is the diffusivity. In forced convection, heat loss is described as

Nu """ Pr m Ren

where Pr = í/ê is the Prandtl number, í is the kinematic viscosity, Re = ud/í is the Reynolds number, and u is the mean wind speed. For laminar flow over a flat plate (used as a leaf analog), the Nusselt number varies locally along the plate and when averaged over a plate, using the Pollhausen equation is

Nu = 0.664 Pr 0.33 Re0.5

For micrometeorological applications in air, where Pr = 0.71, a more general expression is

Nu = A Ren

where A and n are constants that depend on the geometry type (48). An analogous relationship exists for mass transfer in forced convection. For laminar flow over a flat plate, the Sherwood number is

Sh = 0.664 Sc0.33 Re0.5

Here Sc = í/D is the Schmidt number. For heat transfer during forced convection, the ratio of heat resistance to water vapor resistance is approximately 0.93, while the ratio of heat resistance to carbon dioxide resistance is approximately 1.32. During light wind or no wind conditions, heat loss/gain occurs by free convection. In this case, the Nusselt number is a function of the Prandtl number, where the Grashof number Gr represents the ratio of the buoyancy forces times an inertial force to the square of the viscous forces. The Grashof number is determined by agd 3 (Ts " Ta) í2 where a is the coefficient of thermal expansion. In conditions with large Gr numbers, free convection is vigorous, as buoyancy and inertial forces stimulating air circulation are much greater than the viscous forces that inhibit it. The distinction between forced and free convection may be determined by comparing Gr to the square of Re. Forced convection dominates when Gr Re2 .

In the natural environment however, the distinction between forced and free convection is usually based on average wind speed and is sometimes blurred. For example, the heat transfer for a 5-cm leaf that is 5æ% C warmer than the surrounding air is expected to be governed by forced convection when u > 1 ms"1 . For 0.1 < u < 0.5 ms"1 , heat transport typically occurs by a mixed regime of both free and forced convection (48). However, there is some uncertainty associated with the determination of free convection and the resulting use of the Gr number when predicted by the average wind speed. The turbulence-induced fluttering may cause the forced convection mechanism to dominate over free convection for a particular mean wind speed.

Another potential effect of the turbulent flow interacting with leaf surfaces is the generation of a turbulent BL. Heat exchange across a turbulent BL has a different dependence on Re than that of a laminar BL. In forced convection, the Nusselt number for flat plates with a turbulent BL is

Nu = 0.036 Pr 0.33 Re0.8

Thus, the conductance increases more rapidly with increasing wind speed for turbulent BL flows (as compared to laminar conditions). Several studies have found that the laminar theory is valid for leaves in canopy flow as reported in the extensive review on the subject. Other studies suggest that the Re number exponent should lie between 0.5 and 0.8 to account for the variation in the BL structure across a leaf's surface. By contrast, other studies have found the Re exponent for heat transfer from leaf models to be 0.84—i.e. in excess of 0.8.

Development of the LBL with Position on the Leaf

The response of leaves to the wind environment is also a function of the position on the leaf. The development of an idealized LBL may be viewed initially as a laminar free stream flow over a rigid smooth flat plate. Near the leading edge of the plate is a laminar region where the local ä is often taken to be:

ä = 1.72 (íx/u)

where í is the kinematic viscosity of air and x the distance from the leading edge of the plate. Thus, ä increases progressively with distance from the leading edge, with eventual transition to turbulence as the flow becomes unstable and breaks up into turbulent eddies. While, for laminar conditions over flat plates, ä increases as x 0.5, ä increases as x 0.8 for a turbulent BL.

The BL development for the upper surface of leaves in other studies confirmed the earlier work for flat plates. A recent reexamination of published empirical results may shed new light on our understanding of the physics of the LBL. The conventional semiempirical formula for the LBL resistance may have to be corrected to take into account the diffusion in the layer immediately near the leaf (the superstomatal air layer). In this case, the convective boundary layer for leaves is treated as not being in direct contact with the surface, which calls for a correction to the application of the traditional formula to estimate the surface concentration. BL resistance results from published literature, when reexamined to include the pore size and the surface number of stomata, may have been in relative error, up to a maximum (20%) in conditions of low humidity, high wind, small leaf, and elliptic ports.

Such recent studies appear to be an improvement over the laminar Re0.5 relationship and turbulent Re0.8 relationships based on flat plates. The transition from a laminar to a turbulent LBL occurs when the Reynolds number Re = ux/í is of the order of 104 to 105 . Thus higher wind speeds cause the transition to occur closer to the leading edge of the leaf with the implication that in the presence of a BL thickness gradient along the distance from the leaf leading edge (x), the transfer rate is local on the leaf. This is of special interest given that the transfer efficiency is linked directly to the magnitude of the wind speed, as higher wind-speed levels cause a thinning of the boundary layer, or in the case of higher turbulence levels, a periodic wipeout of the boundary layer.

Consequently, the plant response to the wind environment and related exchange rates for carbon uptake, evapotranspiration, ozone damage, and isoprene emissions observed in the outdoor wind environment are substantially higher than those predicted for the laminar BL theory.

Wind-Induced Fluttering, Leaf Structure, and Leaf Sheltering on LBL

The behavior of real leaves in the field differs from idealized flat plates in a laminar free stream. A consequence of both the deviation of leaf shape and motion from the flat plate is that the thickness of the leaf BL ä, determined empirically “ as (íx/u), is smaller than the idealized BL thickness value. Such differences, characterized by higher BL conductances, arise not only from the structural features of leaves that interact with the natural turbulent flow but also from greater fluttering. The transition from laminar to turbulent flow was found to begin at Re with an order of magnitude in the low 104, while in other studies, it was found to occur at much lower values (400 to 3000) than predicted for the flat plate.

This lower Re number may be explained by the geometry, movement, and surface irregularities present in real leaves. Laminar empirical relationships hold satisfactorily for these leaves for a BL conductance value of 1.06 × 10"2 for winds less than 4 ms”1. Morphological differences between leaf types, such as the presence of serrated edges on leaves, were found to trigger turbulence in wind-tunnel studies, while veins and hairs increase the surface roughness. The curled front edge of a Populus leaf was shown to generate a turbulent wake. Typical values of ä will range from 2.8 to 0.28 mm for wind speeds ranging from 0.1 to 10 m s"1 , respectively, while for large leaves in calm conditions, ä may be on the order of 1 cm. Thus, large leaves, by virtue of their generally thicker boundary layer, have lower exchange rates due to the longer diffusion pathways.

Wind-tunnel experiments show no significant difference demonstrated between vine-type leaves and circular replicas of equivalent diameter for wind speed less than 3 ms"1 , while at higher wind speeds, the conductance of the vine-shaped replica seems to increase more rapidly than for the circular replica. Many studies of leaves and leaf replicas have also shown that the conductance for real leaves is frequently underestimated by the engineering values for laminar boundary layers. In contrast to studies suggesting an increase in the laminar Re exponent, it has been found that measured conductances were well described when the predicted laminar transfer rates were multiplied by a constant value. Nusselt or Sherwood numbers are typically larger than predicted by an enhancement factor â between 1 and 2.5. It has been suggested that the predicted conductance values be increased by 50% to better estimate exchange value, although several of the above studies suggest that a higher enhancement factor is warranted. Rather than using an enhancement factor as mentioned above, an appropriate method to characterize laminar boundary layer conditions may be to adjust the Re exponent instead when the leaf boundary layer is partially or fully turbulent.

These enhancements or increased Re exponents are primarily attributed to the leaf characteristics, the response of leaves to wind, and the interaction between leaves in a canopy. The development of an overall plant BL conductance value is complicated by the wind speed's deviation from the free stream velocity within the canopy. Two aspects of this "sheltering" effect give insight into the relationship between BL conductance and free stream velocity within a canopy.

The mean velocity reduction within the canopy causes a decrease in the exchange of mass and heat. This reduction is somewhat mitigated by the increased turbulence in the wake of neighboring plants. The relative influence of the two effects depends on the canopy structure and may be estimated by measures of foliage density and stem and leaf areas. Wind penetration into the canopy structure creates higher turbulence and increased the BL conductance values of leaves, as shown in a study using cladode replicates in an open woody bush, with leaf replicates placed in a plant with a denser canopy exhibiting lower than predicted conductance values.

In realistic canopies characterized by mean leaf area index smaller than 2.5, wide variations of BL conductances, according to leaf location and wind characteristics, are expected due to concentration of the total canopy leaf area within relatively limited volumes. Such studies explain why conductances measured at the upwind edge of a canopy half way up in the canopy layer may differ by as much as 40% from values found at the trailing edge of the canopy. Aerodynamic characteristics of the canopy therefore play a critical role in determining the conductances of individual leaves inside vegetation canopies. Furthermore, LBL conductances are also sensitive to the position along the vertical axis of the canopy layer, with literature reports suggesting that the position of the leaf along a vertical axis can induce variations of up to 80%. This likely mirrors the fact that turbulence levels are height-dependent within the canopy layer.

LBL Atmospheric Decoupling as a Function of Wind Speed

A leaf with a thick laminar BL will have reduced coupling between the canopy and the atmosphere, thus lowering the plant response to the wind environment, so that the exchange of heat and mass is limited. When no exchange occurs, the ambient air and the leaf are considered to be decoupled. The extent of coupling for the exchange of water vapor may be expressed using the "decoupling coefficient" as

= å+1 å + 1 + gb /gc

where å is the dimensionless ratio of the increase of latent heat content to the increase of the sensible heat content of saturated air and gb and gc are the boundary layer and canopy conductances, respectively. That formulation is based on the "big leaf" approximation, a concept that treats the canopy as one single large leaf, with the underlying assumptions of a well-mixed canopy regime and no radiative transfer within the canopy. A modification to Ref. 11 was proposed in later studies incorporating the radiative coupling between the vegetation and the atmosphere. The modified was found to be most important for canopies with low roughness values, such as grasslands, that result in low boundary layer conductance.

Both approaches have values that range from 0 to 1, where the upper limit is valid for a decoupled system while the lower limit is valid for a completely coupled system. The decoupling coefficient also provides a measure of partitioning transpiration control between stomatal conductance and BL conductance. That is, the decoupling coefficient approaches one (completely decoupled) when the BL thickens—a condition in which the vapor pressure at the leaf's surface is nearly decoupled from the atmosphere. In such conditions, the relative importance of the stomatal conductance is small as compared to the boundary layer conductance. The establishment of for different kinds of vegetation is a step toward formally quantifying species intercomparisons and helping to extrapolate results from one situation to another, such as greenhouse studies to field conditions.

This approach is valuable given the growing use of open-top chambers to study questions of great current interest, such as climate change, high atmospheric CO_2 concentration and their impact on plant growth and water use efficiency. Experimental values of have been determined for several types of vegetation and trees under a range of wind-speed and other climatic conditions. Mean values of 0.82 to 0.9 were obtained in studies of transpiration from treetops of four tree species (Crecopia longipes, Ficus insipida,

Luehea seemanii, and Spondias mombin) characterized by moderate to large leaf sizes in wet conditions (rainfall was 250% of normal) with low wind speed (<1 m/s).

These low winds resulted in low BL conductance values, even for species with smaller leaves, and are thought to be largely responsible, in addition to the wet conditions, for the decoupling. The link between measured conductances and decoupling coefficients is evident with a 50% decrease in BL conductance leading to a reduction in the decoupling coefficient to values as low as 0.5. In such conditions, transpiration was only weakly dependent on stomatal conductance (10% change in conductance results in 1.8% change in evaporation). Dry conditions appear to have an inverse relationship on decoupling values in similar tree species, with decreasing to 0.5 for the species above. values as low as 0.28 have been observed in an Amazonian forest at both higher wind speeds and smaller stomatal conductance values (180 and 40% respectively) than in the study above.

The coupling of crops to the atmosphere through the wind speed, has been eloquently demonstrated and isolated from other relevant coupling parameters such as plant density, leaf area index (LAI), and leaf epidermal conductances (63): values ranging from 0.4 to 0.8 for maize before the inception of senescence have been reported with values as large as 0.8 for winds of 4 to 5 ms"1.

Analytical models are showing great promise as tools to determine the effect of partial canopy decoupling to predict transpiration. Models using the "top-down" or "big leaf" approach to estimate transpiration with bulk parameters describing canopy and BL conductances are of particular usefulness. A recent model, calibrated using a year of transpiration from a mature beech forest (Fagus sylvatica L.), showed a seasonal average of 0.28 with the strongest decoupling (> 0.3) during periods of low wind velocities and large canopy conductances.

Overall, experimental results suggest higher decoupling coefficients for closed canopies, which are typically characterized by reduced atmospheric turbulence and larger BL resistances. Lower decoupling coefficients for the beech forest as compared to the tropical forest and crop canopies are attributed to smaller leaves and canopy closure, respectively.

STOMATAL CONDUCTANCE RESPONSE TO THE WIND ENVIRONMENT

The wind speed modifies the stomatal conductance when atmospheric CO_2 and water vapor partial pressure differences are held constant. Studies have found the stomatal conductance to be largest for the lowest wind speeds and to decrease logarithmically with increasing wind speed based on windtunnel experiments on Sitka spruce seedlings. This relationship appears to indicate that increased wind speed results in partial stomatal closure; this effect may also be due to an increased vapor pressure deficit caused by the replacement of moisture in the BL with drier ambient air. The role of the leaf BL in the stomatal response is sometimes examined in a cuvette heat exchanger. Such studies demonstrated that the relationship between the total conductance and the partial water vapor pressure difference between leaf surface and ambient air depended on wind speed, but such relationship between the stomatal conductance and the water vapor partial pressure difference between the stomates and the leaf surface did not.

Other studies have looked at the rate of CO_2 fixation and the role of the boundary layer in stomatal conductance of water vapor and CO_2 for wind speeds that correspond to natural conditions and found the bulk air properties of CO_2 and water vapor to differ from those at the leaf surface because of a significantly thicker BL. This is in contrast with other studies from previous closed-top chamber experiments, which used high wind speeds to reduce these differences. Such experiments are sometimes conducted in a differential gasexchange system and simulations are performed to evaluate the response of stomatal conductance to changes in wind speed (resulting in a change in BL conductance) to properties of CO_2 and water vapor. Results indicate that changes in BL conductance cause stomatal conductance rates to change due to altered properties of CO_2 within the stomata as well as due to changes in the leaf surface water vapor deficit. While such efforts focus on the effect of the BL on stomatal conductance, it also offers a framework for scaling up to the leaf response to these effects.

Field and laboratory experiments support the feedback theory between wind and humidity to determine stomatal conductance, as demonstrated for coffee hedgerows. The apparent partial stomatal closure is thought to be mediated by higher BL conductances, allowing drier air to reach the leaf surface. Experiments in stands of koa, a native Hawaiian tree, suggests a strong interaction between wind and humidity in regulating transpiration rates. This work is consistent with hypotheses from other studies arguing that epidermal transpiration plays a role in the stomatal response to humidity.

OPEN-TOP CHAMBERS: WIND-RELATED PLANT RESPONSE

Scientific studies are increasingly conducted inside open-top plant growth chambers (hereafter OTC) in the field, and with global warming perspective looming, the need to elucidate the effect of ambient increased carbon dioxide emissions on crop and tree above-ground and below-ground biomass production is as pressing as ever. OTCs are gaining popularity, supplanting the more conventional closed chambers, and for good reason: their low cost, hence accessibility, and enhanced microclimate similarity with natural conditions appeal to experimentalists.

Nevertheless, the OTC remains a physical system where wind-related plant response needs to be critically assessed. While there have been numerous studies conducted in OTCs, few studies have evaluated the effect of wind flow on plant response in this semicontrolled environment and compared it with the response of plants grown in natural field conditions. Unintended flow modifications resulting from the design of OTCs can cause changes, among others, in leaf temperatures, transpiration, carbon dioxide, and pollutant uptake.

Impact of the Enclosure on the Flow Field and the Plant Response

In chamber studies, either OTCs or closed-top chambers, the plant response is related to the time-averaged pollutant concentration (dose) measured in the chamber atmosphere. Extrapolation of dose-response relationships from OTCs to field plants ideally requires that the gaseous uptake mechanism from the atmosphere to the plant interior be identical in both systems. As demonstrated below, this is difficult to achieve. This section explores the importance of the representativeness of the OTC flow regime to open-field conditions and examines differences in wind-related plant response between OTCs and open-field conditions. Briefly, the gaseous uptake by vegetation can be described by the "big leaf" model, where the uptake is the product of the atmospheric concentration and deposition velocity (Vd). Vd incorporates the important physical and biological factors that determine the rate of uptake from the atmosphere to the plant interior. Vd , the deposition velocity, can be defined by a series of resistances:

Vd = 1 ra + r b + r c

where ra , rb , and rc are the aerodynamic, boundary layer, and canopy resistances to gas exchange, respectively, and ra describes the ability of the atmosphere to vertically transfer gaseous material from a height z to the boundary layer at the plant surface, as a result of turbulent exchange. This is estimated in natural conditions by

ra = 1 z"d ln ku" z0 " Cm

where k is the von Karman's constant, u" is the friction velocity, d is the zero plane displacement, and z0 is the surface roughness. Cm is the atmospheric stability correction for momentum. The transfer of gaseous material across the plant boundary layer is characterized by rb as seen in the discussion above. The latter is determined by atmospheric, vegetative, and gas concentration characteristics:

rb = 1.5d 0.5 í 0.17 D "0.67 u0.5 for laminar flow or rb = 33d 0.2 í 0.47 D "0.67 u0.8

for turbulent flow. rc represents the resistance to gaseous transfer from the within-canopy leaf exterior to interior. The latter is determined primarily by the stomatal resistance, which varies with the species of interest and is controlled by the plant in response to its water status, the incident radiation, and foliage temperature. However, the stomatal aperture itself varies as a function of wind speed, so that the canopy resistance is itself indirectly linked to the magnitude of the wind speed as well. The effect of an OTC on rc has also been examined in several studies, with varying results. Several studies found no consistent difference between field and OTC rc values in grapes (Vitus labrusca L.), while others have found slightly higher values in the OTC for soybean [Glycine max (L.) Merr.] and slightly lower values for lettuce (Lactuca sativa L.) and others found the chamber reduced rc by 22% for both kidney bean (Phaseolus vulgaris L.) and cotton (Gossypium hirsutum L.).

A high value of rc can be the controlling mechanism in determining Vd when ra and rb are much smaller than rc . The modification of the natural flow properties inside an OTC also gives rise to differences in ra and rb when compared to field conditions. Depending on the value of rc , a significant difference in the deposition velocity between the OTC and the field may then occur. This suggests that gaseous exchange studies and dose–plant response relationships found in the OTC cannot be simply extrapolated to field-grown plants. Given the relations observed in Refs. 12 through 15, it is of little surprise that for OTC grown plants to mimic the response to varying dose-response relationships, a flowfield similar to that observed in field conditions is required. Relationships between OTCs and flows observed in open conditions have been the object of several studies.

In a typical OTC, ports are located at the lower levels of the chamber (<1 m) and exhausted out the chamber top. In calm conditions, the wind-speed maximum is typically found to be at around 25% of the OTC height inside an OTC. Such OTC observations contrast sharply with the ambient flow regime of rapidly increasing wind speed with increasing height just above the ground. Several studies have found that when exposed to moderate winds (1.1 and 2.3 ms"1 in the region corresponding to about 1.1 the OTC height), the OTC flow was less than ambient at upper levels in the chamber and of comparable magnitude at lower levels. The OTC fiow in calm conditions and its implications on ra , rb , and Vd reveal the flow to become increasingly vertical with increasing height up to 50% of the OTC height. This pattern is consistent with mass conservation: inflow at low levels induces a converging horizontal flow at the base, with a vertical exhaust flow, increasing with height up to near the level of the top inflow ports to about 25% of the OTC height.

Above the mid-OTC height, the flow becomes more horizontal, indicating that the vertical flow at mid-OTC height reflects the combination of both an exhaust flow and vertical circulation near the top of the inflow ports. Unlike true field conditions, the vertical velocity in the OTC is in general away from the surface (due to the blower and OTC structure), with intense coherent quasistationary circulation patterns present in specific areas of the OTC. Average OTC flow characteristics provide little useful information because of the large spatial variability. For instance, in one intensive study aimed at quantifying the spatial variability across the chamber, u varied from 0.28 to 1.33 m/s. The average turbulence intensity (defined as the ratio of the standard deviation of the horizontal velocity to the mean flow velocity) of the flow increases with height up to 60%. Field studies suggest that as ambient wind speed increases, there is an enhanced intake of ambient air into the chamber and an associated loss of uniformity of pollutant concentration as well as loss of costly pollutant gas.

The addition of a baffle with a reduced opening, displaced vertically above the test area, appears to maintain the highest uniform concentration in the test area, and the effect of the presence of the OTC on the flow inside the chamber occurred below $z/h < 2$ and at $x/h < 4.2$, respectively. In one study, the Reynolds stresses for the three profiles were uniform throughout the chamber above $z/h > 2$, with turbulence intensities both longitudinal and vertical at x/ h = 0, 1.8, 4.2, greatest below z/ h < 1.5 when the flow system was operating. Lateral variations in the mean wind at x/ h = 1.8 suggest a mean velocity greatest under these conditions (except near the center line, where the reverse was true).

This pattern was maintained at x/ h = 4.2. Such important differences between the OTC flow and that of the openfield conditions result in differences in their respective ra and rb values. Altered flow characteristics within an OTC tend to create aerodynamic and boundary layer resistances (ra and rb) differing from field values, complicating the extension of OTC results to field conditions. In the well-mixed OTC atmospheric environment, the turbulent exchange of gaseous material is rapid, leading to lower ra values than those in the field even in the most turbulent field conditions. A study showed that the variable flow in the OTC results in widely varying rb values within the OTC itself, depending on the actual physical location within the chamber.

In addition, the OTC ra and rb would differ from field values under typical meteorological conditions. For plants subjected to environmental stresses, for the underside of leaves, or with otherwise low stomatal conductance, this could create significant differences in gaseous uptake for individual plants within the OTC as well as for the average plant in the OTC versus that in the field. Values of rb typically decreased with increasing depth in the canopy, since the wind speed maximum is within the canopy rather than at the canopy top. Furthermore, rb values varying by almost as much as 100% can be observed depending on the location within the chamber. In a study using a model soybean canopy, rb values at the canopy top were found to be higher in the OTC than in the field, with lower calculated rb for within-canopy leaves. The OTC ra is often assumed to be insignificant as a result of the efficient mixing in the chamber.

In one investigation of the impact of flow characteristics on plant response, Vd values in the OTC ranged from 69 to 110% of that in the field depending on location and time of the day. Vd in the OTC averaged 6% lower than the predicted field Vd during the windy day because of low field values of ra and rb. Depending on the location, the OTC-averaged Vd was 69% higher than predicted field values during the low-wind day, with OTC Vd values ranging from 125 to 200% of that in the field. For identical ozone concentrations in the field (at 10 m) and the OTC (in the upper half of the chamber), the actual ozone uptake in the OTC was higher than that in the field in low wind conditions and than that in the field in high winds.

In general, periods of relatively high ozone concentration are associated with wind speeds below 3.5 m/s, suggesting that applying OTC results to the field during the typical high-ozone periods are likely to overestimate the ozone dose for the field plant. Since the flow complexity affects all mass exchanges between the plant and the OTC environment airspace, CO_2 uptake, evapotranspiration (ET), and pollutant dose-response relationships will be influenced by the OTC. The uptake of CO_2, ozone, and ET will be enhanced in the OTC relative to an open field during calm conditions and vice versa in windy conditions. This is likely to lead to differences in the growth rate of plants grown in the OTC compared to those in open-field conditions. It should be pointed out here, as a positive note, that the use of controls in OTC-based experiments still provide the cumulative effects of the OTC on the plant growth pattern and rate. The OTC flow creates a condition where the pollutant deposition velocity (Vd) is likely to vary with position in the chamber and differ from field observations.

The differences in Vd would be largest for plant species with low stomatal resistances (such as soybean) and during periods of low ambient winds. As a result, extension of OTC pollutant dose-plant response relationships established in an OTC to plants growing in open fields should account for the differences in Vd between the location in the OTC and the field to prevent overestimates of the pollutant dosage on field-grown plants, leading to incorrect actual or potential plant response to the exchange of pollutants, carbon dioxide, and water vapor. Studies linking the differences between rice plants grown inside an OTC versus those grown in natural field conditions have shown also that the microclimate of vegetation growing in open-top chambers differs from that in outdoor conditions: temperature profiles and carbon dioxide concentrations were found to differ from the open-field conditions, leading to biomass production 12.5% less than the biomass of plants grown in the open. This may be explained by the fact that the air was warmer than in the open field throughout the day, which in turn, is likely a result of the lower air exchange around the plants within chamber walls.

Several designs of OTC provide an air distribution system with controlledventilation open-top chamber (CVOTC) wind speeds above 1 m/s. This leads to LBL resistances comparable with those of plants in open-field conditions. LBL resistance rb in the chamber depends on the rate of ventilation by the fan, on air movement caused by incursion, on position in the chamber, and on the position (shelter) in the crop canopy. Some studies have predictably found that the conductances inside the chamber depend very much upon the position of the leaf inside the chamber with respect to the air inlet. These same studies found that rb values were small compared to values reported in crop canopies, where wind speeds seldom exceed 1 m/s and note that the low effective rb values might cause the deposition of gases on leaf surfaces in chambers to be larger than in the field.

Chamber effects on wind have also been noted above vegetation but not within when ambient wind velocity was very low, as in radiational cooling situations. In such cases, chamber airflow exceeded ambient flow, and dew formation was occasionally reduced or suppressed completely inside chambers, possibly due to the internal airflow as well as the slightly higher air/leaf temperatures resulting from infrared reradiation from chamber walls. Suppression of dew formation could have decreased infection by fungi as was suggested in one of the studies, with a reduced rate of air movement across leaves increasing the boundary layer resistance and leading to increased leaf temperatures and decreased absorption of pollutants inside the stomata.

CONCLUSIONS

The plant response to the wind environment has been explored under its many facets: first in the natural wind environment, examining its impact on variables that are indicators of the modification of the local leaf environment, and its impact on the atmospheric transfer of gases and heat using the concepts of aerodynamic, stomatal, boundary layer, and canopy conductances and resistances. Second, given the resurgence of interest in the plant response to the wind environment, the change of the wind environment brought about by open-top chambers has been discussed along with the applicability and reproducibility in outdoor conditions. Further studies are needed, in particular in the integration on the above information for "scaling up" models of leaf to the canopy to the landscape levels. Further studies are needed to bring the response of OTCs closer to field conditions; meanwhile, a more thorough examination of the characterization of coherent structures superimposed on the overall flowfield modification and on the plant response is urgently called for.

13

Soil Physical Constraints and Plant Growth Interactions

INTRODUCTION

Soil is a medium for plant growth, and its structure should not hinder the movement of water, oxygen and nutrients to plant roots, impede the growth of roots, or allow the buildup of toxic substances around roots. Soil structure can be described as the organization of the particles in the soil—the internal configuration of the soil matrix.

Soil structure is formed by many interacting processes in the soil, especially shrinkage with drying, channel formation by plant roots, faunal activity, and cultivation. Well-developed soil structure is represented by distinct stable aggregations (peds) of soil particles separated by interped pores. The interped pores of an aggregated soil are larger, on average, than pores between particles of unaggregated soil, resulting in a less dense condition.

The larger pores are also critical in terms of allowing movement of air and water through the soil. Unfavorable soil structure, on the other hand, can impart the characteristics of greater soil density, decreased aeration, poor percolation, and mechanical impedance to roots, which can restrict plant growth. There are a number of factors that may result in poor soil structure. Soil texture is important; in fact, very sandy soils are usually classified as structureless due to lack of soil matrix (sand is viewed more as the "skeleton" of the soil).

In sandy soils, size distribution and packing of the grains are considered rather than structure per se.

In loamy and finer-textured soil, clay acts as a cementing agent to provide some level of stability to the particle orientation in structured soil; however, clay can also cement particles in a structurally degraded condition ("massive"). Chemical conditions can be responsible for structurally degraded soil; a relatively high sodium content causes dispersion of particles and elimination of aggregation. These "sodic soils" occur naturally but can also be initiated or exacerbated by human activity. The human-imposed factor that degrades soil structure to the greatest extent is compaction. This chapter focuses on the effects of compacted soil on plant growth, including the direct effect of mechanical impedance as well as the indirect effects that usually accompany compaction. Finally, amelioration of compaction is discussed, with emphasis on the ability of plant roots to effect changes in soil structure and hence modify physical properties.

COMPACTION

Hillel described soil compaction as the compression and densification of an unsaturated soil body, reducing the fractional air volume. The degree to which a soil will compress is a function of the soil moisture content, antecedent bulk density, magnitude of the compactive effort, soil texture, and content of organic matter. Forces that compact soil can originate from natural sources, including rainfall, radial root pressure, cycles of wetting/drying and freezing/thawing, or traffic of people and machinery. The potential to degrade soil structure has increased as modern machinery has become larger and heavier, causing compaction to a greater depth. Compounding this problem is the tendency to tread repeatedly over soil while implementing cultural practices such as seeding, fertilization, pest control, harvesting/mowing, or construction during site development.

Soil compaction on recreational sites is thought to be one of the most challenging issues faced by turfgrass managers. Cultivation implements are generally designed to overcome the bonds stabilizing structure, breaking aggregates into smaller ones for seedbed preparation to maximize seed-soil contact, enhance water infiltration and retention characteristics, and improve soil aeration. Routine tillage of soil, however, can also degrade soil structure by shattering aggregates, eliminating pore networks, and imposing compacting forces, particularly in a subsurface layer of soil.

Soil Responses

Porosity, bulk density, and water retention characteristics are physical properties characterizing soil structure and compaction phenomena. Compaction of a soil decreases soil porosity and subsequently increases soil bulk density. Veihmeyer and Hendrickson showed that the critical soil bulk density needed to inhibit sunflower (Helianthus annus L.) root growth varied with texture; no roots penetrated soil with a bulk density of 1.9 g $cm^{"3}$. The lowest density where roots failed to penetrate was 1.46 g cm"3 for an Aiken clay loam. Air tends to occupy the larger pores of soil, whereas the affinity of water for mineral surfaces creates water films and wedges (menisci) within the small fissures and capillaries of the soil. A reduction in the total porosity of soil, as a result of compaction, generally occurs at the expense of the air porosity, those relatively large pores not filled with water at a given soil water potential (usually "33 kPa to represent "field capacity").

Swartz and Kardos observed a decrease in air porosity from 19.3 to 12.7%, with increasing levels of compaction on several sand-soil-peat mixes differing in moisture content at the time of compaction, whereas capillary porosity increased from 32.2% at the lowest compaction level to 35.7% at the highest level. In aggregated soils, the loss of porosity due to compaction can be attributed to the collapse of interaggregate pores. Water retention and flow characteristics in soil are influenced by alterations of soil porosity. Relative to noncompacted soil, compacted soil will generally retain a greater amount of water at a given soil matric potential as a result of increased capillary porosity. Soil water permeability, particularly at saturated or nearly saturated conditions, is a function of air porosity; as air porosity decreases, so does water permeability. Compacted soils with lower infiltration rates are prone to problems with stagnant water and anaerobic conditions.

Constraints on Root Growth

1. Soil Aeration

Soil oxygen movement to plant roots is critical to maintain adequate respiration for growth. Anaerobiosis, or oxygen stress, occurs in soil when the rate of supply falls below the biological demand. Impeded soil aeration can arise from poor drainage and waterlogging or from compacted soil. One approach to evaluate soil aeration is to measure the composition of soil air. This technique indicates that gas exchange between the atmosphere and soil air is restricted when oxygen content of the soil air falls significantly below that of the atmosphere. An important challenge with this approach is how to extract a representative sample of soil air that avoids mixing of gases from outside the point of sampling or contamination from the atmosphere.

Another approach for assessing soil aeration is to determine the air porosity, or fractional air space, at a standard soil water potential. Work to identify threshold air porosity values below which plant growth is limited has generated values ranging from 5 to 20%. Madison has indicated that 10% air porosity is the threshold level for intensively utilized turf. The United States Golf Association Green Section (USGA) has suggested 15% air porosity at a 3 kPa water tension as the lower test limit for materials used in the construction of root zones for golf course putting greens. The extent to which air porosity in the root zone changes with time under a perennial turf system is a subject of current studies.

The rate of air exchange, rather than the volume of soil air, is the more important factor in soil aeration and therefore limits the usefulness of air porosity as an index of soil aeration. Gaseous movement in the soil occurs by two main processes: convection and diffusion. Convection, where the moving force is a gradient of total gas pressure, is thought to be a minor mechanism of soil aeration except at shallow depths and in soils with large pores. Although convection is not considered an important factor for more deeply rooted plant species, it could be more influential for shallow-rooted turfs. A large fraction of the root system of moderately to highly maintained turfs is found at surface depths of 5 cm or less.

Furthermore, the crown, the major meristematic organ, of turfgrass plants is located near the soil surface. Thus, turfs with a high plant population could have sufficiently high oxygen demands at the soil surface that convection would play a useful role in maintaining adequate aeration for plant crowns and surface rooting. Convection, therefore, could be partially responsible for the observations of improved turfgrass quality after changes in air masses (pressure) associated with passing weather systems. Below the surface, however, diffusion is considered the more important exchange mechanism in soil, and the moving force is a gradient of partial pressure. Gas exchange between the atmosphere and soil is maintained predominantly by diffusion through air-filled pores. In contrast, live tissue is typically hydrated, and the supply of oxygen to roots occurs by diffusion through water films. This is an important distinction, since the diffusivity of oxygen in water is less than its value in air by a factor of 10"4.

The solubility of oxygen in water may be a compounding issue, especially at higher temperatures, where solubility decreases. Methods that measure gaseous diffusion through air-filled pores do not provide information on the impedance to oxygen presented by the water film surrounding a root. It is possible that an inadequate supply of oxygen to roots can occur in a well-aerated soil (i.e., high air-filled porosity and O_2 concentration) if the roots are surrounded by thick water films. Thus, under such conditions, measurement of soil oxygen movement to plant roots would provide a more complete assessment of soil aeration. Lemon and Erickson introduced the method commonly called ODR (oxygen diffusion rate) to measure oxygen diffusion to a root-like electrode inserted into the soil and enveloped in water films of the soil. The ODR technique has been used by a number of researchers to demonstrate the reduction in oxygen supply in compacted soil.

Limiting soil aeration conditions are often transient and strongly affected by wetting and drying cycles in compacted soil. Therefore, the timing of gas composition and ODR measurements is critical for accurate detection of anaerobiosis. Generally, 200 ng cm”2 min”1 has been considered the minimum ODR value, below which plant roots will not grow. Some researchers have reported values ranging from 50 to 200 ng cm”2 min”1 as limiting ODR values for turfgrass root growth. The interpretation of these results has been questioned because, in addition to the diffusion of oxygen, other soil factors and components could have affected the measured ODR. Work by Blackwell has helped to reduce errors associated with reactions other than the reduction of oxygen in the ODR technique. Moreover, early studies of limiting ODR were performed in growth chambers at about 20æ% C, whereas soil temperatures in the field can vary considerably during the growing season. Blackwell and Wells concluded that the effect of oxygen flux on root growth is related to temperature differences and differences in root respiration. Thus, it is plausible that the oxygen flux limiting root growth under high soil temperatures may be greater than values that have been observed at 20æ% C.

When oxygen becomes limiting, some species of bacteria shift metabolic pathways so as to utilize other compounds as terminal electron acceptors. Thus, plants may have not only to survive periods without oxygen but also to withstand toxic substances such as hydrogen sulfide, which are produced during anaerobic microbial respiration. Development of aerenchyma tissue (intercellular spaces) that allows diffusion of oxygen from aerial plant tissue down to roots may be an adaptive response that helps certain species of plants to survive periods of soil anaerobiosis. Agnew and Carrow reported increased root porosity in Kentucky bluegrass (Poa pratensis L.) grown under compacted soil conditions. They observed the greatest root porosity under conditions of both compaction and water stress.

2. Soil Strength

Soil strength can be described as the capacity of soil to resist a force without rupture, fragmentation, or flow. Various methods exist to quantitate soil strength in the laboratory, but the method most used in the field is the penetrometer. It measures the effort necessary to push a thin, cone-tipped probe into the soil. Taylor and colleagues conducted pioneering research demonstrating that the strength of a soil, as measured with a static penetrometer, will increase as soil bulk density increases and water content decreases; consequently, mechanical impedance to root growth is greater. The limiting strength of soil to cotton (Gossypium hirsutum L.) root growth is in the range 2.5 to 3 MPa. For many crops, a 2-MPa penetrometer resistance is commonly encountered under field conditions and can reduce root length and elongation by at least 50%.

Root Morphology

In experiments designed to study the constricted growth of roots, the ability of ryegrass (Lolium perenne L.) roots to enter rigid pores (glass capillaries and sheets of steel) depended on the size of the root cap and the thickness of the stele, which needed to be about one-third of the nominal root thickness. Roots could elongate down long capillaries while constricted, albeit at a reduced rate. Roots can enter pores of diameter smaller than the root tip itself only if the rigidity of the pore structure is weak enough to allow soil displacement. Thus, major root axes typically thicken when soil pores are too small for root penetration. Ethylene production has been linked to this thickening response of roots subjected to mechanical impedance. Abscisic acid, which increases temporarily under conditions of mechanical impedance, has also been shown to induce root thickening as well as increased root-hair number and curling of roots. The thickening of the root compresses soil laterally and minimizes friction with soil as the root extends axially. Additionally, root-hair development aids in anchoring the root as it penetrates compacted soil. Thus these responses can be viewed as adaptive, as they mitigate the effects of axial resistance on growth. Additional contributing factors to thicker roots' relative endurance of compact soil might be greater resistance of thicker roots to bending or higher axial pressures exerted by thick roots. Variation in plant genetics exists for tolerance to high mechanical impedance. Interspecific comparisons have shown differences in root dimensions and the ability to penetrate soils. Greater root thickness and the tendency for roots to expand radially in response to mechanical impedance are correlated with the capacity to elongate in hard soil. Intraspecific studies have also demonstrated genetic variation in characteristics associated with tolerance to mechanical impedance. Two tall fescue (Festuca arundinacea Schreb.) lines with large-diameter roots were able to penetrate a hardpan at the 0.4 to 0.6 m soil depth, extracted more soil water from the 0.6 to 1.2 m depth, and yielded 40% more in dry matter compared to fescues with small-diameter roots.

Development of efficient techniques to screen plant germplasm for greater tolerance to high mechanical impedance could prove to be highly useful. Iijima et al. described the morphological development of rice (Oryza sativa L.) and maize (Zea mays L.) root systems as affected by soil compaction. Elongation of the main root axes of rice and maize was restricted in compacted soil. Seminal roots of maize were much less restricted than those of rice. The root system of rice was characterized by a larger fraction of long, thick laterals with potential to produce higher-order laterals on their axes. Growth of higher (second- and third-) order lateral roots in compacted soil compensated for the restricted growth of the main root axes in both species. The work of Carrow and colleagues indicates that the effects of compacted soil on root growth varies with plant species and management. Total root mass of Kentucky bluegrass decreased in response to compaction treatment, whereas tall fescue and perennial ryegrass root systems were more tolerant to compaction stress.

Subsequent work indicated that the most detrimental effect of compaction on root growth of tall fescue and perennial ryegrass occurred under higher nitrogen fertilization. Although total root mass of a turf may not change under compacted conditions, a redistribution of the root system can occur where root mass increases in the surface 5 cm of the soil at the expense of rooting below the 10-cm depth. Root mass may not provide the most detailed index of a root system's response to compacted soil, since root mass is affected less by bulk density than root length is, primarily because of larger-diameter roots in high-density soil. Thus, the measurement of the number and length of roots growing in soil may be a more sensitive indicator of compaction stress on a root system than root mass. Root length and number measurements, however, are expensive, particularly for experiments evaluating a large number of treatments and for plant systems such as turf, which have extremely high root lengths.

Physical alteration of water and nutrient uptake by a root system can result as the orientation and morphology of roots change. Higher soil bulk density brings more soil, and associated water and nutrients, into contact with the surface area of the root system and thus has the potential to increase availability. This effect is particularly pronounced for nutrients such as phosphorus, which have relatively low mobility in the soil. Greater soil contact with the root system, and thus availability of nutrients and water, could at least partly explain the greater clipping yields of turf growing on heavily compacted plots compared to lightly compacted plots during the spring. The fact that this response was reversed during the summer suggests that the beneficial response of greater soil and root surface contact may be beneficial until environmental conditions become limiting for other essential growth factors under compacted soil conditions. As environmental conditions become more limiting, the reduced total root elongation rate and length in compacted soil ultimately decreases availability of water and nutrients by restricted access.

Shoot Responses

The direct and indirect effects of compaction on plant roots can elicit responses in the plant shoot as well. A number of studies on grasses demonstrate the potential of compacted soil to limit shoot density, verdure, clipping yield, soil cover, and lateral stem growth. Lower dry-matter production and yield under compacted soil conditions is attributed to reduced light interception caused by restricted leaf area development and is not a result of an impaired ability of crops to utilize intercepted radiant energy. Hormonal mechanisms have been proposed through which roots "sense" the mechanical impedance of the soil and elicit anatomical changes in leaf growth. An increase in abscisic acid in the xylem sap appears to be a root-to-shoot signal that lowers stomatal conductance and leaf expansion rates.

PLANT EFFECTS ON SOIL PHYSICAL CONDITION

While soil structure and related properties certainly affect plant growth, it is also recognized that vegetation can modify physical conditions of soil. Species reported to be detrimental to soil structure are maize, soybeans (Glycine max L.), and cereal species in general. Plant species identified as beneficial to soil aggregation include ryegrass, bromegrass (Bromus ssp.), alfalfa (Medicago sativa L.) and clover (Trifolium ssp.). Stone and Buttery found that nine forages differed in their ability to improve structure. Warm-season C4 prairie graminoids appear to promote aggregation better than cool-season C3 grasses, possibly due to differences in total biomass production, length and timing of growth, physiological differences affecting root exudates, root morphology, and/or microbial population (especially mycorrhizal infection). Moreover, land uses associated with continuous plant cover of soil and lack of soil manipulation provide greater opportunity for the development of stable soil structure. Use of land as pasture has been found to increase aggregation of previously tilled soil.

Mechanical Binding

One documented mechanism of roots' influence on soil structure is mechanical binding of soil particles by fine roots and microbial hyphae. Networks of dead and especially living roots resist compactive loads and shear stress; fungal hyphae work similarly within soil aggregates. Rooting patterns (i.e., total root length, distribution, root length density, branching frequency, and root hairs) are thought to be important in explaining differences in soil stabilization by different species. Alfalfa and clover improve soil structure primarily through enhancement of infiltration rate, hydraulic conductivity, or soil water retention/drainage, which might be expected from the channel development under these tap-rooted plants. However, mycorrhizal hyphae associated with the roots of white clover (T. repens L.) have been related to increased stability of aggregates.

Organic Matter

Total soil organic matter content is the soil property most closely associated with soil structure stability. Soil organic matter accumulates over the long term to a steady-state level, which is determined by the amount of biological contributions over time, soil water content and temperature (regulating decomposition), and other factors such as texture. As primary producers in terrestrial ecosystems, plants ultimately can be credited with nearly all of the organic matter added to soil. Direct contributions occur from seasonal shedding of leaves and roots and root exudates as well as the whole plant upon death. The organic compounds added and the microbial activity and products that result greatly enhance soil structure and improve structural stability.

Qualitative differences in soil organic matter and the mechanisms of stabilization involved may account for unexplained differences in aggregate stability associated with plant species. Often much of the short-term increase in organic carbon has been found in the sand-size fraction, which includes fragments of plant tissue. However, the effects of organic matter on the formation, maintenance, or degradation of soil structure are more directly related to metabolic compounds and decomposition products that interact with soil particles, especially clays, on the molecular level. Hydrophobic coatings (presumably waxes from plant roots or associated microorganisms) can cause water repellency of sand-textured aggregates (94) and lead to the development of localized dry-spot formation in turf. Water repellency can reduce the rate of clay-aggregate wetting and therefore increase aggregate stability and contribute to development of preferential flow paths of infiltrating water. Grassland soil aggregates exhibit greater potential water repellency than aggregates of arable (maize) land.

The grassland vs. cultivated comparison, then, may reflect breakage of hydrophobic coatings (exposing uncoated soil) and/or microbial oxidation of the coatings in the cultivated land. Another possibility is a species difference in deposition of hydrophobic coatings on soil particles. Strong correlations occur between soil carbohydrate content, or some fraction thereof, and soil structural indices. Periodate-sensitive materials (polysaccharide and/or polyuronides) have been shown to be stabilizing agents for aggregates in many cases as well as pyrophosphatesensitive materials probably bound to minerals by polyvalent cations. Carbohydrates have been found to constitute 8 to 16% of soil organic matter in some virgin soils, the amount generally increasing with clay content. Soil in agricultural land use generally contains greater carbohydrate content than fallow, and species variability is evident. Some of the soil carbohydrate is contributed by structural components of plants (e.g., cellulose), but soil also gains carbohydrates in the form of soluble compounds released from plant roots.

1. Root Exudates

Roots of many species have been shown to exude metabolic compounds of varying composition and quantity. Barber and Gunn's minimum estimate of exudates released was 9% of the dry matter of the root increment grown. Rovira estimated that 0.1 to 0.4% of carbon assimilated by photosynthesis was released to the soil. Carbohydrates are major constituents of root exudates; for example, Moody et al. found that water-soluble components of root "slime" were mostly (> 95%, w/w) carbohydrate. While some root exudation is considered passive loss of photosynthates by the plant, it is clear that some exuded compounds are produced by the plant specifically to aid root function, induced by environmental conditions.

Therefore, root exudation is influenced by both genetic and environmental factors, including plant species, plant age, temperature, light, plant nutrition, soil moisture, root damage, and foliar applications. Shoot harvest has been shown to affect the amount of alfalfa root exudation. An additional factor that is especially relevant here is mechanical stress, which can increase root exudation of amino acids and carbohydrates. Greater development of secretory organelles in root cap cells under conditions of mechanical impedance presumably ameliorates adverse effects by production of mucilage, wetting the soil. Organic compounds released by roots serve as rich sources of carbon and energy for many soil microorganisms living in the rhizosphere. The term rhizosphere refers to the zone of high microbial activity, compared to bulk soil, that surrounds roots. Further classification of the rhizosphere is defined by root products and abundance of microorganisms.

The microbial community that develops in the rhizosphere may be characteristic of the plant species. These microbial communities produce their own "exudates," which, in turn, can be influential in particle binding. Relative contribution of microorganism- vs. plantderived carbohydrates to soil has been a subject of study. Direct effects of root exudates on aggregate stability has shown variability; for example, extracted bromegrass root exudates increased wet aggregate stability and decreased dispersible clay compared to maize exudates. Quantitative/qualitative differences in root exudates are likely responsible for species' effects on soil aggregation. Soil aggregate stabilization by ryegrass was maximized by shoot harvest, perhaps by increasing root exudates. Maize presents a special case in terms of root contributions to soil and subsequent soil structure effects. Cheshire and Mundie claimed that as little as 0.5% of 14C fixed by maize during 36 days was released as watersoluble substances; however, maize roots are characterized by abundant mucilage or mucigel. Low-molecular-weight components exuded from root cap cells polymerize extramurally and hydrate to form mucilage, which is likely to remain associated with mineral surfaces after dispersion. An SEM study of maize roots indicated a mucilage layer nearly covering the entire length, with soil aggregates embedded in the mucilage at the root cap and on root hairs. However, soil carbohydrate content and soil structure are usually not improved by maize culture. Evidence that maize-root compounds are more readily decomposed may reflect the distinct composition of maize-root exudates and explain lack of soil stabilization. One theory regarding the detrimental effect of maize on soil aggregates suggested that chelating agents released by roots disrupt organic matter–mineral particle bonds. Pojasok and Kay disputed this, finding that the relative degree of aggregate stabilization by bromegrass or maize correlated with the amount of divalent cations released from soil in response to root exudates. Tillage of soil that is common for maize production complicates field studies.

Soil Drying

Soil drying by root extraction of water has been indicated as a stabilizing force in several studies. Reid and Goss speculated that drying promoted adsorption of organic materials onto mineral surfaces. Wetting and drying of molded soil increases the stability of the molded form, which is analogous to the drying of puddled soil in the field. A logical explanation of this phenomenon is optimization of particle position and orientation to maximize bonding forces as water films thin and particles are slowly drawn together. Naturally formed aggregates, however, appear to be more strongly influenced by biological activity than by drying forces.

Time

Time is an important factor in the stabilization of soil aggregates by plant influences. Only 8 weeks were necessary before increases in the aggregate stability with ryegrass could be measured, but the effect leveled off at 16 weeks. In another study, alfalfa and ryegrass caused linear increases in soil aggregation from 1 to 4 years; but a degraded soil, such as has been under continuous row cropping, did not recover aggregation levels equal to a virgin site even 30 years after conversion to meadow. Reduction of infiltration into a compacted subsurface layer under turf could still be seen 12 years after the compacted layer was developed despite a trend toward faster infiltration with age. Biologically and physically significant recovery of aggregation occurred after 5 to 10 growing seasons in cultivated soil restored to tallgrass prairie at a site in eastern Illinois. Rapid recovery in this case was aided by high degrees of initial aggregation, very high production of biomass (1 to 1.5 kg m”2), lack of soil manipulation, and vegetation type with associated microorganisms. Separating the effect of time without disturbance from the effect of vegetation type was not entirely possible, but such effort indicated that the time factor might predominate. A conceptual model of soil-structure dynamics proposed by Gibbs and Reid emphasized macropore (> 100 μm) dynamics; and the direct root effects on macroporosity included in the model were creation and blockage of macropores and roots' decomposition to organic matter. Activities of living roots were cited as indirect influences on organic-matter humification, macropore stability, shrinkage (due to water uptake), and planar micropore expansion by mechanical pressure.

Roots Plugging Pores

Roots potentially can be a contributing factor in the reduction of soil aeration. Substantial external force is applied by plant roots as they grow; the pressure of expanding roots may approach 0.9 MPa, causing a zone of compaction around the root and reorienting soil particles tangential to the root. Bruand et al. also demonstrated quantitatively the reduction of porosity in the radial vicinity of roots. Backscattered electron scanning images of soil porosity around maize roots revealed that porosity was 22 to 24% less within the soil surrounding the root than in the bulk soil, and the bulk density increased up to 1.80 Mg m”3 at the root–soil interface, whereas density of the bulk soil was 1.54 Mg m”3.

Micropore collapse was suggested to be induced through water extraction by the root as well as through root expansion. Dexter developed a simplified model for soil compression around roots, using the assumptions that the root volume is accommodated by loss of porosity in the surrounding soil, that there is a minimum soil porosity below which soil will not be compressed, and that density decreases exponentially with distance from the roots' surface, the exponent being a constant multiple of the root diameter.

Asady and Smucker found that roots occupying more than 5% of the air-filled porosity of a soil resulted in O_2 consumption rates that exceeded the supply rate and increased CO_2 concentrations, because diffusion was decreased by the presence of excessive quantities of O_2 -consuming root sinks.

Thus, soil regions below and adjacent to areas with the greatest accumulation of roots can be prone to reduced aeration, particularly if the soil is also compacted. Studies of turf and forage grasses have reported very high rootlength densities compared to those reported by Asady and Smucker and others working with field crops. Thus, it is appears plausible that plant species with very high root-length density could develop soil oxygen stress due to extensive rooting that plugs air-filled pores and compacts the rhizosphere soil. This condition may be exacerbated under high soil temperatures, when the demand for oxygen by plant roots and soil microbes is greatest.

SUMMARY

Compaction of sōil is one of the more important forms of soil degradation caused by human activity. Cultivation is a reliever of soil compaction in that it breaks and loosens cohesive or compacted soil, but it can also be a cause of compaction due to heavy equipment and repeated traffic over the soil.

Interactions between soil physical conditions and plant growth have been demonstrated by examining research on soil compaction. Soil compaction is detrimental to plant growth when mechanical impedance becomes excessive and restricts the exploration of soil by roots and/or when soil aeration becomes limiting for root respiration and stimulates the production of toxic substances through anaerobic microbial processes.

Soil texture and water content are additional factors, among others, that determine the point of "excessive" impedance or "limiting" aeration. Plant roots are responsive to these conditions and hormonal mechanism are being identified that control adaptive changes in plant growth. In cases of perennial turfs with high plant population, roots themselves can be problematic in that their profuse growth can fill pores, blocking water and air movement. Deposition of hydrophobic organic substances by plant roots can hinder the wetting of soil, thus impacting the availability of water for plant growth. Conversely, the effects of plant roots on soil structure have been examined to demonstrate the important ameliorative potential that exists for physically degraded soil. Plant roots serve to bind soil particles together, thus resisting compactive and shearing forces acting on soil. Organic matter added to soil by plants provides cementing agents for aggregation and stimulates microbial activity, which also contributes to soil structure development. In addition, wetting and drying cycles in soil, enhanced by plant water use, are components of soil structural dynamics. However, research shows the persistence of compactionrelated problems despite ameliorative efforts. Thus, the necessity of preventing or minimizing soil compaction is emphasized.

14

Phytoremediation

INTRODUCTION

Phytoremediation uses living higher plants for cleaning up of environment contaminated with organic or inorganic pollutants by removing, sequestering, or chemically decomposing the pollutant. Microorganisms fostered by plants in their root zone may enhance the availability of the pollutant for uptake by the plant root system and may efficiently contribute to the degradation of organic pollutants. From the point of view of phytoremediation a plant may be viewed as a solar-driven pump-and-treat system, which may contain a contaminant plume and prevent the spread of contamination by reducing the movement of contaminated water and the erosional transport of contaminated soil. The efficiency of plants as detoxifiers, filters, or traps has been proven in the cleaning up soils polluted with crude oil, explosives, landfill leachates, metals, pesticides, polycyclic aromatic hydrocarbons, and solvents. Plants with phytoremediation potential can be chosen from wild species growing on polluted sites, or, alternatively, crop plants may be selected that have specific characteristics determined by the particular environment and pollutant.

At medium or large sites where contamination is shallow and its level is low to moderate phytoremediation is a viable alternative to "traditional" mechanical or chemical cleanup methods. When compared with "traditional" remediation technologies, phytoremediation has two major advantages: it is relatively inexpensive, and it is associated with minimal environmental disturbance. Since it is also an aesthetically pleasing technology, phytoremediation has high public acceptability. On the other hand, phytoremediation is time-consuming (usually several growing seasons are necessary), it is limited to soil depths that are within the reach of plant roots, much research is needed, and there is a possibility that the contaminant will reach the food chain through animal consumption of plant material. The following methods of phytoremediation are applicable:

1. Phytoextraction (also called phytoaccumulation): the uptake and translocation of pollutants from the soil or water by plant roots into the above-ground portions of the plants.
2. Phytotransformation (also called phytodegradation): the pollutants are detoxified in the plant root zone or within the plant tissue via chemical reactions with natural compounds and enzymes produced by the plants. This process may convert the inorganic pollutant into a nonsoluble derivative, thereby preventing its entry into the food chain.
3. Phytovolatilization: the pollutants are taken up by the root system of the plant, are translocated to the leaves (in unaltered form or after [bio]chemical transformation), and volatilize into the atmosphere.
4. Rhizotransformation: soil pollutants are detoxified by microorganisms living in the rhizosphere.
5. Rhizofiltration: contaminated water is cleaned by using the ability of plant root systems to bind contaminants.

THEORETICAL GROUNDS

The environmental fate of pollutants in the plant–soil system is determined by a highly complicated set of chemical, biochemical, physical, and biophysical reactions, elements of which may play significant roles in determining the ultimate success of the solution of a particular pollution problem by phytoremediation. Considerable variation in ability to take up and tolerate environmental pollutants exists between plant species. Only those plants having the appropriate biochemical pathways are effective for phytoremediation purposes. Basic research in the fields of plant physiology, biochemistry, and molecular biology of the preceding processes paved the way for the development of phytoremediation.

Uptake and Translocation of Pollutants in Plants

Bioavailability of soil pollutants is often the fundamental limiting factor in phytoremediation efficacy. Rate and efficiency of phytoremediation of polluted soils depends on the physical and chemical properties of the pollutant and those of the soil: pollutants may be bound to soil particles or taken up by microorganisms, plants, and animals. In the process of phytoremediation the availability of the pollutant for uptake by microorganisms of the rhizosphere and the plant root system is of crucial importance. Although differential uptake between crop and weed plant species has been implicated in the selective phytotoxic action of herbicides, this process usually does not play a role in plant sensitivity to environmental chemical stress. Uptake of inorganic and organic pollutants dissolved in water and their translocation within plant tissues may be mediated by membrane-bound transporter systems or, alternatively, it may be a passive process, regulated by the water transport into the cells. Penetration through the cell membrane of a solute and its transport within the organism is strongly affected by the water solubility of the chemical as well as by its size, shape, and charge distribution. The extent of uptake of some contaminants depends on the relative rates of metal influx and efflux. In mammalian tissues expression of the multiple resistance protein MDR renders cells tolerant to cytotoxic organic chemicals by pumping the toxicant out of the cell. Recently, the existence of similar systems in plants has been described. Synthetic chemicals may also serve as amendments of the phytoremediation process. These are being used for enhancing desorption of pollutants in soils thereby improving the bioavailability of soil pollutants for uptake by plants and microorganisms in the rhizosphere.

Biotransformation and Compartmentation of the Pollutant in Plant Tissues

In living plant tissues pollutants are transformed by a wide variety of chemical/biochemical metabolic reactions. Metabolism of a pollutant is involved in determining sensitivity and tolerance between plant species and has been found to play an important role in the development of stress-resistant plants. Biotransformation reactions of xenobiotics are generally referred to as Phases I and II, where Phase I includes oxidation of xenobiotics and Phase II deals with the conjugation of Phase I products. In plants, the oxidative metabolism in the Phase I system is usually mediated by cytochrome P-450 mixed-function oxygenases. In the Phase II systems activated hydrophobic xenobiotics are converted to more hydrophilic forms via conjugation with sugars or the sulfhydryl (-SH) group containing tripeptide glutathione (ã -L-glutamyl-L-cysteinyl-glycine, GSH). Since cellular -SH groups give protection against toxic metal ions as well as against alkylating organic compounds, it is not surprising that sulfur assimilation is powerfully regulated by pollutants such as the heavy metal cadmium, or the -SH-reactive chloroacetanilide herbicides.

1. Transformation Products

Detailed information on the chemistry of metabolites of inorganic and organic pollutants and metabolic pathways in susceptible and tolerant plants are scarcely available. In tolerant plants heavy-metal ions may be detoxified via chemical transformation into insoluble forms or chelated with cellular thiols or carboxylic acids and are eventually sequestered into the cell vacuole. Of the different Phase II reactions that are most commonly involved in pollutant metabolism in plants, conjugation with GSH or homoglutathione (ã -L-glutamyl-L-cysteinyl-âalanine) in some plants is one of the most important reactions and is often the rate-limiting step in the detoxication of an organic compound. It has long been shown that GSH transferases (GST, E.C. 2.5.1.18) mediate the GSH conjugation of many herbicides according to the reaction: GSTs represent a family of enzymes with usually broad and overlapping substrate specificities, which facilitate the preceding reactions of hydrophobic electrophilic substrates.

Our knowledge of plant GSTs has expanded greatly in recent years. Evidence is accumulating on the regulation of gene expression, molecular characteristics, and specific catalytic action of the multiple forms of these enzymes. Most of the information on plant GSTs concerns enzymes that are involved in the detoxification of a number of herbicides, but evidence is gathering that plant GSTs have a much wider role, and may be involved in general plant stress phenomena. The microsomal fraction of maize (Zea mays L.) shoot extracts contains measurable levels of GST. It has been suggested that microsomal GSTs may be effective in the detoxification of lipophilic electrophilic chemicals. The Phase II conjugation system is regarded as a detoxification process of xenobiotics. GSH conjugates, however, are not devoid of biological activity. Thus, accumulation of the resulting metabolites in cells can lead to a reduction in the detoxification activity of the Phase II system. Several GSH conjugates have been found to inhibit both GSTs and GSH reductase (GR, E.C. 1.6.4.2). Accordingly, rates of biochemical transformations of GSH conjugates of xenobiotics reducing their concentration in the cytosol are important detoxification steps.

2. *Compartmentation*

Plants lack the excretion system of animals. In plant cells toxic metabolites and pollutants are sequestered into the vacuole. This Phase III type process is an active one and is catalyzed by membrane-bound ATP-driven pumps. Recent studies showed the existence of a Phase III system that is involved in the elimination of GSH conjugates from the cytosol. C. Detoxification of the Active Oxygen Species Generated by the Pollutant Oxygen radicals are produced at various electron transfer sites or via different oxidation reactions in plant tissues. Under chemical stress conditions production of these radicals is powerfully enhanced. For example, micromolar concentrations of mercury(II) ions induce lipid peroxidation reactions in leaf tissues of maize plants. Plants contain a variety of defenses to protect against the damaging effects of oxygen radicals that are produced. It has been shown that a critical balance exists between oxyradical-generating factors and the activities of the systems that protect the cell from their harmful effects. Antioxidant defenses belong to three general classes, including:

1. Water-soluble reductants, e.g., compounds that contain thiol groups (cysteine, GSH, etc.), ascorbate, and catechols.
2. Lipid-soluble compounds, e.g., -tocopherol and -carotene.
3. Enzymatic antioxidants, e.g., GSH peroxidase (GP, E.C. 6.4.11.6), ascorbate peroxidase (E.C. 1.11.1.11), catalase (E.C. 1.11.1.6), and superoxide dismutase (E.C. 1.15.1.1). Microsomal and cytosolic GST enzymes in mammals may act as GP by catalyzing the reaction between GSH and lipophilic hydroperoxides, thereby protecting cell membrane polyunsaturated fatty acid moieties against lipid peroxidation. Recently reported in plants, such activity of some GST enzymes may contribute to phytoremediation ability.

INORGANIC POLLUTANTS

Uptake and Translocation

Metal ions are strongly bound to soil particles. To overcome this barrier, plants have evolved strategies to improve the bioavailability of essential metallic micronutrients. These include the production and secretion of metal-chelating natural products, which, by chelation, mobilize iron, copper, and zinc and exude protons to change the pH of the soil in the root zone, thereby solubilizing the adsorbed metal ions. An analogous solubilization-based mechanism is involved in the synergistic action of rhizosphere bacteria in phytoremediation of soils polluted with inorganics. Uptake and accumulation of zinc as well as the tolerance of Arabidopsis plants to this heavy metal is positively influenced by a zinc-transporter protein. In wheat (Triticum aestivum) zinc fluxes at supra-optimum levels of zinc supply (corresponding to a phytoremediation situation) appears to be controlled primarily by zinc efflux and not by short- or long-term regulation of zinc influx. A calmodulin-binding protein (involved in metal uptake across the plasma membrane) has been found to modulate plant (tobacco, Nicotiana tabacum) tolerance and accumulation of lead. In plants metals are transported through the xylem. Metal ion mobility toward the shoots may be strongly retarded by the high cation exchange capacity of the xylem cell walls. Therefore, anionic metal–chelate complexes should be transported more efficiently in the transpiration stream.

1. *The Role of Amendments*

Certain synthetic and natural chelating agents were found to greatly facilitate metal uptake by roots of soil-grown plants as well as metal transport to plant aerial parts. Thus, in the practice of phytoremediation, uptake and accumulation of metals in aerial tissues of plants can be enhanced through the application of synthetic and/or natural chelators to the soil. High shoot tissue concentrations in Brassica juncea of lead were obtained from lead-containing soils amended with synthetic chelates, such as ethylenediamine tetraacetic acid (EDTA).

Tissue accumulation levels were proportional to lead and EDTA concentrations in the soil. EDTA was also found to enhance the accumulation of cadmium, copper, nickel, and zinc. Chelators with higher efficiency in enhancing soil lead desorption were found to have higher efficiency in total lead accumulation in plant shoot tissues of pea (Pisum sativum) and maize plants. Within the plant, lead atoms are transported in EDTA-chelated form, indicating that EDTA increases not only the uptake of metal into the plant roots but also its translocation to the shoot tissues.

The high efficiency of anionic chelators in promoting uptake, translocation, and accumulation of inorganic pollutants has been shown in a comparative study on the effects of organic acids on uranium desorption from soil to soil solution. Of the acids studied (acetic acid, citric acid, and malic acid), citric acid was the most effective in enhancing uranium desorption and subsequent accumulation in plants. In shoot tissues of B. juncea and B. chinensis grown in citric acid–amended soils thousandfold increases in uranium concentrations were found.

Biotransformation

The intrinsic metal uptake systems render plants vulnerable to toxic levels of metals in their rhizosphere. Therefore, plants have evolved mechanisms to tolerate high concentrations of toxic metal ions in their tissues. One mechanism involves metal-chelate formation with thiol-rich oligopeptides (phytochelatins, PCs) and proteins (metallothioneins, MTs) and other low-molecular-weight natural products, such as amino acids and carboxylic acids. PCs are cysteinerich oligopeptides known to bind cadmium and copper in plants. They are synthesized from GSH in an enzyme- (phytochelatin synthase, E.C. 1.2.3.4) catalyzed reaction powerfully upregulated by traces of heavy metal ions in the cytosol. In addition, coordinated changes of gene expression occur for several sulfur assimilation enzymes in response to an increased demand for cysteine during PC synthesis.

MTs, on the other hand, are gene-encoded, lowmolecular-weight, cysteine-rich proteins. MTs are induced by copper and have high affinity for this metal. Accumulation of the essential amino acid proline and the dicarboxylic acid anions malate and citrate in response to exposure to cadmium and zinc has been attributed to metal-complex formation, resulting in protection against phytotoxicity of these metals. Further research is necessary to clarify the importance of the ability to precipitate metals in the forms of phytate or phosphate (zinc) or carbonate (lead) in determining metal tolerance of plants. The toxicity of such metals and metalloids as chromium, selenium, and arsenic can be reduced in plants by chemical reduction of the element and/or by its incorporation into organic compounds.

Selenium, for example, is an essential trace element but is also toxic at higher concentrations, because it is metabolized to selenocysteine and selenomethionine, which replace cysteine and methionine residues in proteins. By channeling selenium into the synthesis of selenium analogs of the sulfur-containing nonprotein amino acids methylselenocysteine and selenocystathione, selenium accumulator species of Astragalus are able to reduce the amount of selenium incorporated into proteins, thereby tolerating higher levels in the shoots. Selenium is also volatilized by plants in the form of dimethylselenide, which is several hundred times less toxic than inorganic forms of this element. Thus, mechanisms increasing selenate reduction may be useful for improving selenate uptake and detoxication. Similarly, the reduction of chromium(VI) to chromium(III) and mercury(II) to mercury(0) is part of a detoxication mechanism in plants. Interestingly, transgenic Arabidopsis plants containing and expressing the bacterial gene merBpe convert the highly toxic methylmercury to mercury(II) and show high resistance to toxic levels of methylmercuric chloride and phenylmercuric acetate.

Compartmentation

Accumulation of metals in plant leaves may not be homogenous among the various tissue cells, as shown in nickel-tolerant Thlaspi montanum. This species shows a preferential nickel accumulation in epidermal cells. In a related study on the cellular compartmentation of zinc in the leaves of Thlaspi caerulescens a greatly enhanced zinc accumulation was found in the epidermis compared with the mesophyll cells. Zinc concentrations in the epidermal vacuolar sap reached 5 to 6.5 times higher levels than those in the mesophyll sap. Within cells, inorganic pollutants accumulate in the vacuole. The process of accumulation is usually driven by a metal/proton antiport. Thus, vacuolar storage of cadmium plays an important role in the mechanism of cadmium tolerance of Silene vulgaris.

ORGANIC POLLUTANTS

The fate of some organic chemicals (e.g., those belonging to chloroacetanilides, sulfonylureas, thiolcarbamates, and triazines) in plants has been extensively studied because of their importance in the selective phytotoxic action of herbicides. Up until recently, however, surprisingly little progress has been made in the field of common organic pollutants. Organic contaminants are present at high concentrations in the soil and groundwater at many hazardous waste sites. Such chemicals may be by-products of agricultural and industrial production or may have leaked from fuel storage tanks or ruptured soil liners at disposal sites. In addition, contamination of some soils as a result of continuous use of agrochemicals (primarily herbicides) has also become a serious environmental problem.

Soil contamination involved in these types of problems is often very dispersed so that conventional soil and groundwater remediation techniques would be expensive or, in some cases, impractical. Phytoremediation is a viable alternative, but it is made highly complicated by the great variation from site to site in the chemistry and the distribution (concentration, depth, etc.) of the pollutant. A. Uptake and Translocation The uptake of organic chemicals by plant roots from soil could be correlated to some physicochemical and structural substance properties. Barley root concentration factors due to root uptake, expressed as concentration in roots divided by concentration in soil, gave a fairly good negative correlation to adsorption coefficients based on soil organic carbon and gave a positive correlation to the n-octanol/water partition coefficients. Both root and foliar uptake by barley could be correlated well with the molecular weight of 14 chemicals.

1. The Role of Amendments

A major problem of organic contamination is the lack of bioavailability of the pollutant for phytoremediation. In comparison with the solubilization of soilbound inorganics, much less is known about the roles of amendments in the phytoremediation of soils polluted with organic compounds. With the aim of maximizing the bioavailability of soil-applied herbicides to weeds, agrochemical companies formulate their products with surfactants to overcome the low aqueous solubilities of lipophilic herbicidal active ingredients by reducing the surface tension at the chemical/water interface. Once solubilized by the surfactant the herbicide becomes bioavailable for uptake by the weed species. Contamination by the aromatic chemicals benzene and its alkyl derivatives (toluene, ethylbenzene, and xylene) seems to be ideally suited for phytoremediation. Being light, lipophilic contaminants, these compounds are often located near the surface at hazardous waste sites. However, removal of these aromatics from soil is possible only by increasing their apparent water solubility. A new and interesting approach takes advantage of the ability of cyclodextrins to increase the elution of organic compounds from soils. These chemicals have dual solubilizing potency, because they may act as surfactants as well as complexing agents that form inclusion complexes with hydrophobic compounds.

A study on the effects of natural cyclodextrins (CDs) and hydroxypropyl-cyclodextrins (HP-CDs) on the apparent solubilities of benzene, toluene, and xylenes found a significant solubilizing effect when HP-CDs were added. Efficiency of solubilization of these aromatics depended on the relationship between the molecular diameters of the compounds, their 1-octanol–water partition coefficient, and the CD cavity size.

Biotransformation

Most of the information available on the biotransformation reactions of organic chemicals in plants deals with the decomposition reactions of pesticidal active ingredients, and excellent reviews have been published on these findings. This paper will attempt to cover studies on the biotransformation reactions of common organic pollutants (aromatic and chlorinated aliphatic solvents, and explosives), with emphasis on phytoremediation-related issues.

The halogenated organic aliphatic compounds, such as carbon tetrachloride, chloroform, and trichloroethylene are widely used organic solvents and are among the most common of the toxic substances found at hazardous waste sites. Plants can play an important role in remediating soil and groundwater contaminated with these chemicals. Axenic cultures of poplar (Populus spp.) tissues were shown to convert TCE to trichloroethanol, trichloroacetic acid, dichloroacetic acid, and a small amount of CO_2. At the whole-plant level TCE was not toxic to the poplar trees at concentrations much higher than those usually found at hazardous waste sites. The trees did not release significant amounts of TCE into the air, because they not only took up the compound, but are also metabolized it within their tissues to a far greater extent than was found in the laboratory studies. Similar results were obtained with carbon tetrachloride (CCl4); that is, about 90% of the material was removed from the water at 20 ppm and no CCl4 could be detected in the transpirate. Thus, in tissues of poplar trees chlorinated aliphatic hydrocarbon pollutants can undergo oxidation and dechlorination processes, and finally, complete mineralization to CO_2.

Soil and groundwater contamination due to explosives such as glycerol trinitrate (GTN, nitroglycerin), hexahydro-1,3,5-trinitro-1,3,5-triazine (RDX), and 2,4,6-trinitrotoluene (TNT) is a problem at many ammunition plants. The presence of plants did enhance removal of these explosives from groundwater. TNT and RDX removal and fate was evaluated using hydroponic batch incubations of aquatic and wetland plant species and substrate treatments with explosives-contaminated groundwater. It was demonstrated that TNT disappeared completely from groundwater incubated with plants, while removal of RDX by plants was slower. Mineralization of TNT and RDX by plants to CO_2 was low, and evolution into volatile organics negligible. The ecotoxicological threshold of TNT in two soils of different properties was investigated by seed germination and early stage seedling growth tests. Four representative species of higher plants, two dicotyledons and two monocotyledons, were assessed.

Oat (Avena sativa) was capable of tolerating as much as 1600 mg TNT kg"1 and demonstrated a potential ability of TNT detoxification in one of the soils tested, suggesting that this plant might be useful in the bioremediation of TNT-contaminated sites. The ability of plants to metabolize the nitrate ester GTN was examined using cultured sugar beet (Beta vulgaris) plant cells and plant cell extracts. Intact cells rapidly degraded GTN with the initial formation of glycerol dinitrate (GDN) and the later formation of glycerol mononitrate. A material balance analysis of these intermediates indicated little, if any, formation of reduced, conjugated, or cell-bound carbonaceous metabolites. Cell extracts were shown to be capable of degrading GTN with the simultaneous formation of GDN in stoichiometric amounts.

The enzyme pentaerythritol tetranitrate reductase of an explosive-degrading bacterium enables it to decompose the nitrate ester and the nitroaromatic explosives. Seeds of transgenic tobacco plants expressing this enzyme were able to germinate and grow in the presence of GTN and TNT concentrations that inhibited germination and growth of wild-type seeds. Transgenic seedlings also showed more rapid and complete denitration of GTN than wild-type seedlings. Contamination of some soils with herbicides has become a serious environmental problem. The chloroacetanilide herbicides, especially acetochlor, alachlor, and metolachlor, are common containants in agricultural settings. Phytoremediation is an attractive option to reduce soil levels of certain pesticides.

Benoxacor is a safener that protects maize from chloroacetanilides by inducing increased herbicide metabolism via GSH conjugation. An integrated model system for phytoremediation using maize, benoxacor, and a rhizosphere-competent Pseudomonas strain capable of catabolizing these herbicides in soil was developed. A combination of chemical and biological safeners (competent rhizobacteria) is a useful novel approach to increase herbicide tolerance in a crop plant for enhanced phytoremediation. It should be noted that the possibility of using herbicide safeners to improve the efficiency of phytoremediation was first raised by Christian Brunold (personal communication, 1991).

CONCLUSIONS

Our knowledge of the factors that determine the efficacy of phytoremediation has expanded greatly in recent years. It became evident that pollutant phytotoxicity is determined by a highly complicated sequence of events, elements of which may play a significant role in promoting or antagonizing plant tissue damage, depending on the plant–pollutant system. Phytoremediation efficiency seems to be strongly influenced by the ability of the plant to escape deleterious concentrations of the toxic form of the pollutant and the active oxygen species that might be generated in the treated tissue.

The key role of the GSH-related detoxification system in the biotransformation of electrophilic pollutants in some tolerant plants and the importance of the antioxidant systems to counteract peroxidative damage has been clearly established. However, much is yet to be learned about these systems in plants, especially, with respect to their specificity and their mechanism of induction. In vivo and in vitro studies to follow pollutant-induced changes in plant biochemistry, biophysics, and molecular biology provide us with intriguing challenges for further research. Given the existing advances in plant molecular biology, the use of transgenic plants in the daily practice of phytoremediation could soon become a reality.

Bibliography

Babe, Robert E.: *Culture of Ecology: Reconciling Economics and Environment.* Toronto: University of Toronto Press, 2006.

Checker, Melissa: *Polluted Promises: Environmental Racism and the Search for Justice in a Southern Town.* New York: New York University Press, 2005.

Gottlieb, Roger S.: *The Oxford Handbook of Religion and Ecology.* Oxford & New York: Oxford University Press, 2006.

Hornborg, Alf, J. R. McNeill, and Joan Martinez-Alier: *Rethinking Environmental History: World-System History and Global Environmental Change.* Lanham: Altamira Press, 2007.

Howard, Sir Albert: *The Soil and Health: A Study of Organic Agriculture.* Culture of the Land Series. Lexington: University Press of Kentucky, 2006.

Lawrence, Henry W.: *City Trees: A Historical Geography from the Renaissance through the Nineteenth Century.* Charlottesville: University of Virginia Press, 2006.

Lear, Linda: *Beatrix Potter: A Life in Nature.* New York: St. Martin's Press, 2007.

Milazzo, Paul Charles: *Unlikely Environmentalists: Congress and Clean Water, 1945–1972.* Lawrence: University Press of Kansas , 2006.

Ott, Riki: *Sound Truth and Corporate Myths: The Legacy of the Exxon Valdez Oil Spill.* Cordova, AK: Dragonfly Sisters Press, 2005.

Smith, Allan H.: *Takhoma: Ethnography of Mount Rainier National Park.* Pullman: Washington State University Press, 2006.

Starnes, Richard D.: *Creating the Land of the Sky: Tourism and Society in Western North Carolina.* Tuscaloosa: University of Alabama Press, 2005.

Index

O

P

R

S

T

W

□□□